E D U C A T I O N A L   S E R I E S

Using Portfolio Management Wisdom
Handbook

Written by Bonnie J. Biafore
for the National Association of Investors Corporation

Published by National Association of Investors Corporation (NAIC)
Madison Heights, Michigan
Copyright © 2005

First published in the United States of America by
National Association of Investors Corporation (NAIC)
711 West 13 Mile Road, Madison Heights, Michigan 48071
1-877-275-6242 • www.better-investing.org

Manufactured in the United States of America
ISBN # 0-9678130-6-9

Publisher's Cataloging-in-Publication
(Provided by Quality Books, Inc.)

Biafore, Bonnie.
    NAIC using portfolio management wisdom handbook /
written by Bonnie Biafore for the National Association
of Investors Corporation.
    p. cm. -- (NAIC better investing educational series)
    Includes bibliographical references and index.
    ISBN 09678130-6-9

    1. Portfolio management.   I. National Association
of Investors Corporation. II. Title.

    HG4529.5.B53 2005   332.6
                               QBI05-200093

NAIC Registered Trademark Rights

BETTER INVESTING®
BI®
BETTER INVESTING BITS®
BETTER INVESTING NATIONAL CONVENTION®
BOND FUND CHECK LIST®
BOND FUND TREND REPORT®
BOND FUND COMPARISON GUIDE©
COMPUFAIR®
COMPUFEST®
COMPUFORUM®
CREATING AMERICA'S NEXT 50 MILLION INVESTORS ®
INVESTING FOR LIFE®
INVESTFEST®
INVESTORS CONGRESS®
INVESTORS EXPO®
INVESTORS FAIR®
INVESTORS TOOLKIT®

NAIC®
NAIC FIXED INCOME MUTUAL FUND COMPARISON GUIDE©
NAIC'S YOUNG MONEY MATTERS®
NAIC...Where Main Street Meets Wall Street® (& stylized sign post)
NATIONAL ASSOCIATION OF INVESTORS CORPORATION®
OFFICIAL NAIC MUTUAL FUND HANDBOOK©
OWN YOUR SHARE OF AMERICA®
PERT®
PORTFOLIO MANAGEMENT GUIDE®
SSG PLUS®
STOCK CHECKLIST®
STOCK COMPARISON GUIDE®
STOCK FUND CHECK LIST®
STOCK FUND TREND REPORT®
STOCK FUND COMPARISON GUIDE ©
STOCK SELECTION GUIDE ®
STOCK SELECTION GUIDE AND REPORT ®

NAIC *Better Investing Book Series*

The Better Investing book series is designed to provide information and tools to help individuals and investment clubs become successful long-term investors. By using the series, investors will follow a self-learning pathway, gaining knowledge and building experience to make informed investment decisions. The series provides information and resources for beginners, intermediate and experienced investors.
For more information contact NAIC:
1-877-275-6242, or visit the NAIC Web Site:
www.better-investing.org

Acknowledgements

NAIC Using Portfolio Management Wisdom *Handbook*

Author/Writer:	Bonnie J. Biafore
Executive Editor:	Jeffery Fox, CFA Director, Educational Development, NAIC
Editorial Consultant:	Barrie Borich
Index Consultant:	Kathleen Paparchontis
Educational Content Consultants:	Kenneth Janke, Chairman, NAIC Richard Holthaus, President & CEO, NAIC Thomas O'Hara, Chairman Emeritus, NAIC Elizabeth Hamm, NAIC Trustee Peggy Schmeltz, NAIC Trustee Robert O'Hara, Vice President, Business Development, NAIC Betty Taylor, Former NIA Director Seymore Zeenkov, Director CGAB Amy Crane, Content Reviewer Jim Thomas, Content Reviewer
Creative Direction & Design:	Michael Bell, Childers Printing & Graphics, Inc. Carol Wyatt, Graphic Designer
Design Consultants:	Ellada Azariah, Graphic Designer, NAIC Pamela Pohl, Graphic Designer, NAIC Mary Treppa, Online Editor, NAIC
Production Coordinator:	Renee Ross, Childers Printing & Graphics, Inc. Jonathan Strong, Director, Corporate Development, NAIC
Printing/Production:	Childers Printing & Graphics, Inc. Printwell Acquisitions, Inc.

Table of Contents

Foreword

Few individuals give much thought to building and maintaining a stock portfolio when they first begin to invest. That is probably not unusual since the initial purchase is usually made with the objective in mind to make some money and little more. However, as different stocks are added and the portfolio becomes more significant, it is vital to pay close attention to what is happening to the fundamentals of the companies and the price of the stock.

For most investors and investment clubs, after only a few short years, the portfolio represents more in total assets than is being invested in new stocks. It stands to reason that more time should be spent monitoring the existing holdings.

What the author and contributors to this book have done is expose investors to the various techniques that are available to keep up-to-date on portfolio holdings.

From the investment aids available to the common sense analysis from looking at quarterly and annual reports, the reader will be able to better understand how to make a portfolio grow.

This book does not advocate trading in and out of stocks, but a practical approach to trying to gain as much from portfolio management as possible. You have already taken the important step of becoming an investor, watching and monitoring the current stocks held is the next logical step. If you read it thoroughly, it should be a great benefit. Your own experience will only help performance in the long-term.

Kenneth S. Janke

CHAIRMAN
NATIONAL ASSOCIATION OF INVESTORS CORPORATION

Introduction

Whether you have big plans for your life or a few modest aspirations, some goals carry big price tags. Sure, you could get lucky and pay for everything with lottery winnings, but you shouldn't count on that. Without good financial planning and management, you're likely to play catch-up: saving until it hurts, taking more risk to chase higher returns, and ultimately laying awake at night worrying whether you will succeed. By planning ahead and keeping your eye on the ball (house, college, retirement, or other objectives), you can grow a nest egg for the future without sacrificing fun for today.

Saving money in order to invest feeds your portfolio and financial goals. But, portfolio management is the vitamin and mineral supplement your investment portfolio needs to grow strong and stay healthy. Sensible portfolio management also acts as the best antacid you can buy, delivering results without a gut-wrenching roller coaster ride.

Go ahead and think big. If you start early enough and work conscientiously toward your goals, you can achieve anything you want. Whether you want to attend a top college, start your own business, or climb Mount Everest, planning how you will achieve your goals increases your chance of success.

Preparing a plan engages your brain—you think about achieving your goal, even when you sleep, and that is a powerful force in itself. With your goal firmly in mind, the second step to success is funding. Big ideas often come with price tags to match. Your plan should include a finance section that outlines your approach to pay for your goals.

As you will learn in this book, an early start paves the way to amassing the money you need. With more time on your side, you can make regular contributions to your portfolio over a longer period, which means each contribution can be smaller and correspondingly

easier on your pocketbook. Longer timeframes also mean that you can afford to take on more risk to achieve higher returns. By earning higher returns, your investment earnings compound faster, helping you reach your financial targets with even more modest or fewer regular deposits to your accounts.

Quality is another factor that does more than produce better investment results. It can save you time. When you own quality investments, whether they are stocks, bonds, or mutual funds, strength, consistency, and dependability can translate into easier

portfolio reviews and fewer changes to your holdings.

Portfolio management is easy; but it isn't automatic. To win, you have to play the game. Playing defense means blocking poor investments before they harm your portfolio. Portfolio offense is working to increase the quality and returns you achieve while reducing your portfolio risk. With a few hours of portfolio management each month, you can both protect your portfolio and score investment points.

No one is better than you at managing your portfolio. You care more about whether you will have money to pay for your goals than anyone else would. You are the one staring at the clock when risky investments keep you up at night. Portfolio management isn't that hard, but it **does** require regular attention. You can do it. Simply make a habit of portfolio management. However, if life seems terminally busy, a financial planner can help you develop a plan, monitor its progress, and suggest course corrections. Of course, you pay for the privilege, but the cost might be small compared to a portfolio gone astray.

George Nicholson developed the investment methodology at the heart of NAIC's education.

The basics of this approach are simple:

- Invest in quality, growth companies that you expect to double in value within five years

- Purchase companies at a good price to increase return

- Invest for the long term

- Reinvest income and capital gains to take full advantage of compounding

- Diversify investments to reduce risk

NAIC offers tools and software to support this investment approach including most of the portfolio management tasks you perform. If you are familiar with the NAIC Stock Selection Guide (SSG), you already know quite a bit about identifying quality growth

stocks and evaluating risk and return. The SSG is equally valuable for portfolio decisions. You evaluate the same information whether you are buying or selling stock. SSG information including your judgment propagates to tools such as the NAIC PERT reports, which shows trends and key information about each of your stocks. These reports help you spot signs of trouble as well as opportunities for improvement. If you own mutual funds, NAIC mutual fund tools help you select the best funds at your disposal, whether you're choosing funds within your employer's 401(k) program or from the entire universe of mutual funds.

For most people, managing a portfolio includes working with both stocks and mutual funds—and possibly other types of investments, such as bonds and real estate. None of the NAIC tools show the big picture of a conglomerate portfolio such as this. However, software applications and online tools fill this gap with a variety of choices to fit investors requirements and pocketbooks.

The Pillars of Your Portfolio

The Dichotomy of Risk and Return

Regardless of whether investment returns stem from price increases, dividends, or interest, the returns you receive on your investments mean that your money is working toward fulfilling your financial objectives. You must remember the relationship between risk and return. When you earn high returns, you also run the risk of large losses. But, you can't play it totally safe, so there's no point suffering through an entire portfolio of low-return investments. Portfolio management means using concepts such as quality, time, and informed analysis to balance the risks you take with the returns you want.

What's So Important About
Investment Returns?

The Relationship Between
Risk and Return

Demand the Best

What's So Important About Investment Returns?

You invest because you want to accumulate money but you don't relish the idea of saving every cent out of your paycheck. Saving a million dollars would be a daunting task even if you earned a six-figure salary and could save tens of thousands of dollars a year. Suppose you saved the 2004 401(k) maximum of $13,000 each year but didn't invest the money. It would take almost 77 years to become a millionaire. So, that's not going to work.

When you invest your money wisely, it should grow—with some basic care and feeding on your part. The investment returns you receive compound your earnings, which exponentially increases your money. Compounding is incredibly powerful, because each year you earn money not only on your original investment but also on the earnings from the previous years. For example, instead of simply stashing that $13,000 a year, suppose you invested your money in stocks that returned 15 percent a year. In this case, it would take slightly more than 17 years to reach a million dollars. By investing instead of stashing, you liberated 60 years of saving from your financial plan. Even if you spent five hours a month nurturing your portfolio, that's only about 1000 hours of effort to eliminate decades of savings.

How Compounding Works

One of George Nicholson's objectives, which has become a tenet of NAIC investing, is to try to double one's money every five years, or in other words, multiplying your original investment by a factor of 2. As a knowledgeable investor, you know that doubling your money in five years is the equivalent of achieving a 14.9 percent return each year. Figure 1-01 shows how this works:

The returns you earn won't be nice and neat like the ones you see in Figure 1-1, but the effects of compounding still hold true. A stock's price might limp along for several years delivering 4 or 5 percent returns, only to jump

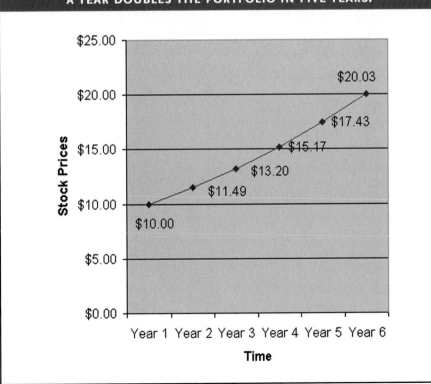

FIGURE 1-01: INCREASING A PORTFOLIO BY 14.9 PERCENT A YEAR DOUBLES THE PORTFOLIO IN FIVE YEARS.

5

30 percent in the fifth year. Still, each year of growth compounds on the year before. Portfolio management teaches you how to differentiate the stocks whose prices are likely to increase from the ones that are simply languishing.

As long as you achieve an average annual compound return of approximately 15 percent, your money will double every five years. After 10 years, your nest egg would be four times your original investment. After 20 years, it would double again to reach 16 times your original contribution. As your timeframe increases, so does the power of compounding.

Because returns vary from year to year depending on the economy and many other factors, you're more likely to see the true power of compounding over periods of 10 years or more. For example, between 1999 and 2004, very few portfolios got close to an average annual compound return of 15 percent.

Why Double Your Money in Five Years?

You might wonder why George Nicholson picked a target average annual return of 15 percent and the goal of doubling your money (total return) in five years. These aren't arbitrary numbers. Trying to grow a portfolio faster than that would increase

risk to an unacceptable level. In the past, the market tended to cycle between bear and bull markets about every five years. And since doubling your money is the equivalent of increasing value by 15 percent a year for five years, doubling your money from one market high to the next was an objective you could spot without any fancy calculations.

Don't Forget Dividends

Reinvesting all dividends is another of NAIC's investment principles. By reinvesting the dividends that your stocks pay into additional shares of stocks in your portfolio, you put the power of compounding to work yet again. Because you own

more shares, you earn more money as the stock price goes up. In addition, for every dividend distribution, you receive more dollars, which you can use to buy even more reinvested shares. If you invested $100 in the Standard & Poor's 500-stock average in 1925 and spent all the dividends you received, your portfolio would have reached approximately $7,140 by the end of 2002. If you reinvested the dividends instead, your $100 would have grown to about $177,000! With results like these, shown in Figure 1-02, it's easy to understand why reinvesting dividends is so important.

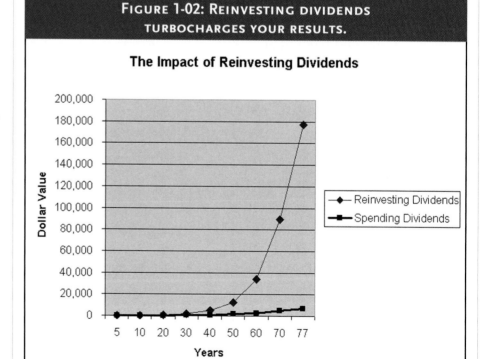

FIGURE 1-02: REINVESTING DIVIDENDS TURBOCHARGES YOUR RESULTS.

The Impact of Reinvesting Dividends

The Relationship Between Risk and Return

From the examples in the previous section, you can see that investment returns are desirable. You might also conclude that the higher the returns are, the better. Not necessarily. The success or failure of your investment plans also depends on factors such as risk, timeframe, and quality.

In investing, risk and return go hand in hand. A small company with a revolutionary new cancer drug has the potential to grow explosively as people clamor for its pharmaceutical product. However, if the FDA withdraws its approval because of adverse side effects, the company might implode, dragging the stock price down as fast as it went up. You can't expect astronomical returns without accepting galactic risks. On the other hand, if you want lower risk, you should also expect lower returns.

If you understand and manage your investment risks well, you will possess one of the keys to good portfolio management. Your tolerance for risk is probably different than your neighbor's. In addition, the events in your life may impact your ability to take on risk. The amount of risk you're willing to accept is likely to change after the birth of a child or the beginning of your retirement. Therefore, you must balance the potential investment returns you seek with the financial risks you can stomach. Higher returns mean your money works hard. Managed risk means your funds are less likely to disappear just when you need them.

Unfortunately, every investment involves some type of risk. Some investors get into trouble because they choose investments to avoid the risks they know and fear, oblivious to the risks that their investment choices carry. Consider the people who feel that the stock market is too risky; they put their money into bonds (or in the case of the perpetually panicked, even certificates of deposit). Unfortunately, while they're hiding from the risk of the stock market, inflation risk could be eating their lunch.

Know Your Risks

Risk represents uncertainty: the chance that things won't turn out as you planned. Probability being what it is, risk could result in better-than-planned performance, but Murphy's Law seems to win out. If you don't manage the investment risks in your portfolio, you probably won't reach your financial goals.

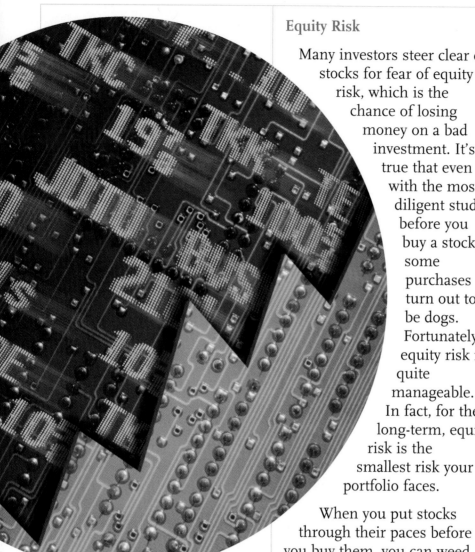

Equity Risk

Many investors steer clear of stocks for fear of equity risk, which is the chance of losing money on a bad investment. It's true that even with the most diligent study before you buy a stock, some purchases turn out to be dogs. Fortunately, equity risk is quite manageable. In fact, for the long-term, equity risk is the smallest risk your portfolio faces.

When you put stocks through their paces before you buy them, you can weed out less vigorous candidates and increase your overall success rate. Diversification (see Chapter 2) is another way to reduce equity risk. If you purchase only one stock and something bad happens to it, your entire portfolio is in trouble. Diversification (another NAIC principle of investing) complements the Rule of Five: out of every five stocks you pick, one (or 20 percent of the stocks in your portfolio) will do much better than you anticipated, one (another 20 percent) will do much worse, and the remaining three (the remaining 60 percent) will perform to your expectations. With proper diversification, one troubled stock affects only a small part of your portfolio.

Time helps diminish equity risk. Stock prices don't increase in lockstep with a company's earnings and, in some cases, drop for no apparent reason. The longer your investment timeframe, the more time you have to recover from temporary setbacks and the more time stocks have to live up to their potential. Of course, if a company shows signs of serious deterioration, no amount of time is likely to help.

Holding period risk is the risk that you might have to sell an investment when its value is in a slump.

Economic Risk

Economic risk is the danger of losing money because the economy tanks, taking your investments with it. Recessions occur at irregular intervals and tend to last months rather than years. But, that's no consolation if you need the money in your portfolio when prices across the board are depressed. Economic risk is the reason that investors focus on stocks for long-term

Risk comes in many forms, and each type of investment carries its own unique combination. Longer investment timeframes reduce the impact of some types of risks, whereas other risks get worse with more time. By understanding the different types of investment risk, you can choose the most appropriate investments for your goals and assume a level of risk in tune with your risk tolerance.

investments, but keep money needed for the short-term in savings accounts or certificates of deposit.

For any one-year period, the return for large-cap stocks as a whole might be a giddy increase of 54 percent, as it was in 1933 or a nauseating drop of 43.3 percent as in 1931. Sufficient time can significantly reduce economic risk. A hypothetical investment in a large-cap stock index with dividends reinvested has produced an average compound annual return of about 11 percent for the past 75 years. Although the market has lost money over a few 10-year periods, it has never lost money over a 20–year period. There's no guarantee that the small portfolio of individual stocks you pick will perform as well as the overall market over 20 years. However, careful portfolio management can help you meet and exceed the market.

When you put your money in foreign investments, currency risk becomes an issue. If the dollar drops compared to the currency in which your investment is based, your investment loses some of its value. Conversely, currency exchange rates work to your advantage when the dollar is strong compared to other currencies.

Interest Rate Risk

Many investors consider bonds to be safe havens for their investment dollars, but bonds are burdened with several types of risk. As a general rule (but not always), both stocks and bonds tend to move in the opposite direction of interest rates. Stock prices frequently drop when interest rates rise because investors move their money into the known return of fixed-rate investments. For bonds, higher interest rates make borrowing for corporations more expensive, thus reducing net incomes of companies that use debt financing. Bond prices also drop when interest rates rise because an already-issued bond with a lower coupon rate is worth less compared to new bonds that offer the going market rate.

At maturity, bonds and other fixed-income investments such as certificates of deposit present another type of interest rate risk: reinvestment risk. This is the risk that interest rates are lower when it's time to purchase a new fixed-income investment, so you earn even less.

Inflation

Many people avoid stocks because of their fear of equity risk. As it turns out, equity risk is small compared to the steady nibbling away of your portfolio from inflation. Putting up with some equity risk is your best

INVESTMENTS AND TAXES

Fixed-income investments suffer yet another blow when you consider the affect of income taxes on the interest earned. Although bonds and CDs generally offer lower long-term average returns than stocks, the interest that they pay out is taxable at ordinary income tax rates. Paying taxes on your interest income reduces the return you receive. To make matters worse, the dollars lost to taxes also are lost to the power of compounding. When you sell a bond before it reaches maturity, you must pay taxes on the capital gains as well.

Taxes work the same way for stocks. You pay taxes each year on the dividends that the company pays out and then you pay taxes on your capital gains when you sell the stock and put the capital gains in your pocket. The difference with stocks is that there is no maturity date. If you hold onto a stock that's growing for decades, you don't pay the tax on the capital gains as long as you own the stock. Meanwhile, the money invested in the stock compounds each year.

defense against the bite inflation takes out of your purchasing power.

Inflation means that you pay more for an item today than you would have paid at some point in the past. In the 1960s, a loaf of bread cost 25 cents. Now, a loaf of bread costs $3. The bread hasn't changed, but the purchasing power of your money has. Inflation is the risk that trips up cautious investors. Unlike equity risk or economic risk, inflation risk gets worse over time. Product prices creep up slowly; you hardly notice the change from year to year. However, over 40 years, 3 percent inflation reduces the purchasing power of a dollar to

about 31 cents. Although the financial world offers few guarantees, inflation guarantees that you will have less buying power when you keep your money in low-return investments for long periods of time.

If inflation is 3 percent and your savings account pays 2 percent interest, you actually lose more than 1 percent of your purchasing power to inflation each year. Although bonds typically pay higher rates than savings accounts, bond returns are hurt by inflation too. If you invest in bonds with a 6 percent coupon rate, 3 percent inflation reduces your actual annual return to

less than 3 percent. Subtracting the taxes you pay on bond income, your return barely stays even, and certainly isn't enough to grow your portfolio in a meaningful way. For the long term, investing in stocks turns out to be the least risky approach for your portfolio.

Demand the Best

Quality can contribute to your investment success. Quality might seem like a subjective measure; everyone seems to recognize it when they see it but often have trouble determining how to measure it. Some heavy hitters in investment circles have placed a great deal of emphasis on the quality of investments and worked hard to quantify investment quality. George Nicholson, one of the co-founders of NAIC, and Benjamin Graham, Warren Buffett's mentor, both used similar approaches for evaluating the quality of potential investments. The factors they considered include the following measures, most of which appear in one way or another on the Stock Selection Guide or the accompanying Stock Selection Report:

- Strong historical growth of sales and EPS

- Consistency of EPS growth

- Strong profitability

- Financial strength

- Strong management

- Business and industry outlook

- Competitive strength (a dominant role in its industry)

- Strong dividend policy

As Benjamin Graham observed, quality often costs more, but also tends to hold (or even increase) its value. Some people buy products with the lowest possible cost and many of these products break down or fall apart quickly. The products might be cheap but they aren't inexpensive. If you buy a product of higher quality, it might even continue to run after you have finished paying for it.

In a bull market, even mediocre portfolio returns often look good. But, a bear market is a better test of your portfolio prowess. True, almost all stocks will suffer in a bear market just as all boats descend when the tide goes out, but high quality stocks typically decline less and rebound sooner. Not only do higher quality companies survive, they often pick up market shares from their lesser competitors. When you buy a quality stock, its price might represent a higher PE ratio, but chances are good that the company's quality will lead to ongoing earning growth and years of stock price increases.

Making your money grow requires knowledge of investing whether you invest in stocks and bonds or entrust your funds to a professional money manager. Whichever route you choose, you must know what your risk tolerance is and what you expect out of your investments. Even a money manager can be more risky than choosing stocks because you trust your whole portfolio to one person...so do your homework!

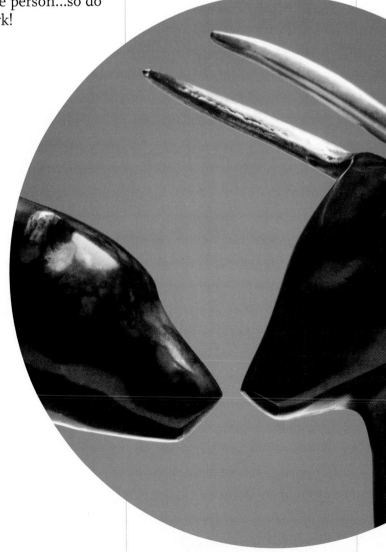

Diversifying Your Portfolio

Spreading the Wealth

Making the most of your investments doesn't mean choosing the one investment whose price blasts past all others in one year. While a shooting star is certainly great for that year's investment return, the next year could be a different story. The idea is to diversify your collection of investments so they meet your financial targets in a way that you can live with. Every financial goal is different, so portfolio management means allocating investments in the right proportions to match the characteristics of your goals. Change is inevitable, so you also must adjust your investments as time passes and your needs change.

The Roots of the Rule of Five

Diversifying a Portfolio of Stocks

Using Mutual Funds To Diversify

Balancing Risk and Return with Asset Allocation

An Overview of Portfolio Diversification Tools

Whether you invest in Fabergé eggs, stocks, bonds, or mutual funds, the maxim *don't put all your eggs in one basket* holds true (and is even more apt for Fabergé's products). If you could accurately predict the future, you would pick the investment that delivers the highest return, sell it when it reaches its peak, and then buy the next big winner. Foretelling the future being what it is (impossible), owning only one investment is a good way to lose most, if not all of your money. You can't pick a winner 100 percent of the time even when you analyze potential investments meticulously.

By diversifying your investments, you can reduce the risk of financial loss. If you own one investment and the company goes under, your entire portfolio goes down the drain. Owning equal amounts of four stocks, your potential loss drops to 25 percent. But, suppose you allocated your portfolio dollars equally among 10 investments. If one of the companies goes under, the damage to your portfolio from that event is limited to 10 percent. Diversification can also reduce the volatility of your portfolio. Investments that exceed your expectations

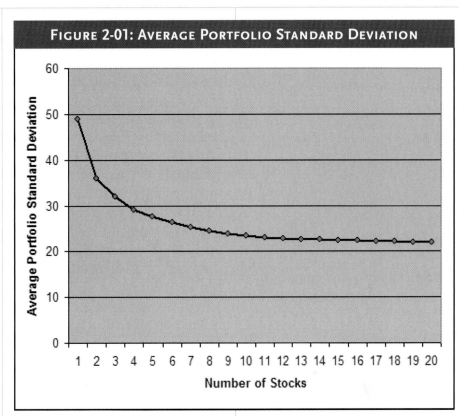

FIGURE 2-01: AVERAGE PORTFOLIO STANDARD DEVIATION

can make up for investments with disappointing performance, smoothing out your overall portfolio's performance.

The Roots of the Rule of Five

As an NAIC investor, you are probably familiar with the Rule of Five, which says that for every five stocks you purchase (quality growth companies at good prices, of course), one will do better than you expect, one will do worse, and the remaining three will deliver about what you expect. The Rule of Five suggests that you

should invest in multiple investments, because, despite your most astute stock analysis, stocks don't always do what you expect them to. By purchasing several stocks, you can limit the damage from an unanticipated corporate crisis in one of your investments. But the Rule of Five doesn't mean you invest in only five stocks for your portfolio. Diversifying your portfolio into different industries and stocks smoothes out the variability of individual stock returns.

Diversifying a Portfolio of Stocks

Many factors affect the stock market and predicting where the damage or exceptional performance will occur next is impossible. Instead of making yourself crazy trying to spot these threats and opportunities, you can diversify your stocks to limit your exposure to downdrafts while still catching the upswings. Regardless of what you invest in, you should diversify your holdings in several ways: by sectors and industries, by companies of varying size, by geographic regions, and by distributing your investments among ten or more individual stocks.

Keeping Individual Positions in Balance

Successful companies often continue to perform well for many years, so you don't want to rush to sell them. Even if you purchase equal dollar amounts of each stock in your portfolio, big winners can gradually assume an overwhelming proportion of your portfolio. When that happens, your portfolio is at risk if something bad happens to that company. So, how do you resolve these conflicting requirements?

Specify a maximum percentage that any one stock can represent in your portfolio. For instance, if your portfolio contains ten stocks, your target

percentage could be ten percent for each stock to equally distribute your holdings. Then, you might limit the maximum for one stock to 15 to 20 percent. When a stock reaches the maximum, sell enough of its shares to bring it back to your target percentage and use the proceeds to buy a new stock or add to another stock in your portfolio with greater upside potential. As you adjust your holdings, always aim to improve both quality and potential return of your overall portfolio. For those flush with funds, another alternative is to add money to your portfolio and invest in the other stocks in the portfolio, which reduces the percentage of the over-weighted stock. The stock portfolio in Figure 2-02 strives to meet these guidelines, but falls shorts in a few cases.

FactSet Research Systems exceeds the 20 percent limit, whereas the 1.7 percent holding in Bed Bath & Beyond hardly seems worth it.

Success Tip!

Very small holdings don't run the risk of decreasing your portfolio return when they drop in value. In reality, they won't make much of a difference to your portfolio whether they do well or poorly. The problem with small holdings is that studying and tracking these stocks takes time away from more influential stocks in your portfolio.

Sectors and Industries

If you navigate to many of the most popular investing Web sites, you know that the definitions for sector and industry vary. In this book,

FIGURE 2-02: A SAMPLE PORTFOLIO OF STOCKS

diversification.xls

Name	Ticker	Shares Held	Current Price ($)	Market Value ($)	Stock Sector	Stock Industry/ Fund	Market Cap (mil$)	Total Return 5 Year (%)	% of Portfolio
Bed Bath & Beyond	BBBY	50	37.02	1,851.00	Consumer Services	Furniture Retail	10,834.32	13.35	1.7%
Cheesecake Factory	CAKE	300	43.29	12,987.00	Consumer Services	Restaurants	2,183.36	28.64	11.7%
Chico's FAS	CHS	300	43.04	12,912.00	Consumer Services	Clothing Stores	3,726.96	71.6	11.6%
FactSet Research	FDS	600	41.41	24,846.00	Business Services	Business Support	1,378.68	11.31	22.3%
Harley-Davidson	HDI	200	56.67	11,334.00	Consumer Goods	Recreation	17,029.31	14.23	10.2%
Medtronic	MDT	100	50.76	5,076.00	Healthcare	Medical Equip.	61,094.99	8.12	4.6%
Microsoft	MSFT	300	26.44	7,932.00	Software	Business Appl.	284,074.37	-7.83	7.1%
Pfizer	PFE	200	36.82	7,364.00	Healthcare	Drugs	279,391.15	0.4	6.6%
PolyMedica	PLMD	350	27.927	9,774.45	Healthcare	Drugs	720.70	43.99	8.8%
Synovus Financial	SNV	700	24.8	17,360.00	Financial Services	Regional Banks	7,437.46	5.08	

a sector represents a broad category of business, such as health care or finance. An industry is a segment within a sector. For example, drugs, medical equipment, and hospitals are all industries within healthcare. Industries and sectors react differently to the economy and interest rates, cycle through peaks and valleys at different times, and carry varying combinations of risk and return.

Sectors and industries fall in and out of favor, such as the way tech stocks went from darlings in the late 90s to dogs in the early 2000s. Government regulations can topple a sector as the threat of health care reform did in 1991. Some industries (such as autos) might languish when the economy is in the trough of a cycle, whereas others (such as grocery stores) stay the course because people have to eat.

By selecting stocks from a number of industries and sectors, you reduce the chance of unexpected events taking a big bite out of your portfolio. Combining investments from these segments often results in more consistent returns through up and down markets. For example, when tech stocks soared in the mid- to late- 90s, some investors held onto their tech stocks even though the sector percentage ballooned in their portfolios. When tech stocks tanked in 2000,

these portfolios got clobbered. Portfolios that were diversified evenly among several sectors felt a little pain, but in many cases still achieved a positive return.

Success Tip!

Experienced investors use relatively flexible guidelines for sector percentages. A red flag for sector representation might be values more than 20 to 30 percent.

Approximately ten industries from four to eight sectors is a good diversification target. Of course, a young club won't have ten stocks at first, but it can continually increase its diversification by studying different industries and sectors for each new stock purchase. For example, Figure 2-03 shows a portfolio's allocation over six sectors and ten industries. (This portfolio isn't perfect. As you'll learn in more detail as you read this book,

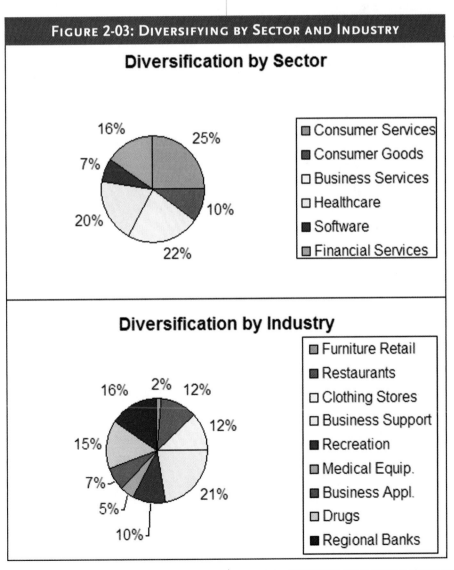

FIGURE 2-03: DIVERSIFYING BY SECTOR AND INDUSTRY

Diversification by Sector

16% 25%
7%
10%
20%
22%

- Consumer Services
- Consumer Goods
- Business Services
- Healthcare
- Software
- Financial Services

Diversification by Industry

16% 2% 12%
12%
15%
7%
5%
21%
10%

- Furniture Retail
- Restaurants
- Clothing Stores
- Business Support
- Recreation
- Medical Equip.
- Business Appl.
- Drugs
- Regional Banks

some of these allocations are too small to make a meaningful difference in portfolio performance.) An individual investor might never own ten stocks if he doesn't have the time to follow that many companies. But stocks that represent different size companies and five different sectors may provide reasonable levels of diversification.

Searching Sectors for Growth

Growth stocks pop up in numerous sectors and industries, although growth characteristics vary based on the nature of the business. Consider the following sectors as a starting point when you're looking for ways to diversify your portfolio, but remember that many other sectors offer opportunities for growth.

The **healthcare** sector is a prime candidate for growth with the aging of the baby boomer generation in the U.S. Strong investment in research and development as well as successful track records bringing new and improved products to market are critical elements for success in these typically high-tech companies. The healthcare sector comprises numerous industries from high-fliers like biotechnology to cost-conscious generic drug manufacturers.

The **financial** sector includes industries such as banking, insurance, and brokerage, although mergers and acquisitions in this sector have blurred the boundaries. Many companies in these industries are sensitive to interest rates; earnings generally drop as interest rates rise and vice versa. Banks and insurance companies must set aside money for potential losses. Banks must be ready to handle loans that are not repaid, whereas insurance companies require money to pay claims. Companies estimate the potential losses from past experience and create reserves out of current earnings. There's no way to know whether the reserves are sufficient until a loss occurs. But the stock price will drop if reserves turn out to be inadequate.

The **clothing** industry isn't high-tech, but it is a high-risk, high-return arena. When products sell well in the retail market, the results can be quite lucrative. But, consumer tastes in fashion are fickle and short-lived, so clothing companies struggle with keeping clothes in stock as well as liquidating unpopular inventory at bargain basement prices.

Retail stores and **restaurant chains** can grow by building more units or by selling more at each store (called same store sales). Look for growth in same store sales, because building

additional capital. Funds from operations rather than the conventional method of after-tax earnings are the data investors typically analyze for REITs. Look for REITs that keep their construction projects on time and within budget, and maintain high occupancy levels in existing buildings.

Success Tip!

As a member in an investment club, keep your treasurer's sanity in mind. Tracking REITs is one of the more challenging aspects of club accounting.

Diversifying by Company Size

Companies of different sizes can help balance the risk and return of a stock portfolio. Just as draft horses can move at a slow but steady pace from dawn to dusk, large blue chip companies typically deliver slow but dependable growth, often for decades. Small-cap companies can be more like race horses: fast for a short distance with risks of a broken leg or other maladies at every turn. Blue chips usually grow too slowly to increase a portfolio 15 percent a year on their own. (For this reason, many experienced investors wait for blue chips to go on sale. By purchasing blue chips when prices and PEs are lower, the stock returns get a boost as the

new stores or restaurants requires a lot of capital, and raising prices eventually prices the store out of the market.

The **information technology** sector went sky-high through the 1990s when people paid exorbitant share prices for companies with no earnings. Then tech stocks crashed in 2000 as people came to their senses. Investors are still cautious about investing in this sector, but this segment of the market still includes some companies that deliver NAIC-style quality growth.

Real estate investment trusts (REITs) own income producing real estate such as office buildings and shopping malls.

An equity REIT is an easy way to invest in real estate, without a lot of money or the headaches of property management. Although equity REITs are adversely affected by increasing interest rates, mortgage REITs are even worse. They make money on the spread between rates paid to borrow money and interest rates earned from mortgages, which can create problems when increasing interest rates pinch the spread. REITs often pay out at least 90 percent of their earnings, making them good candidates for income investments. However, because they pay out so much in earnings, they also often borrow money or sell more shares of stock to raise

(or even no-caps). The NAIC guideline for company size is that large companies are those with sales greater than $5 billion; small companies have sales less than $500 million; and medium companies are somewhere in between.

Large-cap stocks represent high quality blue chip companies with annual sales of at least $5 billion and earnings growth usually between 5 to 7 percent a year. When companies such as these also pay significant dividends, the payouts provide additional return and may support the stock price during a bear market.

Demanding high quality and excellent management is critical when purchasing slower growing blue chip companies. Look for dependable growth as well as signs that management can continue the company's growth in the future. Otherwise, you might be buying no more than a bloated and aging also-ran.

Small companies are more agile, but also more risky. Small companies can maneuver in many ways to grow their sales and earnings rapidly, but might not have the resources to recover from problems or fight off competition. If a small company has only one product and it fails, the company is likely to follow suit. Investors expect growth of at least 15 percent a year to offset the added risk of investing in small companies. Medium-sized companies are the compromise. They can grow faster than large companies, but aren't as risky as small companies. Investors typically expect earnings growth from 8 to 15 percent.

PEs expand to their typical levels. Small companies can deliver growth, but a portfolio comprised only of small companies jacks up the portfolio risk to unacceptable levels.

Annual sales, or assets, are a better gauge of company size than capitalization. For example, in the late '90s, some "dot com" companies appeared to be large- or medium-capitalization stocks, but quickly became small-caps

WHEN SMALL COMPANIES ACT LIKE GIANTS

Sometimes, companies don't act as you would expect based on their market-cap or annual revenues. For example, if a small company commands the lion's share of a small and stable market, its growth rate might be more like that of a large company. Conversely, large companies can grow rather quickly when they expand into major new markets.

NAIC suggests diversifying into 25 percent large-cap stocks for stability and moderate growth, 50 percent in mid-cap stocks for a good mix of risk and return, and 25 percent in small-cap stocks to boost return. Diversification by size can be tough. Good small companies are difficult to find and can be tricky to analyze. Then, if they are successful, they become mid-size or even large companies. Fortunately, diversification by size is the least important diversification target. Many mid-size and large companies provide sufficient growth to reach your portfolio return target.

Depending on your tolerance for risk, you can adjust the percentages to increase or decrease the overall risk and potential return for your portfolio.

Attaining Geographic Diversification

With Russian teenagers wearing Levi's and McDonald's opening in Japan, you might question the importance of diversification beyond U.S. borders. Many experts still recommend that you further diversify your portfolio with international investments. Investing in individual, foreign stocks is quite difficult in practice. Consider the effort you expend obtaining dependable information about U.S. companies. Compound

that with the risks of currency exchange rates and political uncertainty and you can see that evaluating foreign companies is a challenge.

One way to simplify foreign diversification is to invest in U.S. companies that generate significant business in foreign countries. These companies provide the diversification you seek, manage currency risk for you as part of doing business, and yet report financials as required by the SEC. Read a company's annual report to determine how much of its business comes from overseas.

Mutual funds are another method for adding foreign investments to your portfolio.

Mutual fund managers do the legwork for evaluating foreign companies as investments and also implement strategies to mitigate currency risk. Because of the costs of investing overseas, fund expenses for international funds tend to be higher than the average stock fund.

Success Tip!

International mutual funds come in several flavors, so categories are important for mutual funds that invest overseas. According to Morningstar, a foreign mutual fund invests no more than 20 percent in U.S. stocks. World funds are international funds

Many people own mutual funds through their 401(k) or 403(b) plans and many more own them for the convenience. Mutual funds offer instant diversification because they usually hold hundreds of individual investments. Depending on the fund objective, a mutual fund might diversify by company size, sector and industry, geographic region, and asset classes. Each share of a mutual fund represents a small piece of every investment in the fund, so you obtain diversification whether you invest $10 or $10,000.

fees nonetheless. By choosing well-managed mutual funds and then adding stocks in well-managed companies, you can diversify from the beginning and eventually achieve the market-beating performance of a portfolio of quality individual stocks.

With over 14,000 mutual funds to choose from, you can diversify with mutual funds in many ways. For example, some asset allocation mutual funds invest in fixed percentages of stocks and bonds to provide a combination of growth and income. Total stock market funds attempt to reproduce the performance of the entire stock market. If you want to choose the percentages in your portfolio, select a combination of mutual funds that focus on segments of the market: large-cap, mid-cap, and small-cap stocks, international stocks, domestic bonds, and others.

The SEC requires funds whose names suggest a concentration in a particular type of investment, Bogle Small Cap Growth, for instance, to invest at least 80 percent of their assets in those investments. Make sure that the other 20 percent isn't too aggressive or tame for your liking.

Although some mutual funds charge exorbitant fees, low-cost mutual funds are convenient and can be cost effective. Investing $1000 in three stocks would cost $21 through one of the lowest discount

that invest more than 20 percent in U.S. stocks. A regional fund such as a European fund invests at least 75 percent of its assets in Europe.

Using Mutual Funds to Diversify

If there are any hard-core NAICers out there who don't own a single mutual fund, raise your hands. OK, the two of you can skip this section.

![Success Tip!]

Investors just starting out often lack the funds to purchase enough individual stocks to diversify their portfolios. Mutual funds are one way to diversify when you have only a few dollars to invest. However, mutual funds charge fees that put a damper on their performance; there are plenty of funds that underperform the market, but charge exorbitant

brokers. Using a dividend reinvestment program is inexpensive, but buying, selling, and keeping track of your shares might require more time than you want to spend. Investing $1,000 in a low-cost index fund such as the Vanguard 500 Index fund (VFINX) with a .2% expense ratio would cost $2 the first year. (The minimum investment in this fund is $1,000 for a Vanguard IRA account; otherwise, you need $3,000 to get started.)

Balancing Risk and Return with Asset Allocation

Risk is a personal issue. Some people like skydiving and bungee jumping while others prefer a quiet evening with a good book and a cup of tea. Regardless how long it is until you need your money, it's important to match your portfolio risk to your personal taste. After all, you want to be able to sleep at night while your money is hard at work.

Stocks have delivered long-term average annual returns three times that of inflation or Treasury bills, so they are ideal investments for long-term goals. When you have financial goals that are closer at hand, a total stock portfolio may not be the answer. Remember, longer time frames provide the luxury of higher-risk, higher-return investing. Higher average annual returns over long periods often represent volatile segues between great gains and alarming losses in the short term. You need time to recover from bad news or the bottom of an economic cycle. Imagine how frustrating it would be to reach 99 percent of your target only to see your portfolio fall to 80 percent right before you want to withdraw your money.

Different types of investments, also called asset classes, present different types of risk and provide different average returns. For example, traditional bonds are extremely interest rate sensitive and provide moderate total returns. You can take advantage of these differences to build a portfolio that provides acceptable levels of both return and risk for your needs. Using asset allocation, you identify a target percentage for each asset class based on the risk and return you want. As time passes and some asset classes do better while others do worse, you move money between the asset classes to

HOW MUCH IS TOO MUCH?

Moderation is as good for diversification as it is for so many other activities. Performance for an over-diversified portfolio is unlikely to match, let alone exceed, that of a stock market index. Too much diversification is more common in mutual fund portfolios, but some investors have never met a stock they didn't like, which can lead to dozens of holdings in every conceivable industry. This distribution across numerous industries and stocks gradually transforms your focused portfolio into a shadow of the broad market. In addition to requiring more of your time to manage all these investments, you will probably pay more than you need to in brokerage commissions and mutual fund expenses.

Compare measures such as the percentages by sector and company size, the average PE ratio, and average annual total return for your portfolio and an index such as the S&P 500. Excessive similarity in sector and size weightings could be a red flag that your portfolio follows the index too closely. If your portfolio is tracking an index, but its returns are below the average total return for the index, you have two potential choices. Either spend some time weeding out your stocks and funds to build a better portfolio or move your money into a low-cost index fund.

maintain your asset allocation percentages (see Chapter 6).

Suppose you have a portfolio worth $500,000 and you want 80 percent in stocks and 20 percent in bonds. After some time, your stocks grow to $600,000 while your bonds increase to $120,000. Your new asset allocation is 83 percent stocks and 17 percent bonds. To bring your portfolio back to your 80–20 target, you would sell $24,000 worth of stock and use it to buy bonds.

You might run across other techniques calling themselves asset allocation. For instance, some fund companies offer asset allocation mutual funds that adjust the percentage of money in stocks, bonds, and cash, but they change the percentages based on the types of investments they think will perform better in the future. This is simply a form of market timing, which is ill-advised under any circumstance.

In the 1980s, stocks averaged a 17.6 percent annual return. Missing the best 40 days during those 10 years reduced the average annual return to less than 4 percent. Unless you can be right all the time, market timing is a loser's game. And, as Jane Bryant Quinn said, "The Forecaster's Hall of Fame is an empty room."

Choosing an Asset Allocation Plan

If you start investing early, the powerful combination of time and compounding growth can turn a modest stock portfolio into a nest egg you can live on without any need for asset allocation. As your stocks' earnings increase, so do the stock prices and the cash dividends you receive. Reinvesting those dividends grows the portfolio even more. Then, when it's time to retire, your portfolio might be large enough that you're comfortable keeping it in stocks. The dividends from your portfolio can pay for a significant part of your living expenses. The key is starting early.

For those of you who didn't start early, asset allocation is a compromise between growing your portfolio and protecting it. The problem with asset allocation is that the experts disagree. Some financial advisors recommend subtracting your age from 100 to determine the appropriate percentage of stocks in your portfolio. At 20 years of age, you would invest 80 percent of your money in stocks. When you're 90, you would have only 10 percent in stocks.

Other experts recommend different allotments. For example, *Quicken*, the personal finance software application, includes portfolio models developed by TeamVest, a

financial information provider. When you select a level of risk and return, the application shows the allocation that should provide that return with the lowest level of risk. For example, a medium-risk portfolio with a 9 percent return target comprises 31 percent large-cap stocks, 12 percent small-cap stocks, 19 percent international stocks, and 38 percent bonds. But, you might have trouble connecting these recommendations to the reality of your situation. How much risk can you tolerate? How does a level of risk translate into danger for your portfolio and your financial goals? What return do you require?

If you are sold on the long-term outlook for investing in growth stocks, consider another approach to asset allocation. Place enough money in lower-risk lower-return investments to meet your financial requirements for the typical time it takes stocks to recover from temporary setbacks. For example, when you're 30 and you're reasonably tolerant of risk, invest all of your retirement money in stocks. (Remember, you can reduce the risks of owning stocks by diversifying your stock portfolio in various ways and by choosing the stocks you purchase carefully.) When you're 65, invest enough of your portfolio in bonds to cover

10 years worth of expenses. This approach keeps most of your portfolio growing for the future and fighting inflation, while providing some protection from the short-term volatility of stocks. To take into account different tolerances for risk, you can adjust the years you estimate for stocks to recover. To be more conservative in your asset allocation plan, estimate a longer recovery period. Chapter 3 digs into the details of planning for a specific financial goal.

Understanding Different Types of Investments

NAIC focuses on investing in stocks to build a portfolio. However, if you combine different asset classes in your portfolio, it's helpful to understand the contributions that each asset class provides.

Stocks and stock funds can deliver higher returns that accelerate the growth of your portfolio, not only fighting inflation but helping you obtain the money you require.

Invest in stocks for the long haul (no less than five years) to reduce the damage of short-term drops. Careful selection of a diversified portfolio of individual stocks can do a lot to reduce the risk you assume with stocks. Quality stock funds offer diversification for any size portfolio and professional management. Stocks are the only asset class whose long-term average returns

Traditional bonds pay interest that you can use as current income. Bonds offer mid-range returns to provide a few percentage points of return over inflation and they can provide capital gains if interest rates drop. Diversify to reduce the impact of a default. If interest rates increase and your bond prices drop, simply hold the bonds to maturity to receive the coupon rate offered when the bond was issued. Keep in mind that interest income and dividend income are taxed differently.

Bond funds are good for diversification, investing small contributions, and reinvesting dividends. However, bond funds are subject to more interest rate risk than individual bonds because you can't choose to hold the bonds in the fund portfolio when interest rates increase.

exceed the rate of inflation by several percentage points

Zero coupon bonds pay your principal and earned interest at a specific time in the future. You can buy zero coupon bonds that mature when you need the money. Zero coupon bonds offer mid-range returns to combat inflation and provide a bit of growth. Diversification helps reduce the risk of default (equity risk).

CDs offer low risk and low returns. Use CDs only to earn some interest on money you will need in the next six months to two years. Do not put money into CDs that you might need before the CD matures, because withdrawal fees are steep. The rates on CDs, particularly short-term CDs, often fall below the rate of inflation, so these investments do not help your portfolio grow for the long-term.

Savings and money market accounts also offer low risk and low returns, but provide more flexibility for withdrawals. Use these accounts to earn some interest on money you will need in the next six months and as a storehouse for the cash you set aside for emergencies.

An Overview of Portfolio Diversification Tools

You can choose portfolio tools based on the level of assistance you want planning and tracking your portfolio. Some of the tools that are available are quite sophisticated, which is both good and bad. Using a software program or Web site to perform your investment calculations saves you time—time that you can spend making important portfolio decisions that no computer can handle properly. For example, in a few seconds, a computer can crank out hundreds of calculations that would take you hours with a hand calculator. But, the computer can't evaluate a company's annual report to determine whether future prospects look rosy. On the other hand, too many bells and whistles might distract you from the task at hand. For example, fine-tuning your diversification percentages to within a tenth of a percent is a waste of time and would cost more in commissions than you're likely to gain in portfolio returns.

Portfolio Diversification with NAIC Software

When you purchase NAIC stock analysis software such as *Investor's Toolkit Pro* or *Stock Analyst,* you receive a few features for checking portfolio diversification (see Chapter 10). The Portfolio Trend Report shows the percentage that stock represents in a portfolio. At the bottom of this report, you can see the percentages you own in small, medium, and large companies. In addition, *Investor's Toolkit 5* includes great portfolio management tools that you'll learn about in Chapter 10.

None of the standard reports indicate diversification by sector and industry, or by geographic region. In addition, these tools show only diversification for stock holdings, so you can't evaluate

your overall portfolio if you invest in both stocks and mutual funds.

Success Tip!

NAIC Stock Analyst *includes some diversification features. Another NAIC program,* Portfolio Record Keeper *provides numerous tools and views for analyzing diversification.*

Tools for Portfolio Diversification

Many online and software tools evaluate portfolio diversification by asset classes and company size. For example, *Quicken* software includes an Asset Allocation Guide, which evaluates your portfolio using large-cap stocks, small-cap stocks, international stocks, bonds, and cash for asset classes. Online allocation tools do much the same, for example *Smart Money's* One Asset Allocation System *(http:// www.smartmoney.com/tools).*

Success Tip!

Before you decide to ask a Web site or personal finance application for portfolio advice, remember that your requirements are unique while the advice you receive is generic. Evaluate the recommendations you receive and modify them to fit your needs.

FIGURE 2-04: A SAMPLE PORTFOLIO OF STOCKS

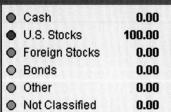

Cash	0.00
U.S. Stocks	100.00
Foreign Stocks	0.00
Bonds	0.00
Other	0.00
Not Classified	0.00

Portfolio Composition

- 50-100 (%)
- 25-50 (%)
- 10-25 (%)
- 0-10 (%)

Not Classified   0%

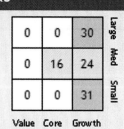

Size	Value	Core	Growth
Large	0	0	30
Med	0	16	24
Small	0	0	31

Valuation

Stock Sector | ⊞ Holding details

	Portfolio (% of Stocks)	S&P 500 (%)
Information	7.07	23.73
Software	7.07	4.67
Hardware	0.00	11.46
Media	0.00	4.15
Telecommunications	0.00	3.45
Service	82.78	46.48
Healthcare	19.97	13.17
Consumer Services	25.22	8.73
Business Services	22.07	3.87
Financial Services	15.52	20.71
Manufacturing	10.14	29.79
Consumer Goods	10.14	9.42
Industrial Materials	0.00	11.76
Energy	0.00	5.94
Utilities	0.00	2.67
Not Classified	0.00	0.00

Stock Type | ⊞ Holding details

	Portfolio (% of Domestic Stocks)	S&P 500 (%)
High Yield	0.00	13.26
Distressed	0.00	2.78
Hard Assets	0.00	6.52
Cyclical	10.14	10.95
Slow Growth	0.00	31.28
Classic Growth	67.62	26.97
Aggressive Growth	22.24	3.15
Speculative Growth	0.00	4.84
Not Classified	0.00	0.23

World Regions | ⊞ Holding details

- >50 (%)
- 10-50 (%)
- <=10 (%)

	Total Exposure (% of Stocks)
North America	100.0
UK/Western Europe	0.0
Japan	0.0
Latin America	0.0
Asia ex-Japan	0.0
Other	0.0
Not Classified	0.0

Fees & Expenses | ⊞ Holding details

Avg. mutual fund expense ratio (%)	---
Expense ratio of similarly weighted hypothetical portfolio (%)	---
Estimated mutual fund expenses ($)	0.00
Total sales charges paid ($)	0.00

ROBERT MANN

Robert Mann's investment club doesn't keep all their eggs in one basket. The club's diversification rules include no stock representing more than 20 percent of the portfolio or less than 5 percent. In addition, no industry represents more than 30 percent of the portfolio. According to Robert, "Breeding for desired traits may be good for food; it's not good for portfolios. Diversify."

Morningstar's Portfolio X-Ray tool is unique in the thoroughness of its evaluation of portfolio diversification. Portfolio X-Ray, shown in Figure 2-4, provides an analysis of asset allocation like other tools, but it also shows the composition of your portfolio by sector and industry, stock type (for example, classic growth, aggressive growth, or cyclical), company size, investment style (value, core, and growth), and geographic region. For investors who use both stocks and funds, Portfolio X-Ray analyzes the diversification of your entire portfolio. It evaluates the stocks and bonds held by the mutual funds in your portfolio and categorizes them within each type of diversification.

The free version of Portfolio X-Ray is called Instant X-Ray and requires that you enter the ticker symbols and number of shares for each holding every time you view an X-Ray. Repeating data entry when you want to experiment with what-if scenarios isn't productive use of your portfolio management time. By subscribing to

Morningstar's Premium Services, you can run a Portfolio X-Ray on a saved portfolio.

- To access Instant X-Ray, on the Morningstar.com Portfolio page *(http://portfolio.morningstar.com)*, choose Instant X-Ray from the Portfolio Manager drop-down list. Follow the instructions to enter your portfolio information.

- To use Portfolio X-Ray, choose one of your saved portfolios on the Morningstar.com Portfolio page. Click X-Ray this Portfolio in the toolbar immediately above the portfolio table.

If you're handy with a spreadsheet, you can build your own diversification tool. You must download or type the sector, industry, the annual revenues, the current price, and the number of shares you own.

Planning: The Path to Reaching Financial Goals

Success and Sleep

Whether you have big plans for your life or a few modest aspirations, some goals carry big price tags. Sure, you could get lucky and finance your goals with lottery winnings, but you shouldn't count on that. Without good financial planning and management, you're likely to play catch-up, saving until it hurts, taking more risk to chase higher returns, and ultimately laying awake at night worrying whether you will succeed. By planning ahead and keeping your eye on the ball (house, college, retirement, or other objective), you can grow a nest egg for the future without sacrificing fun for today.

Making the Most of Your Life *and* Your Money

Getting Started with Financial Planning

Saving for a Goal

What to Do if Things Go Wrong

Making the Most of Your Life *and* Your Money

Do you know what your goals in life are? If you answered yes, you are already on your way to success. You can't expect to achieve goals if you don't even know what they are.

Have you written your goals down and do you scan them frequently? This might seem silly, but committing your goals to paper makes those goals more tangible. Reviewing your goals regularly focuses your mind on them. Your subconscious will work on achieving those goals whether you're aware of it or not.

Have you developed a plan for achieving your goals? In most cases, you need knowledge, be it reading, writing, 'rithmetic, business finance, or mountaineering techniques. Achieving goals usually requires some effort. Identify the steps you must take. Document your steps; a simple checklist is usually enough.

With a goal firmly in mind, the second step for success is funding. Big ideas often come with big prices. Your plan should include a finance section that outlines how you plan to pay for your goals. No, borrowing money from your

relatives is rarely the correct option. As you will learn, an early start paves the way to obtaining the money you need.

Unfortunately, things don't always run according to plan. In fact, events rarely follow your plan. Eisenhower once said, "In preparing for battle I have always found that plans are useless, but planning is indispensable." If plans are useless, why prepare them? Because you need a road map to know when you have gone off course.

When you prepare a financial plan, you identify the goals you want to achieve, how much they cost, when you will need the money, and your ability to stomach risk as you implement your plan. Change is inevitable. Events occur that can change your objectives (you're appointed diplomat to Burundi and don't need to buy a house), your view of risk (you and your spouse become the proud parents of triplets), and time frame (your triplets turn out to be over-achievers and

plan to start college at 15 years of age). As long as you have a plan in place, you can calmly reappraise the situation and adjust your financial plan accordingly. Without an existing plan, you're likely to overreact, which can lead to disastrous results.

Getting Started with Financial Planning

If you have avoided planning your finances because you're afraid it's too complicated, fear not. To start planning for a financial goal, you need answers to only three questions: what, when, and how much. But, let's face it. Regardless of the type of goal,

planning amounts to a guessing game, because you don't know what the future holds. Planning is easy enough as long as you can accept that uncertainty.

What do you want to achieve?

Money doesn't influence your decisions for some goals, although such goals are more rare than you might think. For example, you might decide to stop working on the weekends. But, if that decision could threaten your employment, money has an impact. On the other hand, if you think money has something to do with being a better person, your problems lie elsewhere. Of

course, the therapist who helps you sort this out charges for her assistance.

When you're paying off college loans, the goal is simple. Continue writing those monthly checks until you receive the paperwork that says the loan is paid off. Buying an item such as a car, house, or boat, has clear financial connections. If you're fortunate, you can buy the item outright. If you're like most people, you put some of your money down and borrow the rest. The goal in this case is scraping together the necessary down payment and making sure that you can afford the loan payments.

For goals such as starting a business, sending your children to college, retiring early, or taking a sabbatical to sail around the world, defining your goal might be more complicated. For example, college educations can range between a few thousand dollars a year to $50,000 a year depending on the type and quality of the school. Retiring early requires that you think about of how early you want to retire and the lifestyle you want to lead. In these examples, the "what" is tightly coupled with the when and how much.

When do you want to achieve it?

Timeframes can measure in months, years, and even

decades. Saving money to buy a birthday present might take only a few months, unless the birthday boy or girl is incredibly fortunate. Investing money to pay for your next car might require four or five years. College education and retirement fall into the decades category.

The investment timeframe is a biggie—it determines the level of risk you can afford, which influences the types of investments or asset allocation you should consider, which in turn establishes a typical annual return you might expect from your investments. Of course, the longer the timeframe, the more your investments benefit from the power of compounding.

You can nail down some timeframes. For example, investing for your newborn's college education is likely to be a 22-year endeavor (18 years to college and four years during college.) For less specific timeframes, a rough guess is sufficient for the first pass. You can fine-tune the plan later. You must revisit your plan every so often (see Chapter 6) to adjust for returns that don't match your estimates, changes in timeframes, or other variances. As you get older, your job becomes even easier as the "when" gradually compresses to "now."

Success Tip!

To be conservative, use slightly shorter estimates for timeframes. A few less months or years won't change your risk level or investment allocations, but shorter timeframes will require slightly higher monthly contributions.

How much is it going to cost?

The cost of many financial goals is another exercise in estimation. For goals many years in the future, inflation increases the future costs of those goals, but even the inflation rate is an estimate. The rate of inflation changes all the time from the double-digit inflation nightmare in the early 1980s to recent rates less than two percent per year. One approach to estimating inflation is to use the long-term average annual rate of inflation, which is 3 percent. However, if you think that inflation will be higher or lower on average during your investment timeframe, you can choose

another value for inflation in your calculations.

Unfortunately, some items increase more than the inflation rate. College tuition, for example, often increases twice as fast as inflation. Recent average tuition increases have been 5 percent, but ran as high as 9 percent during the 1980s and early 1990s. To complicate the matter, tuition increases at

If you're thinking about purchasing a house in the future, contact a real estate agent in the area you're interested in to find out how much houses cost and how much they increase or decrease each year. For college tuition, read articles about the cost of college or use cost calculators from Web sites such as the College Board (*http:// apps.collegeboard. com/fincalc/ college_cost.jsp*) and SavingforCollege.com (*http://www.savingforcollege .com/college_planning_ resources/calculators*). The Internet provides numerous resources for estimating prices and identifying typical price increases for college educations, houses, and even expenses during retirement.

Saving for a Goal

Contributing some money each month to a savings or investment account is a relatively painless way to save for a goal. Automatic paycheck deduction plans, in which a contribution is subtracted from your paycheck, are truly magical. Psychologically, you don't realize you earn more money, so you adjust your habits to the net amount of your paycheck. Most companies offer automatic deductions for 401(k) retirement contributions and many companies also offer plans for transferring money automatically into a savings account. Mutual funds and brokerages are usually happy to set up automatic contribution plans, which transfer to an investment account the amount you specify on the schedule you request.

Calculating a Monthly Contribution

To set up a savings plan with one of these services, you need to know how much you must save on a regular schedule. You don't have to work this out with pencil and paper. *Microsoft Excel, Quicken, Microsoft Money,* financial calculators, and hundreds of Web sites offer tools that perform the calculations for you. But, to ensure that you use the tools correctly, it's always a good idea to understand the concepts behind the calculations. To calculate the monthly contribution, often called the payment, you need only a few bits of information:

different rates depending on the type of college you're considering. Tuition at community colleges and four-year public universities has risen recently at an average of approximately 14 percent a year. At that rate, by the time your child is 18, college would cost ten times as much as it did when she was born.

Before you specify the amount you need, do your homework.

- Future value—The amount of money you need at a time in the future. For an investment plan, the future value is usually shown as a positive number, because it represents the money you receive at the end of your plan.

- Periods—The number of months or years until that time in the future.

- Present value—The amount of money, if any, that you plan to contribute at the start. The present value is usually shown as a negative number, because it represents money coming out of your pocket into the investment plan.

- Return—The return you expect to achieve with your investments for each period. If you contribute money each month, approximate the monthly return by dividing the annual return you expect by 12.

Table 3-01 lists some tools that calculate the monthly contribution for you.

Saving for Retirement

Determining your nest egg needs for retirement is another story. Unlike a goal in which you need a pile of cash at a specific time, retirement represents years of withdrawals from your savings and investments. You might

FIGURE 3-01: TOOLS THAT CALCULATE A MONTHLY CONTRIBUTION

Quicken personal finance software	Choose Planning|Financial Calculators|Savings to open the Investment Savings Calculator. The Opening Savings Balance input is the equivalent of the present value. The Ending Savings Balance is the future value, which you can specify in today's dollars or future dollars. You must specify an annual yield, which is the annual return you expect. Choose Weeks, Months, Quarters, or Years as the frequency of your contribution. Specify the number of periods until your goal (such as 120 if you plan to contribute monthly for ten years.) Choose the Regular Contribution option to calculate the money you must contribute. This calculator can take inflation into account and show the result in future dollars.
Excel	Insert the PMT function into a spreadsheet cell with the following parameters: = PMT(rate,nper,pv,fv,type) Rate equals the return per period. Nper is the number of periods you plan to contribute. Pv and fv are the parameters for present value and future value. For a savings plan, enter 1 for the type parameter, which indicates that the contribution occurs at the beginning of the period. For example, to reach $125,000 with a monthly contribution for eight years, an annual return of 9 percent, and an initial investment of $10,000, the formula is: = PMT(.09/12,96,-10000,125000,1) = -$741.71 contribution per month
The Motley Fool Web site	Navigate to *http://www.fool.com/calcs/calculators.htm* and click the "What will it take to save for a vehicle, home, etc.?" link. The Amount you need to input is the future value. The Amount you have invested is the present value. Omit the Amount you can save monthly to calculate that value. Specify the number of months you plan to contribute. Your savings rate is the annual return you expect. This calculator can take your income tax rates into account. This Web page also includes a link to calculate college savings.

continue to work part-time and earn some income for several years. Inflation continues to decrease your purchasing power so you'll need more money as the years pass. The remaining principal in your accounts continues to grow while you are retired.

For retirement planning, you must estimate a larger number of items:

- Current retirement savings

- Average annual return

- Annual contribution to tax-advantaged retirement accounts such as IRAs and 401(k)s

- Annual contribution to taxable retirement accounts

- Number of years until retirement (how long you have to save)

- Number of years of retirement (how long your savings must last)

- Retirement income (Social Security, pensions, part-time work)

- Inflation rate

- Tax rate before retirement

- Tax rate during retirement

- The annual income you want during retirement

- How much you want to leave behind

Clearly, estimating the regular contributions you need to fund retirement is a complicated calculation. Fortunately, many financial companies offer retirement calculators on their Web sites to entice you to invest with them. Table 3-02 lists some tools that perform calculations for you.

You can also rough out the retirement war chest you need with a few simple calculations. Suppose you invest your portfolio to achieve a target total return of 10 percent a year (that's return from capital gains, cash dividends, and interest.) Leaving 5 percent of each year's increase to offset inflation, you have an additional 5 percent to use for living expenses. To determine the value of the portfolio you need to provide the income you require, you must calculate the gap between your expected annual living expenses and other retirement income you receive:

Income from portfolio = Expected annual expenses – Social Security – Pension benefits – other income

For example, if you want $100,000 each year for retirement expenses and expect to receive $12,000 in Social Security, and $20,000 from a pension, your portfolio must provide $68,000 a year from a combination of capital gains, dividends, and interest. Because you plan to use only 5 percent of your portfolio, the value of the portfolio is calculated as follows:

URBAN RETIREMENT MYTHS

Many experts talk about your expenses being lower in retirement. Sure, you'll spend nothing for commuting or work clothing, but you might spend more having fun. In addition, the costs of health care continue to increase at a rapid pace and Medicare won't cover all the cost of your health care. You'll want a health insurance policy that helps pay for the things Medicare doesn't. You might want long-term care insurance if you want to protect your assets for your spouse or heirs. If you think the value of your house will be gravy for your retirement plan when you move into smaller (and you assume less expensive) digs, you're better off reserving those potential funds to help cover your health care. Considering real estate, rising real estate taxes often take a chunk out of retirees fixed budgets. And, the biggest myth of all—your children will take care of you. Well, they might, but you shouldn't count on it.

Portfolio value = Annual portfolio contribution / 5 percent

= $68,000 / 0.05 = 1,360,000

What To Do if Things Go Wrong

Because your financial plan is based on estimates and assumptions, things rarely turn out as you planned.

FIGURE 3-02: RETIREMENT PLANNERS WORTH EVALUATING	
Quicken personal finance software	For an easy but limited tool, choose Planning| Financial Calculators|Retirement to open the Retirement Calculator. This calculator doesn't consider income you might earn during retirement and other potential retirement situations. For a comprehensive planner, choose Planning|Retirement Planner.
Motley Fool Web site	Navigate to *http://www.fool.com/calcs/calculators.htm* and click the "Am I saving enough? What can I change?" link. This online calculator includes options for almost every conceivable retirement assumption such as your monthly expenses during early retirement, intermediate retirement years, and the remaining years. The calculator includes two one-time investments, such as the money from selling your house or receiving an inheritance from a relative.
MSN Money Web site	The MSN Money retirement planner *(http://money.msn.com/retire/planner.asp)* is a comprehensive tool. However, make sure you are comfortable with the privacy policy because it requires that you enter personal information.
Vanguard Group Web site	Vanguard is one of many financial companies that offers planning tools to attract new customers. Navigate to *http://flagship3.vanguard.com/web/ planret/PlanningAdvicePublicOverview.html* and click the Invest for Retirement link to walk through the steps of planning for retirement. This Web page also includes a "Rescue Your Retirement" link for people who are worried about whether they can afford retirement. The "Manage Your Retirement" link includes advice for managing your retirement assets after you have retired. Check your broker's site for a retirement planning tool.

For example, you don't save as much as you planned or your timeframe changes. If you review your progress regularly, say once a year, you can catch these variances early and adjust the plan to get back on track.

Short term stock returns aren't particularly dependable, which is why investors focus on average long-term returns for their stock investments. If your portfolio return falls short of your estimate one year, don't panic; another year's above estimate return will balance things out. However, if your portfolio returns are lagging behind your estimates for several years, start looking for ways to save more money. If your budget is totally tapped, you can try to push out the date. That might work for retirement, but your children might chafe at the idea of going to college when they're 30 years old. If you're thinking about the symbiotic risk-return relationship and considering increasing your risk to earn higher returns—don't.

For stymied savings or shorter timeframes, the only sensible option is to dig deeper to save more money. Surf to *http:// www.cheapskatemonthly.com* or search the Web with the keywords "frugal living" to find tips on relatively painless ways to cut corners.

Rounding Out Your Financial Plan

What, me worry?

Looking at the typical topics that a financial plan covers, you would think that people do nothing but worry about their money: how to get it, how to keep it, and how to keep it away from Uncle Sam. But, that's why a financial plan is so valuable.

By spending time up front on how you plan to make money and what to do if something goes wrong, you can spend most of your time doing something more fun than worrying about your money.

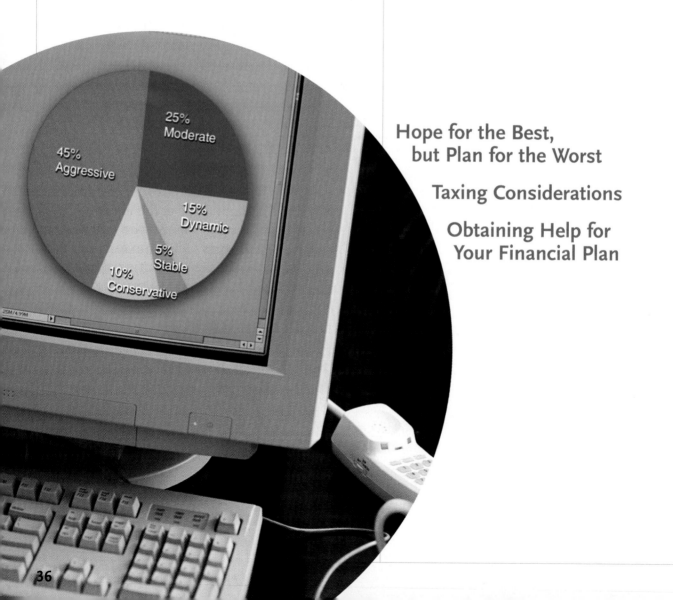

Hope for the Best,
but Plan for the Worst

Taxing Considerations

Obtaining Help for
Your Financial Plan

Hope for the Best, but Plan for the Worst

You have already learned that you must deal with risk when you plan your strategies for making money (see Chapter 1). It doesn't seem fair that you must do more work on your financial plan because of risk. Unfortunately, investments aren't the only risks that can affect your plans, so a well-rounded financial plan considers the most consequential obstacles that you might face.

You work hard to make money and you work hard to protect it. Although taxes pay for important services (as well as some silly ones), paying them doesn't help you reach your financial goals. Sad to say, taxes are complicated and don't appear likely to get easier in this millennium. In response, your financial plan should include tax planning so you don't lend Uncle Sam money for free or get unpleasant surprises come tax time.

How to Handle Financial Trouble

Disasters small and large—crashing your car, losing your job, getting sick, or getting sick enough that you can't work—

can affect your physical, mental, and financial health. A crisis is painful enough without adding financial woes to the mix. Seat belts and surgical masks can help safeguard your health, but how do you protect against the financial ramifications of catastrophe? Well, it's called insurance, one of the products you love to hate. When nothing goes wrong, insurance seems like a waste of money. But, just let that policy lapse and something bad is bound to

happen. Another facet of insurance is that it can be wretchedly complicated and that often means you pay more than you need to. Consider this a review of the insurance you should consider. To work out the details, look to one of the books, Web sites, or other planning resources listed at the end of this chapter.

Property insurance is essential to protect what, for many, is their largest investment—their homes. If you carry a mortgage on your house, the mortgage company

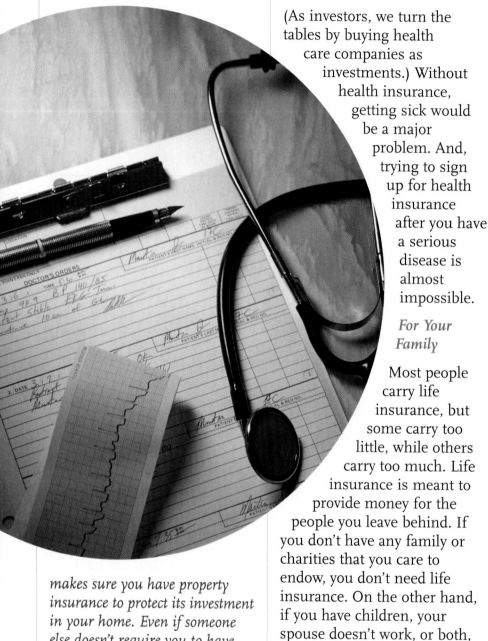

(As investors, we turn the tables by buying health care companies as investments.) Without health insurance, getting sick would be a major problem. And, trying to sign up for health insurance after you have a serious disease is almost impossible.

For Your Family

Most people carry life insurance, but some carry too little, while others carry too much. Life insurance is meant to provide money for the people you leave behind. If you don't have any family or charities that you care to endow, you don't need life insurance. On the other hand, if you have children, your spouse doesn't work, or both, you need life insurance and plenty of it. Your life insurance policy should be large enough to pay off the mortgage, fund a college education fund, and cover living expenses for as many years as necessary. Life insurance can be complicated, but simplicity is not only possible but preferred. Term

insurance is easy and cheap, but it usually does the trick.

Whole life insurance and other more complicated offshoots combine life insurance coverage with investments. These alternatives might be the right solution for some folks, but NAIC investors don't need an insurance company to invest for them.

For Your Piece of Mind

Two types of insurance that people often ignore are disability and liability, but these holes in your armor can be fatal. Disability insurance covers what is possibly your most valuable asset—your ability to earn a living. Consider the consequences of foregoing disability insurance. If you are disabled and can't work, you're alive; your living expenses continue; your earning power has stopped; your hard-earned savings start flying out the door.

Liability insurance kicks in if you are responsible for someone's injury or property damage and they sue you. Liability insurance is essential because, unfortunately, lawsuits become more common every day and judgments against you are often based on how much money you have. The more assets you own, the higher the liability coverage you need. Auto and home owner's policies often provide liability coverage up to $100,000 for

makes sure you have property insurance to protect its investment in your home. Even if someone else doesn't require you to have property insurance, you should insure your home to protect your asset.

For Your Health

Most people wouldn't think of foregoing health insurance. The cost of health care is increasing faster than just about everything else.

each person who is injured with a maximum of $300,000. If your assets add up to more than that, first congratulate yourself, and then look for an excess liability policy that covers $500,000, $1,000,000, or more.

Creating Your Own Safety Buffer

Perhaps you've heard of companies self-insuring. This means that the companies set aside reserves of cash to cover the costs of possible problems. For most individuals and most types of insurance, the do-it-yourself option isn't feasible. But, an emergency stash of cash is one form of self-insurance everyone should and can implement.

Before you begin an investing plan, you should save enough money to cover three to six months of living expenses and keep it in a very safe place (like a savings account). These funds keep you afloat in case you lose your job or while you're waiting for long-term disability to kick in. If the need arises and you raid your emergency fund, take a deep breath, restore your resolve, and replenish those funds as quickly as possible.

DIG YOURSELF OUT OF DEBT

If you ran up debt in your younger, more wayward days, begin your financial plan by ditching your debt before you start saving and investing. Many credit cards charge interest rates as high as 22 percent. Simply eliminating this debt is like earning a 22 percent return, which is tough to beat even with the best of stock investments. Move your debt to lower interest credit cards or consolidate the debt into a home-equity loan or other lower interest option. Start a regular monthly contribution and pay down your highest interest debt first. When that debt is paid, apply the contribution to the next highest interest debt. When all your debts are paid off, depositing that monthly contribution into a savings or investment account will be painless.

Taxing Considerations

You work hard to earn money and then you spend your valuable spare time trying to make your money work hard for you. Paying taxes isn't optional, but the money you pay in taxes means less to feed the power of compounding in your savings and investment accounts. So, paying your fair share of taxes, but not a penny more, is the way to go.

The government isn't totally clueless. With baby-boomers approaching retirement and fewer company-funded pension plans every day, people need as much help reaching their financial goals as they can get. These days, you can choose from a number of tax-advantaged accounts that help you save for your retirement or for education. In addition, smart portfolio management can minimize the tax bite in your taxable investment accounts.

LEAVING A LEGACY

If your assets amount to a few thousand dollars and your collection of the World's Best Books Written by Engineers, you might not have to worry about estate planning. However, if you have children or you possess more than $625,000 in assets (this amount increases each year), planning the distribution of your assets after you're gone helps get your money and property to the people and organizations you want it to. Preparing a will also ensures that you communicate your plans for the care of your children after you're gone. If you don't have a will, state law determines who gets what of the assets you own that don't have beneficiaries defined. Always consult an attorney for preparation of a will or trust document.

Furthermore, it's bad enough that you have to pay taxes as you earn money while you're alive. Some people chafe at the idea of their estate paying taxes a second time after they go. Planning your estate helps to minimize the estate taxes your estate must pay before distributing your assets. As with insurance, estate planning can be a complicated business. Work with your tax advisor, accountant, attorney, financial planner, and refer to the resource section at the end of this chapter for sources of information on estate planning.

Choosing the Right Type of Account

When the government offers you the chance to save on taxes, that's an offer you shouldn't refuse. Of course, the benefits of different options vary, so you must decide which type of tax-advantaged account is the best for your situation. In most cases, any type of tax-advantaged account is better than its taxable alternative.

Suppose you earn $10,000 that you want to invest. If your annual earnings are high enough, the $10,000 goes into your 401(k) before taxes. Right off the bat, the taxable account is at a disadvantage, because in a 25 percent tax bracket you end up with only $7,500 to deposit. In addition, suppose you had to pay taxes on half of your return each year and that your capital gains rate is 15 percent. Table 4-1 shows that the 401(k) balance is about 25 percent greater than the taxable account after 20 years.

Success Tip!

Because of the power of tax-deferred investing, withdraw money from your taxable retirement accounts first, leaving the tax-deferred accounts to grow as long as possible.

The following are some of your tax-advantaged account options and a brief description of their benefits:

- 401(k) plan or 403(b)—
  If your employer offers a 401(k) or 403(b) plan, and most do, you can contribute 15 percent of your salary before taxes up to $13,000 in 2004. The maximum increases by $1000 per year until 2006 after which it is adjusted annually for inflation (at least until the tax laws change.) If you leave your employer, you can transfer the funds in your 401(k) or 403(b) into a rollover IRA to continue enjoying tax-deferral on gains.

Success Tip!

If your employer offers company matching, do your best to contribute enough to earn every penny of matching money. That's the easiest 100 percent return you'll ever earn. Beware if the employer's contributions are in company stock. If the company

TABLE 4-01 COMPARISON OF TAXED VERSUS TAX-ADVANTAGED RESULTS		
Assumptions	**Taxable account**	**401(k) account**
Initial investment	$10,000	$10,000
Effective annualized return	9.25%	10%
Ending balance	$44,003	$67,275
Ending balance after taxes	$44,003	$56,184

goes under, you lose your job and a chuck of your retirement savings, too.

- SEP-IRA—If you are self-employed or run a small business, a simplified employee pension IRA (SEP-IRA) is the easiest way to create a pension plan. You can contribute up to 25 percent of your income up to $41,000 in 2004. You can set up a SEP-IRA for a side business, even if you contribute to a 401(k) at work.

- Traditional IRA—Anyone with earned income (adults or children alike) can contribute to a traditional IRA. Contributions are tax deductible depending on your level of income. The maximum contribution is $3,500 in 2004. Taxes on gains are deferred until you withdraw funds, although you'll pay penalties if you withdraw money before you turn 59 1/2. If you've reached the maximum on your 401(k) contributions but want to save more for retirement, use this type of account to boost compounding on your gains.

- Roth IRA—The contributions to a Roth IRA are not tax-deductible, but you can continue to contribute money after you reach age 70. Unlike traditional IRAs, there's no mandatory annual distribution, so it's a great way to achieve tax benefits for later years in your retirement. In addition, you can withdraw your contributions at any time without paying taxes or penalties and you can withdraw gains tax-free after the age of 59 1/2. Income limits do apply.

- Education savings account—Investments grow without taxes and withdrawals are tax-free when you use them for qualified educational expenses. An adult creates the account for a child and manages the assets until the

child turns 18, at which point the child can accept ownership of the account. Note: These types of accounts can affect student loan eligibility.

- 529 College savings plan— Investments grow without taxes and withdrawals are tax-free when you use them for qualified educational expenses. The owner of the account makes contributions, but can use the money for his or her own educational expenses or name a family member as the beneficiary.

Tactics for Taxable Accounts

After you have exhausted your options for tax-advantaged accounts, there's still hope for tax savings—if you play your cards right. Consider the following approaches to reduce the impact of taxes on your investment returns:

- Use taxable accounts to hold growth stocks that you intend to own for years. As long as your wealth grows in unrealized capital gains you won't pay taxes. If possible, keep income-oriented investments in tax-deferred accounts so you don't have to pay taxes on the income immediately.

- If you've owned a stock for years and don't need the money it represents, consider giving the stock as a gift to a child, relative, or to charity.

- Don't forget to consider the taxes you'll pay on capital gains before you decide to sell a stock (see Chapter 12.)

- Don't buy mutual funds just before a distribution. When a mutual fund makes a distribution, the share price decreases by the amount of the distribution. The new share price and the amount of the distribution equal the pre-distribution price, so the shareholder has the same amount of money. However, the distribution is taxable. For example, suppose you buy a mutual fund whose share price is $10. The next day, the fund distributes $1 in dividends. The share price drops to $9. You receive a taxable distribution of $1. If your tax rate is 25 percent, in effect, your new investment value is $9.75: the $9 share value and the $.75 that remains after paying taxes on the distribution. That's a 2.5 percent drop simply from buying one day too soon.

- Sell mutual funds before distributions. When you sell a mutual fund, the increase in fund value is taxed as capital gains. Although the tax rates for dividends have dropped under some circumstances, if you sell a fund right after a distribution, you might pay regular income tax rates on the dividend portion of the distribution.

Success Tip!

Time mutual fund purchases to distributions only when the distribution date is close at hand. When a distribution is months away, you stand to gain more by owning the fund than you avoid in taxes.

Obtaining Help for Your Financial Plan

As your assets grow, so does your financial plan—in complexity, not dollars. If you don't want to become an expert in every facet of investing, taxes, insurance, estate planning, and more, there are plenty of financial professionals willing to help. Most professionals set a minimum portfolio amount that you must meet before you can hire them. On the other hand, if you're willing to do the work, but don't know how, you can turn to books, educational Web sites, or online financial planning services for the answers.

Choosing the Right Type of Financial Professional

Your Aunt Thelma can call herself a financial planner, but that doesn't mean her advice will make the most sense for you. Even professionals with impressive sounding certifications might not have experience in the areas of financial planning that you need. For example, your accountant can help you do your taxes and track your finances, but a Personal Financial Specialist designation indicates proficiency specifically in financial planning. A Chartered Financial Consultant might sound good, but the title means only that the person has completed eight financial planning classes and has some experience in the field. No test is required. Another alternative is a Certified Financial Planner, who must pass a certification test and continually update his knowledge with continuing education.

Financial planners use different methods for calculating how much they charge. Each method has its pros and cons, so unfortunately, some homework is in order before you sign up for someone's services. Compensation plans fall into the following three categories:

- Commission-based— Planners are paid through commissions on the financial products they sell

such as stocks, bonds, and mutual funds. These fees can be costly and are only too easy to ignore when they are embedded in your transactions. In addition, an unethical planner could generate more income for himself by selling you the products with the highest commissions or recommending that you switch investments.

- Hourly rate—Planners charge only for the time they work on your finances. This is the most flexible approach, because you can decide how much of the work you want to do to limit your financial planning costs.

- Percentage fee—Planners charge a percentage of the dollar value of your assets that they manage. Beware of fees more than one percent.

Fee-based means that a financial planner earns compensation with hourly or percentage fees only.

Finding the Right Professional

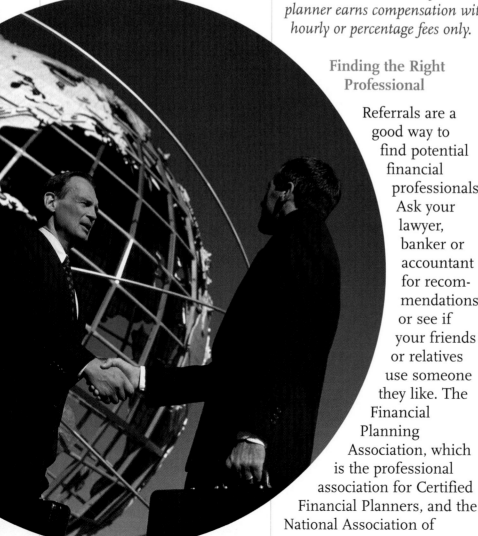

Referrals are a good way to find potential financial professionals. Ask your lawyer, banker or accountant for recommendations or see if your friends or relatives use someone they like. The Financial Planning Association, which is the professional association for Certified Financial Planners, and the National Association of

Personal Financial Advisors (NAPFA), which represents fee-only financial planners, both offer search functions on their Web sites.

The Financial Planning Association search tool (*http://www.fpanet.org/planner search/plannersearch.cfm*) helps you find a planner by zip code, city, state, or within a specified radius of your zip code. You must enter personal information, including your e-mail address, to use the NAPFA search feature (*http://www.napfa.org*) and you must specifically opt out of sending your personal information to planners.

You can research a planner's client base, compensation method, background, and whether the planner has ever been disciplined or investigated at the Securities & Exchange Commission web site (http://www.adviserinfo.sec.gov/ IAPD/Content/IapdMain/iapd_ SiteMap.asp). *The state in which you reside might also have a department which tracks financial professionals.*

Before you select a planner or advisor, interview each of the candidates. (Planners usually provide an initial consultation at no charge. Prepare a list of questions for the interview, but also evaluate whether you feel comfortable with the person. The Motley Fool Web site includes a sample questionnaire as well as a checklist of documents your should bring to your meeting *(http://www.fool.com/fa/fin advice03.htm?source=famp).* After you choose a planner, prepare a written agreement that defines the services the planner will provide, estimated costs, responsibilities for you and the planner, and a termination clause.

Success Tip!

Even if you go with your Aunt Thelma, don't provide your planner (or your broker for that matter) with total power over your finances. Require your approval for any investment as well as regular account statements prepared by a third party. **Note:** *See Chapter 1 of NAIC Official Guide for a detailed discussion of financial professionals.*

Online and Software Resources

Financial planning education and advice is available online or through some software tools. Many Web sites offer information for free. But, financial planning advice specific to your circumstance typically costs money. Although the price tag might be lower than that of a financial planner, these Web services are often more generic and less comprehensive than the planner's offerings. If you are

interested in less expensive options and are willing to roll up your sleeves a bit, check out the following online and software-based resources:

- The Motley Fool TMF Money Advisor *(http://www.fool.com/fa/finadvice.htm)*—Includes an online financial planning tool, phone consultations with a financial planner, access to Motley Fool personal finance seminars and discussion boards. After a 30-day free trial, the annual subscription is $199.00.

- Morningstar Clear Future *(http://www.morningstar.com/Cover/ClearFuture.html)*—When you subscribe to Morningstar's Premium Service ($12.95 per month or $115 per year), you can use ClearFuture, which provides a tool to calculate your retirement needs, develop a plan to meet those needs, and recommend mutual funds that fit your plan.

- MSN Money *(http://money.msn.com/planning/home.asp)*—Access educational articles and calculators for every aspect of your financial plan. Although the planning tools are reasonably comprehensive, you must provide mPower with personal information to receive advice.

- Your broker's Web site— Your broker might offer online financial planning tools or discounts on a personalized financial plan.

- Personal finance applications—*Quicken* and *Microsoft Money* include tools to help you plan and manage your finances.

Many other Web sites include articles about different aspects of financial planning. Try searching for keywords such as "financial planning," "retirement planning," "estate planning," or "college saving."

Developing Your Strategy

Nothing Lasts Forever

No investment automatically earns a permanent place in your portfolio. Even the Dow Jones Industrial Average contains only one of its original companies. Management changes, regulatory changes, competition, new technology, and other factors can adversely affect company fundamentals. These downturns in fundamentals often lead to downturns in stock price, which damages portfolio performance.

Even the winners in your portfolio might wear out their welcome. Increasing stock prices, maturing companies and industries, and slowing growth can reduce the potential return for some of your investments to the point that they no longer meet your objectives. Lower returns might not harm your portfolio the way losses do, but they leave room for improvement.

It's Not About Price

Playing Defense

Playing Offense

It's Not About Price

Portfolio management does not mean watching stock prices every moment that the markets are open. Monitoring short-term price fluctuations won't help your portfolio, but it can hinder your concentration, productivity, and overall well-being. Portfolio management is more than just tracking portfolio performance.

Portfolio management also is not buying or selling stocks based on their price performance. Without evaluating the underlying company fundamentals, buying on a price drop could be buying bad news. Selling stocks simply because their prices have dropped, reached a plateau, or hit an arbitrary target price is often portfolio mismanagement.

Success Tip!

Over long periods of time, the stock market is quite efficient: sooner or later, a company's stock price adjusts to reflect its earnings and dividend potential. During short stretches, prices can fluctuate wildly for little or no apparent reason. Stock prices can drop due to over-reactions to news. They can languish because

a stock or industry is out of favor because of the market's prediction of the future. Prices can increase based on speculation. Don't go by the vagaries of short-term price performance. Decide for yourself what a company is worth and then buy it when the price represents a good value.

If portfolio management isn't about price, then what is it about? One part of portfolio management means regularly evaluating the prospects of the companies in your portfolio, looking for both potential

problems as well as room for improvement. The other part of portfolio management is seeing whether the components that make up your portfolio work well together.

Portfolio management is a two-pronged approach, similar to football. Playing defense shields your portfolio from harmful losses, while playing offense adds points of investment return to your portfolio's performance. Playing defense doesn't take much time, but you must remain on guard. A deteriorating investment can run with the ball while you aren't looking and put numbers in the investment losses column. Offense often receives more attention because its results are more obvious and exciting. Spectacular returns are fun and great for bragging rights.

But, playing offense isn't actually more important than defense. For long-term success, you must build both strong defense and offense.

Your financial plan and stock studies must be up-to-date before you begin your portfolio management tasks. Although your financial plan won't change frequently, you need to know the risk you can afford to take with your portfolio and the overall diversification you're striving for. In addition, your SSGs, mutual fund studies, and any qualitative analyses you have prepared must be up to date, so you can evaluate whether a company or fund is performing at an acceptable level.

Playing Defense

Believe it or not, the defensive team can do more for your portfolio return than the offense. For the same percentage change, a loss is far more damaging than its corresponding gain. For example, you might assume that you need a 20 percent gain to recover

from a 20 percent drop. In reality, it takes a 25 percent increase to salvage a 20 percent loss. Suppose your $100,000 portfolio dropped 50 percent to $50,000. Yes, you need the same dollar amount, $50,000, to get back on track. However, $50,000 represents 100 percent of the new portfolio value of $50,000. Just like hiking up or down a hill, 50 percent drops seem easier than 100 percent gains.

As an NAIC investor, you buy companies that can grow sales, profits, and earnings per share, because increasing earnings should lead eventually to increases in stock price. Therefore, to protect your portfolio, you watch for the opposite behavior: deteriorating growth in sales, profits, and earnings, which by the way is even more dependable at dropping the stock price quickly.

Although playing defense is a key to successful portfolio management, you don't have to play it constantly. Since defensive strategy looks for deteriorating growth, a company's quarterly report is the primary resource for signs of deterioration. Generally, the defensive team takes the field once every three months, when the quarterly report is published. Although you want to analyze companies' quarterly performance, you don't want to react too quickly to quarterly information. One bad quarter

doesn't automatically mean you should sell.

In addition to evaluating recent fundamentals each quarter, keeping an eye on company news is good defensive strategy. Factors that might affect a company's future, such as new technologies or government regulations, can pop up at any time. If company performance falls below your expectations, news stories might explain what happened and help you understand whether the problem is short-lived or around for the long haul.

Defensive plays consist of the following steps:

1. Evaluate qualitative aspects of the company to check for deterioration in the business or industry outlook. For example, look for changes such as increased competition, less effective research and development, product obsolescence, expiring patents, or lawsuits.

2. Look for poor management trends in sales, pre-tax profit, and EPS growth, such as slowing growth rates, losses, or EPS growth that has dropped below your estimated rate. This information is available on the PERT-A graph and report, the PERT report, and the PERT Trend report.

3. If the business outlook and/or fundamentals have deteriorated and don't appear poised to improve over the next year, sell the stock.

SuccessTip!

Once you've decided to sell a stock, sell it, whether or not you've found its replacement. If you wait until you find another stock to buy, the one you own might have already dropped like a rock.

4. Move on to playing offense to find a company to purchase with the proceeds of the sale.

SuccessTip!

Mutual funds can harm your portfolio, too. A new fund manager, a proposed fund merger, significant increases in fund assets that can force a change in fund philosophy, expense and fee increases, increasing investment turnover, or wrongdoing on the part of the fund manager or fund company can all adversely affect the returns you receive from a mutual fund. Read Chapter 14 to learn what to look for and what to do about it.

Playing Offense

Playing offense means putting more points on the scoreboard—by increasing returns, reducing your overall portfolio risk, or improving the overall portfolio quality. Unlike with defensive plays, the failure to react quickly on offense doesn't damage your portfolio. You can ply your offense when you have the time. That doesn't mean you can let offense go for years. Regardless how many points you block with defense, you can't really win unless you score some points of your own. Although quick response is not required for offense, regularly paying attention to improving your portfolio may improve your results.

High prices and the low potential for return that they often bring are one reason to bring in the offense. Quality growth stocks whose prices are too high don't contribute much toward achieving the return you want. The Portfolio Summary report (see Chapter 11) is a great tool for spotting overvalued companies. Total return, relative value, and the upside-downside ratio columns each provide a different view of the value of a stock:

- A total return that drops below five percent is a boat anchor on your overall portfolio return.

- When PEs are high, you can count on them to drop to more moderate levels—taking the price down with them if earnings remain the same. Relative value greater than 150 percent might be a red flag that the PE ratio is poised to retreat to the average PE.

- And, an upside-downside ratio close to or less than one tells you that the stock price could fall farther than it might rise.

When these indicators scream "overvalued", it's time to look for another company that can offer better returns.

When the stocks look fine both defensively and offensively, you might find value by improving the quality of companies in your portfolio. When you have the time and the inclination, you can try to increase quality without sacrificing your investment returns (see Chapters 12 and 13). For example, for higher quality, look for companies that deliver the same average annual growth rate but with more consistent growth from year to year and quarter to quarter. And when you increase quality and returns, you often achieve the added benefit of lower portfolio risk.

When you're ready to improve your stock holdings, begin by updating your stock SSGs and reviewing the company outlooks as you would if you were reviewing fundamentals for defensive portfolio management. Modify your SSG judgment if necessary. Playing offense consists of the following steps:

1. Examine the overall results of your portfolio for return, risk, and quality (see Chapter 10.) *Toolkit 5* calculates these measures for you, but knowing the characteristics of your overall portfolio is worth a few keystrokes on a hand calculator.

2. Look for signs of overvalued companies (see Chapter 10) on the PERT report, which includes relative value, upside-downside ratio, and compound annual rate of return. The PERT Summary report shows total return, relative value, and upside-downside ratio. The PERT Trend report shows projected average return and total return.

3. Review your current stocks for return, risk, and quality (see Chapters 7 and 8).

4. For each company whose return, quality, or risk you would like to improve, screen for companies to pit against your existing holdings (see Chapter 12). If your portfolio diversification is where you want it, screen for companies in the same industry and of the same size. Otherwise, look for companies that can help rebalance your diversification at the same time.

5. Analyze potential replacements and prepare an SSG for each of them.

6. Compare current holdings to contenders using the Stock Comparison Guide and the Challenge Tree (see Chapter 13) and decide whether to replace your existing holdings.

7. Review your portfolio diversification. If it needs adjusting (see Chapter 6), review your current holdings in the segments that are over-represented and consider selling some or all of the stock with the least potential for the future. Review your current holdings in the segments that are under-represented and consider buying more of a stock with the most potential for the future. Or, repeat steps 2, 3, and 4 to find a new stock to purchase for that segment of diversification.

IMPROVING ON MUTUAL FUNDS

Improving the funds in your investment portfolio is a bit different from tweaking stocks (see Chapter 14). Many actively managed funds perform very well one year only to lag the field the next. Therefore, switching funds because of one year of lagging returns can become a game of chase the returns. Instead, look for mutual funds that have outperformed your current fund as well as its category average for the past three-, five-, and 10-year periods.

The Fine Art of Portfolio Management

Profit from Good Habits

Some tasks are quick and easy when you stay on top of them. Let them slide and the same tasks become slow and hard. Going through your mail every day, throwing out the junk, and sorting the remainder for action or filing takes a few minutes at most. When you return from a two-week vacation, catching up on the mail is enough to undo all the good your

vacation did. You realize that two dozen catalogues arrive each week; your filing is two inches thick; and you owe late payments on three bills. Portfolio management doesn't have to be like that. By getting in the habit of caring for your portfolio, you maintain an attractive portfolio return and reduce the time it takes to produce it.

Forming Profitable Habits

Portfolio Management for Individuals and Clubs

Portfolio Management Step by Step

The Ins and Out of Diversifying Your Portfolio

Caring for Portfolios of Different Ages

Forming Profitable Habits

The bad news is that good habits are hard to form—eating right, exercising regularly, and managing your portfolio are tough to transform into second nature. The good news is that habits are hard to break as well. So, the hard work is ingraining portfolio management into your schedule. Just like eating right and exercising regularly, the results of good portfolio management don't appear immediately. In fact, with portfolio management, the benefits might not become apparent for a year or more. The key is to facilitate your portfolio management tasks while you develop them into habits.

Scheduling Time for Portfolio Management

The first step to developing the habit of portfolio management is to reserve a regular time in your schedule each month—the third Tuesday evening, the second Sunday afternoon, whatever works best for you. If you belong to an investment club, it's easy, because the club meeting can become that time as long as all the members agree. For individual investors, motivation can be difficult in

the face of other pressing matters. Choose your portfolio management meeting with yourself at a time that is rarely interrupted by other duties. Then, provide incentive by visualizing the best part of reaching a goal. Picture your child walking up to receive her diploma. Imagine sitting on the deck of your retirement home enjoying the scenery.

Making Portfolio Management Easy

Sometimes, it costs money to make money. NAIC software, NAIC's Online Premium Services, and many online tools simplify portfolio management tremendously. And, if portfolio management looks like less of a chore, you are more likely to perform it when you should.

One key to portfolio success is simply taking the time to manage your portfolio:

evaluating stocks to see what you need to fix and what you might improve. NAIC software tools alleviate some of the time it takes to calculate the values you need to manage your portfolio, which means you have more time to apply your all-important judgment to your stocks.

NAIC stock analysis tools, such as *Investors' Toolkit, Stock Analyst,* and *NAIC Classic,* take care of calculating values for you. You're more likely to update your stock studies or apply judgment when you don't have to face a hard 30 minutes of calculator time to do it. Similarly, Online Premium Services downloads

stock data into your stock analysis tools, which means you can create or update a stock study whenever you want—without having to head to the library. *Stock Prospector* makes quick work of finding stocks that meet the criteria you're looking for in new stocks for your portfolio.

The idea of spending several months' worth of investment money on software tools might seem excessive when you're anxious to see the benefits of compounding for yourself. Over time, the growth of your well-managed portfolio will completely overwhelm the cost of purchasing these tools (see Chapter 17).

A small set of applications, data sources, and Web site subscriptions can speed up and improve your portfolio management activities. That's no excuse for pigging out on every financial newsletter, software tool, or subscription that's touted. Apply the same techniques to your tools that you use for stocks. If you find a new tool that looks promising, challenge the ones you currently use to determine whether to continue with the tools you use or replace one tool with another.

Portfolio Management for Individuals and Clubs

Other than division of labor and group dynamics, portfolio management for the individual investor and the investment club is the same. In each situation, portfolio management means buying, selling, and holding investments to achieve financial objectives with an acceptable amount of risk.

In an investment club, each club member can follow one or more stocks and summarize the company performance and the stock outlook for the other members. With a dozen members, a club can follow a dozen holdings and a dozen stocks on a watch list with an hour or two of time from each member. On the other hand, an individual investor has to limit her holdings and watch list entries based on the amount of

time she is willing to spend on her portfolio each month.

Club members can take turns learning an investment topic and teaching it to the other members. By explaining a topic to others and answering their questions, club members obtain a deeper understanding of the topic. Individual investors must learn on their own or attend classes.

Members in an investment club must reach consensus on buying, selling, or holding. You might think that the individual investor has the advantage here, but individuals can argue with themselves, second-guess their decisions, or rationalize the course they want to take. The discussion and even the disagreements between club members might lead to better investment decisions. Even if a club doesn't buy a recommended stock, any club member who sees its positives is free to purchase it on her own.

Portfolio tracking and accounting for an investment club is a little more complicated than tracking an individual's portfolio (see Chapter 16). Club members should take turns as club treasurer, but that doesn't always happen. Software applications and online tools can help reduce the workload here as well (see Chapter 17).

Portfolio Management Step by Step

Doing your homework when you buy is clearly an important step to successful investing. But, portfolio management can continue and even enhance your investing success. Portfolio management suffers the same fate as the elephant described by a group of blind men. Depending on whether you feel the elephant's skin, tusks, or tail, your perception will be different from your peers. However, each of you is sure you're right! Over time, you will have a chance to inspect the entire portfolio management animal, develop your unique view of the beast, and determine how to put it to best use. Until then, you can try out the portfolio management procedures outlined in this section.

As you learned in Chapter 5, a good chunk of portfolio management is about protecting your portfolio from investments that aren't working out and also working

to improve your portfolio to try to achieve even better results. The steps in this section begin to break down those high-level objectives into more digestible pieces. And you'll learn even more about detail in the remaining chapter in the book.

For now, here's what you'll read about over the next several pages.

- There are a few things you **must** do before you think about selling or buying investments in your portfolio. For example, to make informed decisions, your investment data must be up to date.

- With the portfolio management prerequisites completed, it's time to weed out the investments that aren't working out. Whether a company's or mutual fund's future prospects look poor to you or the investment no longer fits your overall plan, clean house if necessary.

- Finally, take some time to try to make your portfolio even better than it is. Many companies that you invest in strive for continuous improvement; you should follow suit with your portfolio.

Chapters 7 through 14 describe each of these steps in detail.

Prerequisites for Portfolio Management

When a financial goal is imminent (your twins have entered high school and college is only a few years away), your first step is to consider whether to move money out of growth investments into safer havens such as bonds or savings accounts, and if so, how much. If your growth portfolio diversification needs rebalancing, consider selling stocks or funds in areas that are over-represented.

After that, whether you are ready to defend or go for the goal line, managing a portfolio always begins with updating the SSGs and qualitative analyses for your portfolio. If your judgment about a company isn't up to date, the company's current performance might look better or worse than it really is, which could lead you to make the wrong choices about buying, selling, or holding. Therefore, the portfolio management process kicks off with the following steps for each company you own.

1. For the stocks you own, update your SSGs with the most recent quarterly numbers. This step is necessary only when a company publishes a new quarterly or annual report.

2. Update your SSGs with the current stock prices. Perform this step whenever you re-evaluate a stock or your portfolio.

Investor's Toolkit 5 includes features that remind you that new data for a company is due or that a stock price is stale.

3. Review the company's qualitative and quantitative performance by reading the quarterly or annual reports, the 10-K or 10-Q filings (see Chapter 8), and by looking

over the SSG. Review your previous assumptions and judgment for the company and modify your SSG judgment if necessary (see Chapter 7).

Success Tip!

The information and judgment on your SSGs drive all of the results that appear in the NAIC portfolio management tools. Skipping these early steps jeopardizes the prudence of your portfolio management decisions.

Mutual funds don't require updating as frequently as stocks. Typically, an annual update of a fund's performance and characteristics is sufficient (see Chapter 14).

Defending Your Portfolio from Harm

The stock market doesn't take deteriorating performance lying down. As long as a company continues to grow at the same or a faster pace, the stock price is usually safe. But, watch out when a company begins to grow at a slower pace or, even worse, the company delivers a negative growth rate—its sales, pre-tax profit, or EPS are less than that of the previous period. The stock market often reacts to these events with a steep drop in stock price, because no one likes uncertainty and surprises. When a stock that was a

dependable performer stubs its toe, investors begin to wonder how bad the injury is. For example, will the company bounce back or is this the beginning of a falling earnings trend? Will the 15% expected returns become 10%? Fortunately, the market sometimes takes a few quarters of less than desirable performance to punish the offender. By playing defense in your portfolio conscientiously, you can spot the warning signs of deterioration and remove a company before a price drop hurts your portfolio too badly.

Defensive Steps for Stocks

When you own individual stocks, perform the following steps for each company in your portfolio:

1. Compare the current growth rates (sales, EPS, and pre-tax profit) for each stock to its forecast growth rates to see whether the company is meeting your expectations (see Chapter 10). Flag any stocks that aren't for further research.

2. Review the PERT reports to see if any companies that you flagged show significant deterioration in company fundamentals. Dig deeper to try to determine whether any problems are likely to continue (see Chapters 8 and 9).

3. If a company's outlook looks grim over the next three to five years, consider selling the stock.

Steps for Mutual Funds

For each mutual fund that you own, reevaluate its performance once a year. The fund's prospectus and most recent annual report contain the information you need for the following steps:

1. If a fund's returns have lagged for two years or more within its category or are lower than the most representative benchmark index, flag the fund for further analysis.

2. Make sure that the fund's investment objectives and philosophy still fit your objectives and tolerance for risk. For example, a fund might achieve better than average returns by using derivatives or currency exchange techniques that are too risky for your situation. Or, you might find that a small-growth fund invests more money in large companies than you want to see (although the SEC limits the percentage of dollars that funds can invest in other segments of the market).

3. Check for increases in fees and expense ratios, which make it difficult for a fund

to do better than the benchmark or its competitors. Also, check fund turnover for above-average numbers. The brokerage commissions generated by excessive turnover show up nowhere in fund data other than below-average returns.

4. Check whether the fund manager is still at the helm. If the manager has changed, evaluate the new manager's experience and performance at his or her previous fund.

Persuading Your Portfolio to Do Better

With the losers weeded out, your portfolio is a collection of good companies whose performance meets, exceeds, or at least comes close to matching your expectations. Stocks like this aren't likely to tank, taking your money with them, but sometimes their prices fly so high that you're not likely to make much money with them either. Even when all your investments are doing just great, you should try to do even better. You're ready to play offense!

Steps for Your Overall Portfolio

Your portfolio is a melding of your individual investments. Although the performance of individual investments is important, the results from the combination of investments with different levels of return,

REVIEW DIVERSIFICATION OCCASIONALLY

Portfolio diversification by individual stock or fund, by industry, by company size, and by geographical region helps reduce the risk in your portfolio. Taken to the extreme, for instance rebalancing your portfolio based on daily stock price gyrations, diversification turns into trading, not investing. Consider check your portfolio diversification once a year. If your portfolio is significantly unbalanced in one or more ways, document the types and dollar values of adjustments you would need to rebalance your portfolio. You can use them to focus your attention on the right types of stocks and funds to bring your diversification back on track. See the section "The Ins and Outs of Diversifying Your Portfolio" later in this chapter.

quality, and risk tell an important story. The statistics for your overall portfolio might highlight areas for potential improvement. Your financial plan should include targets for diversification, return, and risk to fit your needs. Once a year, evaluate the measures for your **entire portfolio**:

- Check the annual return to see whether it meets your target return. If it doesn't, make a point to look for individual stocks and funds whose returns aren't pulling their weight, as described in the following sections.

- Some NAIC investors use the forecast high and low prices of stocks to determine the overall Upside/Downside ratio for a portfolio. If this ratio is less than 2.0 to 1, stocks whose Upside/Downside ratios are very low could be targets for

replacement to improve the risk profile for the portfolio.

Playing Offense on Stocks

Basic offense for individual stocks means looking for potential future returns that don't live up to your expectations or risks that are too high for the potential return. Improving your portfolio can represent either of the following objectives:

- Find a company with significantly better potential return and equal or higher quality than your current investment.

- Find a company with equal or better return but significantly less risk.

For each stock in your portfolio, follow these steps:

1. Review potential return for each stock looking for returns that you'd like to try

to improve on. You can find return on the PERT report (shown in the % Compd Annual Rate of Return column) or PERT Trend report (shown in the Total Return column. If you use *Toolkit 5*, you can view return in the Overview shown in Figure 6-1.

2. Review risk and return on the PERT report by examining relative value and the Upside/Downside ratio (both described in detail in Chapter 7).

Success Tip!

The calculations for relative value are not the same on the PERT Report and the SSG. Relative value on the SSG compares the current PE to the five-year average PE. On the PERT Report, relative value compares the current PE to the future average of high and low PEs based on your forecast high and low prices in Section 4 of the SSG.

4. If one or more of the return and risk measures disappoint you, flag the company for possible replacement through the challenge process.

Success Tip!

Determining the minimum return that a stock should provide takes some judgment. Your goal is to achieve an annual return for your entire portfolio. That doesn't mean that each company in your portfolio must provide that same return. In fact, as prices change after you purchase stocks, the returns are almost never the same. When some companies have the potential to exceed your target by a wide margin, other companies can deliver a return less than your overall target.

If the potential return for your entire portfolio meets your goal, you might decide to keep the low-return stocks that you own. However, when that overall potential return drops below your target, you should begin scrutinizing the stocks with the lowest potential returns as candidates for replacement. See Chapters 10 and 11 for instructions on calculating overall portfolio return.

5. Challenge each existing stock that you flagged for possible replacement with one or more companies. If your portfolio diversification needs rebalancing, look for companies in industries that help rectify your diversification percentages or are of the right size. Always consider the tax consequences when you decide to sell.

Remember, a replacement company should offer a

SPEND YOUR TIME WHERE YOU HAVE THE MOST MONEY

Many investors and investment clubs spend their time looking for new investments to buy when they add money to their portfolio. Potential companies seem so exciting and brimming with opportunity. But, when it's time to look at the stocks already in their portfolios, they scatter faster than children who are supposed to do chores. There's nothing wrong with scouting the markets for better investments. A problem arises when you keep all your existing investments and simply add your new investment find to the portfolio pile.

Think about it. You study, dig, analyze, and evaluate a new stock or fund from every angle as a potential purchase with your monthly contribution. Meanwhile, the $100,000 already invested in your portfolio could be limping along with some slow growers. The bottom line: spend your time putting the bulk of your money to work. For a young portfolio that means studying stocks and funds to buy. But, soon after it means managing your portfolio.

If you add money to your portfolio regularly, you must choose the best way to invest that money. You can invest in new companies or add to your existing holdings. If you decide to add money to a stock you already own, take advantage of price dips to boost your portfolio return. Check whether the price dip is due to poor EPS performance, and, if so, wait for EPS to recover before you invest. Regular contributions can help rebalance portfolio diversification. When your portfolio is unbalanced, focus your new contributions on companies of sizes or industries that are under-represented in your portfolio.

significantly better return with equal or higher quality, or it should offer at least the same return and quality but with significantly less risk. Also, there's no rule that says a replacement must be a company that you don't already own. As long as it meets your return, risk, and diversification objectives, you can

use one of your existing stocks as a challenger.

Investment clubs typically don't invest in mutual funds and thus evaluate only individual stocks in the club portfolio. But individual investors might build a portfolio with stocks and mutual funds. Investors such as these should evaluate both their stocks and funds.

6. Check the percentage that each company represents in your portfolio. If the percentage exceeds the maximum you're comfortable with, consider selling some of the shares you own to bring the company within your diversification guidelines.

Take Care Playing Offense with Mutual Funds

Improving on your mutual funds is a great idea, but you must restrain yourself from chasing returns. Actively managed mutual funds have a tendency to run hot and cold.

Mutual fund companies are fond of touting the funds on hot streaks to attract new customers, while keeping their losing streaks to themselves. Therefore, beware of mutual funds that wildly outperform their peers. They could be poised for a period of below average performance.

If you want to improve on the mutual funds that you own (see Chapter 14), focus on the following steps:

- Look for mutual funds in the same category that charge lower expenses. Expenses and fees reduce the return you earn as a fund shareholder. Because of this, funds with very high expenses must perform better to make up for the expenses they charge. In reality, high-expense funds rarely beat the competition over long periods of time.

- Look for mutual funds in the same category that offer the same level of return with lower risk. The Sharpe ratio is a theoretical measure of return for unit of risk. A fund with a higher Sharpe ratio delivers its return with less risk.

WHEN TO SAY GOODBYE TO BIG WINNERS

Big winners are a blessing and a burden. On one hand, you shouldn't rush to sell your big winners. After all, they have produced much of your portfolio's performance and are the rewards of all your hard work studying investments. When a big winner appears to be overvalued, be sure to update your SSG before you decide to sell (as you should for any stock you sell.) Higher earnings translate into a lower PE for the same price. You might find that the company is fairly valued after all.

However, the run-up in price for a big winner can transform it into an excessively large holding in your portfolio. And you might succumb to the temptation of keeping a stock that's been good to you when it's no longer a good investment. If something both detrimental and unexpected happens to the company, your portfolio has problems—big problems. You might sell some of your shares to bring your diversification back in line or, if you have cash, you can add to your portfolio, or you can buy more of other investments to adjust their percentages. Consider buying a smaller company with great prospects, or a similar company that offers a better value and return. But, don't sell a winner to buy a loser.

The Ins and Outs of Diversifying Your Portfolio

Bringing portfolio diversification back on track requires a delicate touch. Because the ideal diversification is unique to your goals and risk tolerance—and represents a balance of company size, sector and industry, geographic region, and individual investments—a change that corrects one imbalance might create several others. You shouldn't expect to maintain perfect diversification—that will lead only to obsessive behavior and excessive brokerage commissions.

Here are a few hints for attaining reasonable diversification without going crazy.

- If you invest in both stocks and mutual funds, be sure to take all of your investments into account when evaluating diversification. If you invest only in stocks, consider NAIC tools such as *Investor's Toolkit, Stock Analyst,* and *NAIC Classic.* NAIC's *Portfolio Record Keeper* software *(PRK)* can handle mutual funds and stocks in a portfolio.

- If your diversification is close to your target percentages (for instance, within 5 to 10 percent,) consider leaving things as they are. For example, some large companies can deliver above average returns, so a portfolio with 50 percent invested in large-cap stocks isn't that bad if your overall portfolio return exceeds your target.

- When you're early in the process of building your portfolio, you might consider using mutual funds to diversify by company, by industry, and by company size. For example, any stock index fund delivers industry and company diversification. Or you might consider purchasing index funds that represent large-cap, mid-

cap, and small-cap market segments to diversify by company size. Mutual funds might even help more sizable portfolio with some types of diversification, such as foreign investments.

- To diversify a young stock portfolio, strive to add new stocks regularly until you own as many stocks as you can follow and have achieved some reasonable diversification.

- Apply new contributions or dividends to investments that improve diversification. If you own too many small-cap stocks, add to your holdings in a mid- or large-cap stock. Turn off dividend reinvestment programs so that your mutual fund dividends and distributions

go to your cash account. Then, use that money to buy more of the areas that are under-represented.

Success Tip!

Dividends are one way to adjust diversification, but dividend reinvestment programs are a great way to buy stocks without commissions. Before you cancel your automatic dividend reinvestments, see if there's another way to alter your portfolio diversification.

- When you decide to sell a stock for defensive reasons or to improve your portfolio, use the proceeds to purchase one or more stocks that improve your diversification.

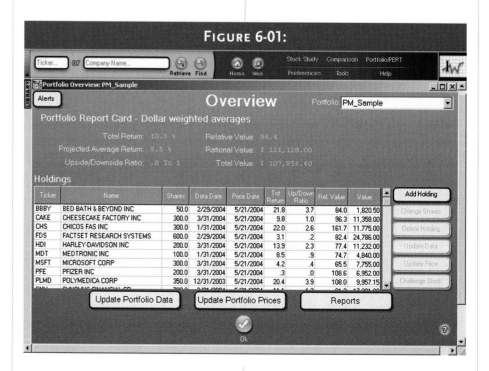

FIGURE 6-01:

Deciding Where to Move Your Money

Determining the adjustments required to rebalance your portfolio diversification can be easy, hard, or impossible. Figuring out the changes that result in a perfect match for your diversification percentage is possible—it's simple math. But it's a waste of time. After one day, your perfect diversification will be gone with the wind of stock price changes along with even more money spent on brokerage commissions. Diversification rules are targets to aim for, not precise numbers you must achieve.

Some online tools such as Smart Money's One Asset Allocation System (*http://www.smartmoney.com/oneasset/*) calculate how much money you should add or subtract to different categories of assets. These tools typically make recommendations based on broad categories of assets and model allocations, which might not offer the type of investments you want or the detail you need. Some NAIC programs show diversification by sector, industry, and company size.

If you want to play with all aspects of diversification and don't mind typing some information, a spreadsheet similar to the one in Figure 6-02 can highlight portfolio values that break your rules. With columns for what-if values, you can try different changes to see their effects on diversification.

Don't grab a stock listed in Figure 6-02 and call your broker with buy or sell orders. That spreadsheet is an example and uses data that's old, obsolete, in the past. No matter what you call it, that data is no good for today's investment decisions. For example, after this book was printed, Pfizer could have announced a drug that cures cancer and increased in price a gazillion times over.

The dollar values and total return forecasts in Figure 6-02 are fictional, but they work as an example for making adjustments. Begin with an overall review of the existing issues with diversification. The spreadsheet in Figure 6-02 highlights the following areas for improvement.

FIGURE 6-02: A SPREADSHEET WITH CURRENT AND PROPOSED VALUES CAN HIGHLIGHT NEEDED ADJUSTMENTS.

	A	B	E	F	G	H	I	J K	L	M	N
1	Investment	Ticker	Value	Industry	Size	Total Return	Current %	What If %	What If Value	Action	# of Shares
2	Bed Bath & Beyond	BBBY	$1,851.00	Retail	Large	21.8%	1.47%	15.00%	$18,901.27	Buy	341
3	Cheesecake Factory	CAKE	$12,987.00	Restaurants	Medium	9.8%	10.31%	10.31%	$12,987.00	None	0
4	Chico's FAS	CHS	$12,912.00	Clothing	Medium	22.0%	10.25%	15.00%	$18,901.27	Buy	20
5	FactSet Research Systems	FDS	$24,846.00	Business Support	Small	3.1%	19.72%	0.00%	$0.00	Sell	41
6	Harley-Davidson	HDI	$11,334.00	Recreation	Large	13.9%	8.99%	8.99%	$11,334.00	None	0
7	Medtronic	MDT	$5,076.00	Medical Equip.	Large	8.5%	4.03%	4.03%	$5,076.00	None	0
8	Microsoft	MSFT	$7,932.00	Business Appl.	Large	4.2%	6.29%	0.00%	$0.00	Sell	26
9	Pfizer	PFE	$7,364.00	Drugs	Large	0.3%	5.84%	0.00%	$0.00	Sell	37
10	PolyMedica	PLMD	$9,774.45	Drugs	Small	20.4%	7.76%	15.00%	$18,901.27	Buy	26
11	Synovus Financial	SNV	$17,360.00	Banks	Medium	11.1%	13.78%	14.65%	$18,460.24	Buy	2
12	Fremont Microcap	FUSMX	$8,250.00	Diverse	Small	18.0%	6.55%	12.00%	$15,121.01	Buy	23
13	Mairs & Power Growth	MPGFX	$6,322.00	Diverse	Large	12.0%	5.02%	5.02%	$6,322.00	None	0
14			$126,008.45				100.00%		100.00%		
15								11%	17%		
16								Port. Total Return	What If Return		
18				Industries	Current	What If	Size	Current	What If		
19				Retail	1.5%	15.0%	Small	34.0%	27.0%		
20				Restaurants	10.3%	10.3%	Medium	34.3%	40.0%		
21				Clothing	10.2%	15.0%	Large	31.6%	33.0%		
22				Business Su	19.7%	0.0%		100.0%	100.0%		
23				Recreation	9.0%	9.0%					
24				Medical Equi	4.0%	4.0%					
25				Business Ap	6.3%	0.0%					
26				Drugs	13.6%	15.0%					
27				Banks	13.8%	14.7%					
28				Diverse	11.6%	17.0%					
29					100.0%	100.0%					

H ◄ ► H\ Portfolio ⟨ Div /

- The total return for several of the companies is less than 10 percent, which results in an overall portfolio return of only 11 percent, when the goal is 15 percent. Consider replacing these companies or selling some of your shares in them and buying companies with better return and quality characteristics.

- Some companies represent too little of the portfolio, while others represent too much. A company that is less than 2 percent of your portfolio, such as Bed, Bath, and Beyond in the example, won't hurt your portfolio much, but won't help it much either. If this company increase 50 percent in value, that represents an increase of only half of one percent in your portfolio. Conversely, FactSet Research, taking up 20 percent of the portfolio could put a dent in your portfolio if that company runs into unforeseen problems. A 50 percent drop in this company would represent a 10 percent drop in your portfolio value. Consider increasing ownership in the small holding of Bed, Bath, and Beyond.

- Although diversification by size isn't as important as other types of diversifica-tion, this portfolio is off the target. You might consider decreasing shares in small-cap stocks and increasing shares in mid-caps, but not at the expense of your overall portfolio return.

These focal points help target potential changes in the portfolio. You can begin by trying to increase the total return of the portfolio and balancing ownership across all the individual investments. Then, if diversification by industries and size is significantly skewed, you might take additional passes to fine-tune the results. **Remember, this is an example of the process. You must use your own guidelines for diversification percentages.**

- Focus first on small-cap companies whose total return is below par. FactSet Research fits that description. Consider replacing it with a company that offers a higher potential total return.

- Look for companies of any size whose total return is below par. Microsoft and Pfizer are large-cap companies whose total return is less than 5 percent. Consider replacing both of them with companies that offer higher potential total returns.

- Cheesecake Factory and Medtronic are the

remaining two companies with total return below 10 percent. If the total return for this what-if scenario is still below 15 percent after you've replaced the lower return companies, you might consider replacing these two companies in a second pass.

- To increase the mid-cap percentage, look for mid-cap companies with attractive total returns. Chico's FAS and Synovus match those criteria, although Chico's FAS offers a more attractive total return. Consider increasing the ownership in both Chico's FAS and Synovus to the target 15 percent for one company.

In this example, Synovus is already close to the 15 percent maximum. You might decide to use dividend reinvestment to help increase this holding instead of a brokerage purchase to save on commissions.

- Now, look for other companies with attractive total returns.

  - Bed, Bath, and Beyond is a large-cap company with railroad tracks in Section 1 of the SSG and a total return of 21.8 percent. It was initially under-represented at 1.47 percent, so consider increasing its percentage because of its quality and growth rate.

- Polymedica is a small-cap company, but it also has an attractive total return. With the elimination of FactSet Research, Polymedica can help bolster the small-caps in the portfolio. Consider increasing its percentage.

- Fremont Microcap is a small-cap mutual fund with an attractive long-term historical growth rate. Increase it to 12 percent.

After making these changes, all of the individual investments meet the guidelines for minimum and maximum percentages. The overall portfolio total return has increased to 17 percent. Diversification by size is within striking distance of guidelines with small-caps at 27 percent, mid-caps at 40 percent, and large-caps at 33 percent. Diversification by industries is also acceptable. The portfolio comprises 10 stocks and 2 mutual funds.

Caring for Portfolios of Different Ages

Portfolios go through phases as they age, just like their owners. The financial objectives may change from long-term growth to income. The risk that is acceptable in a young portfolio might seem foolhardy in a portfolio for a retiree who started investing only a few years previously. In addition, the emphasis on portfolio management tasks changes,

although none of the tasks ever disappear entirely.

Managing a Young Portfolio

A young portfolio faces several hurdles. First, a young portfolio doesn't have much money, and it doesn't have many stocks. The lack of diversification is a big risk. But, with few dollars in the portfolio, brokerage commissions would consume your contributions if you were

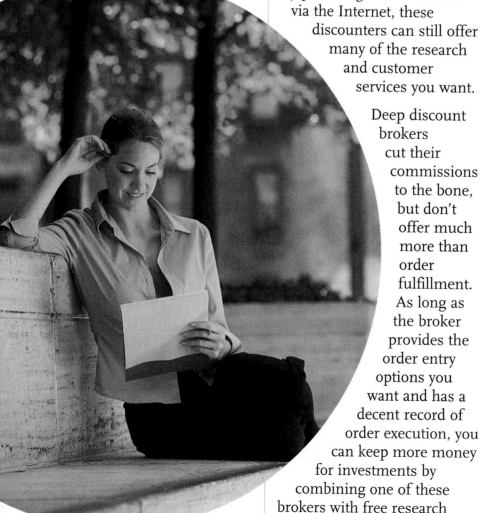

to try to buy several stocks even through a discount broker. A young portfolio is always looking for ways to invest the money that's added on a regular basis. What's a portfolio manager to do?

Contain Costs

Pay as little as possible in commissions and other sales fees. Fortunately, this is much easier to do these days. Discount brokers offer commissions much lower than full service brokerage prices. By providing more features via the Internet, these discounters can still offer many of the research and customer services you want.

Deep discount brokers cut their commissions to the bone, but don't offer much more than order fulfillment. As long as the broker provides the order entry options you want and has a decent record of order execution, you can keep more money for investments by combining one of these brokers with free research

at the library or online (see Chapter 16 for investing resources).

Several brokerages have introduced portfolio services, which act like your own personal mutual fund. You specify the amount of money you intend to contribute and the frequency of your contributions. Then, you designate the stocks that you want to purchase and how to allocate your contributions to those stocks (by dollar or percentage). The brokerage pools folio investors' purchases into buckets of buys to save on fees. For example, FOLIOfn charges a flat $19.95 a month for purchases made during their two daily trading windows. Sharebuilder.com has programs that offer the equivalent of $1 or $2 per trade.

Dividend reinvestment programs (DRIP) and direct stock purchase programs (DSP) are another alternative for ultra-low-cost commissions. These programs are a direct link between you and the company whose shares you want to buy. Many companies create them so they can distribute dividends in additional shares of stock instead of cash. Usually, they also enable you to buy additional shares for little or no additional fees. DRIPs and DSPs are great for cost containment, but they do make portfolio management more difficult. Each investment is in a separate account, so selling one stock and then purchasing another takes some time—and effort. To learn more, navigate to the DripCentral Web site *(http://www.dripcentral.com)*. Be wary of any DRIPS and DSPs with high fees.

Diversify

Once you've got the costs buttoned down, you can start working on your portfolio diversification. If you're an individual investor just getting started with investing, index funds are a low-cost approach to achieving both diversification and market-matching returns with the most modest monthly contribution. If you're like most Americans, the company you work for probably offers a 401(k) retirement plan with a choice of several mutual fund investment options. Contribute as much as you can afford to your 401(k), because your 401(k) contributions reduce your taxable income. The reduction in your take home pay is smaller than the contribution you make to your retirement.

Even if you can't contribute the maximum to your 401(k), be sure to contribute the percentage that your company matches. Every dollar of company matching immediately earns a 100 percent return, which is too good to pass up.

If you want to get started investing in individual stocks, an investment club is a great way to accelerate diversification. With several members contributing $30 or more each month, the club collects enough money to purchase stock regularly (i.e. monthly).

In addition, investment clubs are under less pressure to quickly achieve diversification. As an individual, you want to reduce your risk as quickly as possible, so you don't lose the money you are earning for your financial goals. Although club portfolios can grow to millions of dollars, most clubs begin life as educational efforts. This means that a club is better able

to handle the ups and downs of a less diversified portfolio for a year or two. (Club members might even remember more readily the lessons they learn from mistakes if the errors cost the club a little money.

Play Tough Defense

When a portfolio is small or large and contains only a few investments, a poor performer really hurts. A significant loss in one of your investments carves a big percentage out of the value of your portfolio. It also carves a chunk out of your confidence, which leads to uncertainty, second-guessing, and less chance of success in the future.

When you're starting out, be discerning about the investments you keep. Consider buying only the highest quality companies even though their returns might not be as exciting as others. High quality companies are easier to study, easier to follow, and tend to produce more dependable results.

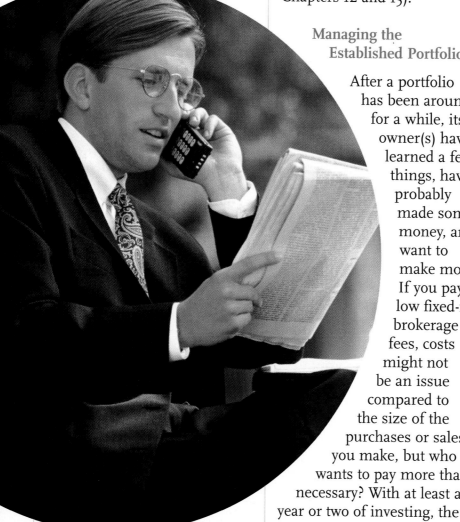

As soon as you own one investment, you must remain vigilant for signs of significant deterioration in the stocks (and funds) that you own (see Chapters 7 through 11). If signs appear, such as significant slowdowns in forecast EPS growth, and seem unlikely to go away quickly (for instance, the one product that a small company produces has become obsolete due to a competitor's new technology,) remove the investment from your portfolio and buy something else (see Chapters 12 and 13).

Managing the Established Portfolio

After a portfolio has been around for a while, its owner(s) have learned a few things, have probably made some money, and want to make more. If you pay low fixed-rate brokerage fees, costs might not be an issue compared to the size of the purchases or sales you make, but who wants to pay more than necessary? With at least a year or two of investing, the portfolio is probably diversified. It sounds like things are well in hand. But, you still have portfolio management tasks to perform.

Play Tough Defense

Regardless of the age of a portfolio, a poor performer hurts. A significant loss in one of your investments might not hurt an established portfolio as much as a young one, but it reduces your overall returns. Continue to perform defensive evaluations when companies release their quarterly results or when new regulations, competition, or market situations change the company outlook.

Seek Continuous Improvement

As your portfolio grows up (in maturity and dollar value), your focus changes to honing its abilities. In addition to protecting it from losses, you spend more time looking for investments that are better than the ones you already own.

A larger, more diversified portfolio also enables you to take higher risks on occasion, because the impact on your portfolio is mitigated if the investment doesn't turn out as you expect. For example, you might decide to put 5 percent of your portfolio in a risky but attractive young company. If the company fails, only five percent of your portfolio is at risk. If the company turns into a Microsoft, your risk will be rewarded. The trick here is to keep the risk, return, and quality of your overall portfolio within the guidelines you've defined.

Buying stocks in a larger portfolio is different from small portfolio purchasing. In addition to adding more stocks to your portfolio for diversification, you will also buy more shares of some of the companies you already own. With time and dividend reinvestments, you can end up with many more shares than you originally purchased. When you decide to sell one investment to buy another, you might have to remind yourself to purchase 500 or more shares instead of the blocks of 10 you started with.

Make Adjustments

Time passes. Some investments produce spectacular results. Others do well. And, still others fall behind. These varying results mean that the diversification that you crafted so carefully in the beginning gradually morphs into something else. So, you not only look for ways to improve your portfolio, you must tweak your holdings to bring your diversification back in line.

During the many years of portfolio middle age, your financial objectives are likely to change. And your portfolio must change in response. For example, if you are investing some of your portfolio to build

EVERYTHING IN MODERATION

Some portfolios suffer the same symptoms as their owners—a thickening around the middle that often comes with age. Investors and clubs can't bear the thought of parting with an investment that has served them well. Unfortunately, this leads to a bloated portfolio, which often means below-average returns. Too many mutual funds in a portfolio increase diversification to the point that your portfolio acts more like a market index, albeit one that charges much higher expenses. Too much money in one mutual fund can be just as bad. Too many stocks make it tough to stay on top of company performance. Poor performers drag down the performance of the portfolio.

a college fund, you'll probably want to move that money into safer investments as your child approaches college age. Many Section 529 plans automatically do this for you. On the other hand, if you win the lottery, you might decide that you can take a little more risk to achieve higher returns.

Managing the Mature Portfolio

The mature portfolio isn't necessarily one that has been around for decades; it's a portfolio that you are finally calling on to pay for your financial objectives. The asset allocation in a mature portfolio should change to protect the money you need over the next few years. Most experts advise you to start moving money out of stocks five years before your target date into secure savings or bonds that mature close to your target date.

Retirement portfolios are more complicated, because you need income to live on but retirement can last for decades, which means you need growth to combat the effects of inflation. Although some people automatically think of income as dividends, you can acquire income by increasing the value of your portfolio with higher returns from both capital gains and dividends.

Scrutinizing Stock Studies

Update, Update, Update!

Buy and hold doesn't mean buy and forget. A company might represent a good investment when you buy it, but that won't last forever. In the worst case, the company's fundamentals deteriorate; its growth rates decline, usually followed by its price, not to mention the value of your portfolio—unless you get out before it's too late. In the best case,

the stock price increases so much that the potential return no longer meets your requirements. The company has been good to you, but it might be time to move on. The only way you'll know whether to say goodbye is with an up-to-date Stock Selection Guide, an important tool for portfolio management.

Being Selective with the Stock Selection Guide

Understanding Data Differences

Evaluating Investments in the SSG Header

Getting Tough with SSG Visual Analysis

Examining Management Quality

The Importance of PE Ratios

Judgment for Stocks that Pay Dividends

Judging Risk and Reward

The Bottom Line: Potential Return

Being Selective with the Stock Selection Guide

Quality, growth companies are easy to understand. They generate their own growth, and also benefit from the growth of their industry and the overall economy. High quality companies are dependable so they help reduce the risk in your portfolio. However, the greatest growth company in the world can still be a lousy investment if you pay too much. Initially, the Stock Selection Guide helps you identify quality, growth companies selling at a price that makes them attractive investments. As you delve deeper into portfolio management, the Stock Selection Guide doesn't just help you decide whether a stock is worthy of investment; it can act as a spotlight to single out the potential winners and losers in your portfolio. Furthermore, by applying ever more discerning judgment to your SSGs, you can identify the most promising winners for additional investment in your portfolio. You're probably familiar with the SSG as a tool for evaluating stocks for purchase. This chapter shows you how to use the SSG to manage the stocks you already own.

Growth and quality are must-have characteristics for an investment. Section 1 of the SSG emphasizes growth and quality characteristics—or their absence. Strong, consistent growth in sales, pre-tax profits, and EPS bodes well for future EPS growth. EPS growth increases the value of a share of stock and that usually leads to an increase in share price.

Section 2 of the SSG uses a few critical measures to show the quality of management and the potential for further growth. Good management can fend off problems and find opportunities in almost any environment. Strong and consistent growth in pre-tax profit margins and returns on shareholders' equity show that management has the right stuff.

If you bought a stock, you saw quality and growth in the first two sections of the SSG. Once a stock is a part of your portfolio and you no longer see quality and growth in the first two sections, consider looking

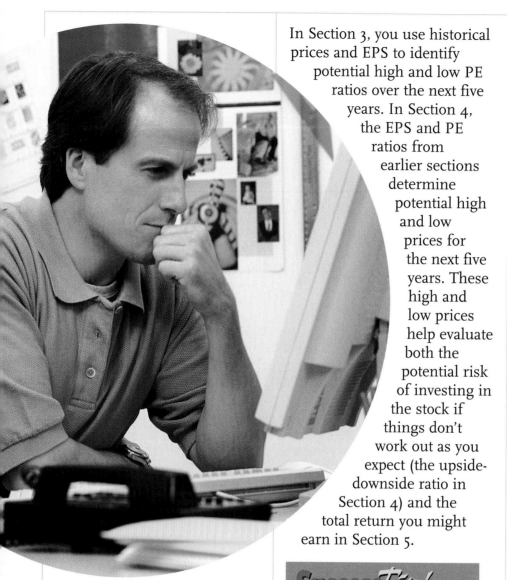

In Section 3, you use historical prices and EPS to identify potential high and low PE ratios over the next five years. In Section 4, the EPS and PE ratios from earlier sections determine potential high and low prices for the next five years. These high and low prices help evaluate both the potential risk of investing in the stock if things don't work out as you expect (the upside-downside ratio in Section 4) and the total return you might earn in Section 5.

Success Tip!

Investors don't pay much for companies of poor quality or slow growth. Unfortunately, low prices can make the results in Sections 3, 4, and 5 look fabulous. However, a dog is a dog at any price, so you must learn to stop studying a new stock when you don't find quality and growth and seriously consider selling the stock if you already own it.

for a replacement. When a company still passes the quality and growth tests of Sections 1 and 2, you can move on to evaluating whether the company is still a good investment for the future. Sections 3, 4, and 5 of the SSG work together to show you whether the current price provides an attractive total return and a reasonable level of risk.

Whether you are adding a stock to your portfolio or replacing one stock with another, the best results come from being tough but fair in your evaluations. Being too optimistic can make almost any company look like a good buy. Being too conservative could leave your money sitting in a savings account, because you rarely find a stock that can overcome the obstacles you place in its path.

When you update your SSGs, be on the lookout for warning signs. Major problems such as deteriorating fundamentals often signal a reason to sell. If a company exhibits minor warning signs, make a point of watching the company carefully, so you can act quickly if the red flags begin to wave frantically.

When you're considering replacing one stock with another, be fussy about quality, the performance you expect, and the price you pay. All the stocks you're considering might offer quality and growth, but you want to pinpoint the one with the best combination of these characteristics. The rest of this chapter discusses techniques to choose a winner when the competition is tough.

Understanding Data Differences

Data differs depending on your source, whether it is a data provider such as Value Line or Standard & Poor's or company provided data in annual reports and SEC 10Ks. The best approach is to obtain data from the same source for stock studies that you plan to compare with one another. However, understanding the possible differences also helps you to interpret the stock studies you prepare.

Financial data comes in many flavors each with its own name. Although distinguishing characteristics can become subtle, the basic differences between these types of data are simple:

- **As reported**—This is the financial data **as reported** by the company.

- **Original as reported**—Original data is the financial data as originally reported by the company at the end of a financial period.

- **Restated as reported**—Companies sometimes modify past financial reports to reflect current accounting practices as defined by the Financial Accounting Standards Board. Restated data is an estimate of what past performance would have been had the company run in its current form (with or without new businesses, discontinued operations, or other organizational changes).

- **Standardized**—Data providers categorize income and expense items into standard categories to simplify company comparisons. Standardized data sometimes moves information shown only in the footnotes of financial reports into the standardized categories.

- **Normalized**—Data providers remove non-recurring income and expenses to better reflect the ongoing performance of the company.

Companies report earnings in several ways. Basic earnings per share represent the net income of the company divided by the number of outstanding shares. Fully diluted earnings are the net income divided by the outstanding shares plus additional shares that the company could issue based on stock options and warrants. Companies report pro forma earnings for several reasons. Pro forma means that the numbers you see include assumptions or a condition that doesn't exist in the real world. For example, when companies merge, pro forma

earnings show the operating results of the two companies as if they had been combined in the past. For mergers (see Chapter 15) pro forma results can help you evaluate future growth and quality, but value judgments are out of reach because you can't generate combined price or PE ratios. Sometimes, companies report pro forma earnings to show their results in a different light (usually flattering to the company). Do not use pro forma earnings unless the company has changed its organization significantly.

Other data differences can affect your stock evaluations. Dividends might be reported based on the date the company declared the dividend or as of the date paid. Book value can include or exclude intangible assets (both Value Line and S&P Stock Reports show book value per share). Return on equity uses EPS and book value so differences in EPS and book value also affect ROE. Chapters 7 and 8 discuss finer points of book value and ROE.

Evaluating Criteria in the SSG Header

The SSG header contains a grab bag of measures that might eliminate a company before you put too much effort into it. You can preview the risk and potential volatility of the stock and consider selling if the risks are too high.

Insider Ownership

The percentage of shares held by insiders such as directors and management tells you whether management's interest is aligned with that of the shareholders. If insiders own a controlling interest the company (51 percent), they might consider the company "theirs" and make decisions for reasons unrelated to providing value to the other shareholders. Conversely, if insiders own too little of the company they might not have an incentive for making sure the price rises. If management's wealth is connected to the stock price, they are more likely to make decisions that are in the shareholders' best interest.

What's the right amount of insider ownership? It depends. Some investors look for insider ownership somewhere between 10 and 40 percent. But, in large companies, as little as 1 percent ownership could represent millions of dollars. Read the annual report to find out how much money insiders have at stake in the company. Look for officers and directors that gain a significant part of their compensation from ownership in the company.

Institutional Ownership

Institutions are organizations such as pension plans and mutual funds. Large percentages of institutional ownership can lead to price volatility. Mutual funds are particularly impatient for results, so they are quick to sell if a company stumbles and less forgiving if the company recovers.

If you prefer a smooth ride, look for institutional ownership of 60 percent or less with that ownership divided among a large number of institutions. (Institutional ownership like this has become harder to find as the assets invested in mutual funds continues to grow.) Finding companies with reasonable levels of institutional ownership becomes more difficult as the dollars invested in mutual funds grows, but stock screens (see Chapter 12) can use institutional ownership to pare down the field.

The Debt to Total Capitalization Ratio

Debt is often a good thing. Without debt, most of us would never be able to buy a house. When companies are just getting started, they don't generate enough earnings to grow quickly. But, by borrowing money, they can grow their operations, increase their profits, and pay off the debt that made it all possible.

Debt can also be a burden, because it must be paid back whether times are good or bad. If a company is struggling, debt payments can consume much of the company's income, leaving little to fund the growth that shareholders expect. When the worst happens and a company goes under, debt holders get paid back first and shareholders get whatever is left.

The ratio of debt to total capitalization shows how much a company relies on debt to fund its operations. This ratio usually uses the company's long-term debt, because short-term debt is payable within a year and shouldn't represent a burden to the company's finances. NAIC's Online Premium Services provides long-term debt in its data files. You can find the percent of debt in the capitalization sections of Value Line and Standard & Poor's stock reports, as well as in company annual reports.

For this ratio, capitalization represents the assets used to fund company operations, not the market capitalization (number of shares outstanding multiplied by the share price) of the company.

A company with debt isn't automatically bad. If the company management can earn more with the money than it pays in interest, the debt benefits the shareholders as well as the bond owners.

NAIC suggests a debt to capitalization ratio of no more than 35 percent. Yet, companies in some industries, such as utilities, have learned to live with much higher levels of debt. Therefore, compare a company's debt to capitalization ratio to the industry average before dismissing the company for excessive debt. Also, compare the company's debt level to its historical debt to see if the company has handled that level of debt successfully in the past.

Success Tip!

When companies carry debt, the interest coverage measure (see Chapter 8) shows the ratio of pre-tax profit to interest payments for long-term debt. Interest coverage of 6 to 7 times should enable a

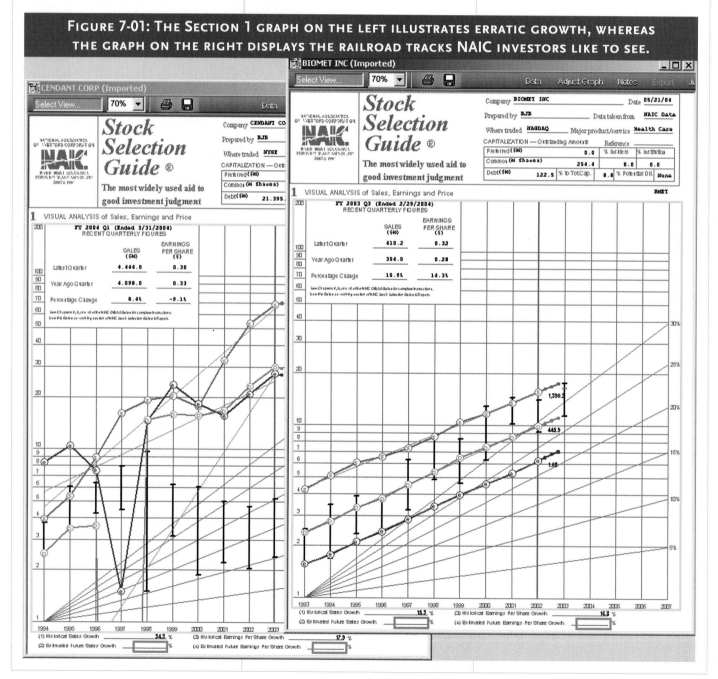

FIGURE 7-01: THE SECTION 1 GRAPH ON THE LEFT ILLUSTRATES ERRATIC GROWTH, WHEREAS THE GRAPH ON THE RIGHT DISPLAYS THE RAILROAD TRACKS NAIC INVESTORS LIKE TO SEE.

company to make its interest payments even if business slows.

Getting Tough with SSG Visual Analysis

The Visual Analysis in Section 1 of the SSG makes it easy to identify the growth characteristics of a company. Historical data is plotted on a logarithmic chart, so you can determine the growth rate of a company. On a logarithmic chart, consistent compound growth rates appear as straight lines radiating out at an angle from the bottom left corner of the page. The steeper the angle, the faster the growth. You must see quality and growth before you take another step. With those prerequisites in place, your estimate of future sales and EPS growth is the key to a company's potential as an investment.

Figure 7-01 compares the Section 1 graphs of two companies: Biomet produces orthopedic medical devices and has been growing consistently and strongly for at least the last ten years—a classic example of an NAIC quality growth company. The consistency and parallel tracks of the sales, pre-tax profit, and EPS growth lines make it easier to estimate the company's performance in the future. Cendant Corp provides travel and real estate services. Its growth lines bounce all

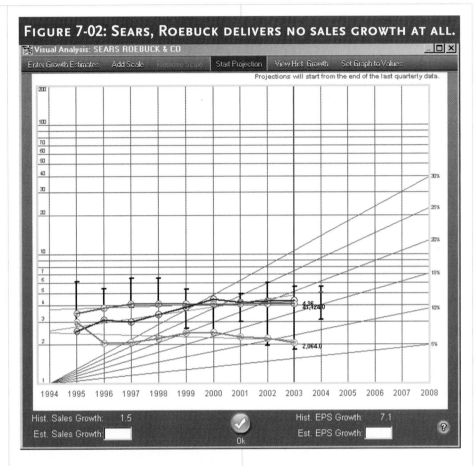

FIGURE 7-02: SEARS, ROEBUCK DELIVERS NO SALES GROWTH AT ALL.

over the map. How could you forecast future performance with any kind of confidence?

On the other hand, Sears, Roebuck and Co. in Figure 7-02 shows consistency all right. It consistently delivers no growth whatsoever. Its sales growth line is flat and pre-tax profit and EPS share growth isn't much better. This company's future performance is easy to estimate, but the results won't help your portfolio increase in value.

What to Look for in Section 1

The desirable characteristics for a quality growth stock don't vary depending on whether

you are buying a stock for the first time or reviewing a stock as you manage your portfolio. Whenever you review a company's performance, ask yourself the following questions:

- Does the company generate sales, pre-tax profit, and EPS growth that is stronger than that of the overall economy? Ideally, look for an annual growth rate of sales greater than 7 percent for large companies, 10 percent for mid-size companies, and 15 percent for small companies.

- Is the company's growth consistent? Consistent

performance is more likely to continue in the future with management that is effective at running the business.

- Are the sales and EPS growth rates similar? All things being equal, EPS derives from sales. If the growth rates diverge, research the company's financials to find out what is driving sales and EPS apart.

The earnings of cyclical stocks respond to the whims of the economic cycle. Investing successfully in these stocks is a matter of accurately timing the market, which is impossible to do consistently. Investing in growth stocks is easier and more profitable.

- Was the last quarter's performance equal to or better than historical and forecast growth rates? If the last quarter compares unfavorably to the same quarter of the previous year, read the footnotes of the quarterly report to find out why. Then, try to determine whether the cause is short-term or forewarns of long-term problems.

Success Tip!

Remember to compare the most recent quarter to the corresponding quarter a year ago. Many industries sell more during one

quarter than others. For example, retail stores often sell the most during the Christmas season.

Determining the Historical Trend

With the historical values for sales, pre-tax profit, and EPS plotted in Section 1, the next step is to identify the company's historical growth trend. As the graph for Cendant in Figure 7-01 demonstrates, the trend line isn't always easy to spot. In fact, sometimes you can't see a trend line, because company growth shows no trend at all! In addition, some of the data

might not represent the true performance of the company. Therefore, before you choose a historical trend line, you must remove any irrelevant data— called outliers.

Outliers can take the form of deficits, small dips, or spikes in values. For example, an acquisition often generates a small dip in pre-tax profit and EPS without an accompanying dip in sales, as illustrated by 1996 in Sungard Data System's SSG in Figure 7-03. The costs of an acquisition are deducted from revenues and depress EPS in the year that the acquisition occurs. Unless

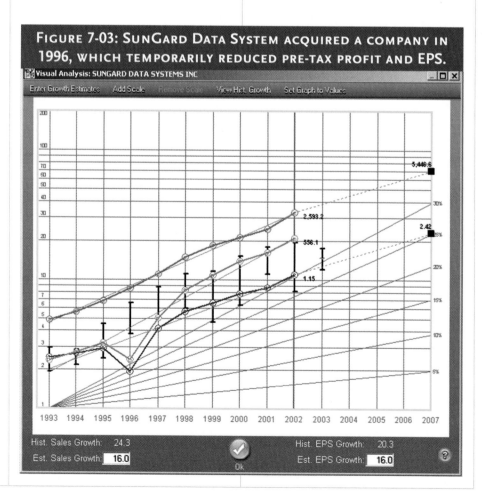

FIGURE 7-03: SUNGARD DATA SYSTEM ACQUIRED A COMPANY IN 1996, WHICH TEMPORARILY REDUCED PRE-TAX PROFIT AND EPS.

the company completes an acquisition every year, the pre-tax profit and EPS should bounce back the following year.

Value Line and Reuters Investor remove one-time events such as acquisitions or divestitures from their data. Value Line describes the adjustments to data in the notes in the lower margin of a stock page. NAIC's OPS uses data from continuing operations, which adjusts data to remove the effect of discontinued operations.

An outlier is a number that is not likely to repeat, but you can't determine whether an outlier will repeat just by looking at Section 1 of the SSG. Before removing a year as an outlier, determine the cause of the blip. If the event might reoccur, it's not an outlier and you should leave the data as it is.

Success Tip!

To be conservative, only remove outliers if the result is a lower growth rate. In addition, if performance in recent years is different than that of earlier years, the more recent performance might be a better indication of the future. In fact, if a company's growth has been slowing as the company size increases, all but the last few years of data could be irrelevant.

If you prepare SSGs manually, you can choose from several methods to select the historical growth trend. In reality, eyeballing a trend line onto the graph works quite well and is quick to perform. When you use NAIC software such as *Investor's Toolkit* or *Stock Analyst*, the software uses a mathematical formula to calculate the historical growth rate and draw the historical trend line in Section 1 of the SSG.

Inputs for Estimating a Future Growth Rate

Estimating the rate at which a company could realistically grow sales and EPS in the future is the bedrock of your stock study. This estimate drives much of the judgment you apply to an SSG and is one of the most important aspects of evaluating whether the company is a good investment and at what price.

Choosing an estimated growth rate isn't just removing outliers from the historical trend and accepting whatever rate the

company has produced in the past. Just as mutual funds like to remind you that past results are no guarantee of the future, a company's future growth derives more from its business outlook and trends in its industry than what happened during the last ten years. Certainly, past results can help. Steady growth in the past indicates that management tends to handle the challenges and opportunities thrown its

way. Slowing growth almost always signals more of the same in the future.

The best estimates of future growth rates come from understanding what drives a company's growth. Yes, you must do some homework on both the company and the industry (see Chapter 17), but your assignment isn't difficult. Peter Lynch, the legendary former manager of the Fidelity Magellan fund, prefers companies that are easy to understand. The following are some questions you can ask to begin your research:

- Do demographic trends imply faster or slower growth in the future?

For example, medical services and pharmaceuticals might grow faster as the population in the U.S. ages.

- Is the market saturated such as that for cell phones or computers?

- How much does the company spend on R&D? What is the success rate of new products and services?

- Does the company keep refilling its pipeline with new products and services?

- Does the company have patents, brand name recognition, or other characteristics that give it a competitive advantage?

- Is the company gaining or losing market share to the competition? Does the size of the market leave room for the company to increase market share?

- What strategies does the company use to compete: innovative products and services, higher quality, lower cost, creation of barriers to other companies entering the market, and so on.

- For retail, does growth come from same store sales or by building new stores? Building new stores requires a great deal of capital. Increasing same store sales is less costly, but growth that exceeds that of the population can be difficult to sustain.

- Does the company grow by acquiring other companies? If so, is the market large enough for this strategy to continue? Have past acquisitions been successful?

With a better understanding of what makes a company tick, you can incorporate the techniques in the following sections to choose an appropriate estimate for future growth. If you find yourself struggling to figure out what a company does, that might be a warning sign to find a company with a simpler business model.

Growth Trends

Analyzing the growth trends for a company and its industry can provide valuable insights into future growth. Past performance doesn't guarantee a repeat performance in the future, but at least it's a place to start. Industries that spawn innovation as a matter of course, such as health care and information technology, often demonstrate rapid growth. Other industries such as those related to food are dependent primarily on population growth. (Otherwise, we would all be very fat.) However, competent management can often generate growth even in industries that are stagnant.

For example, Wal-Mart practically reinvented the retail market with its Supercenters. It used innovative business practices to offer low prices and improved services that took business away from competitors. By doing so, the company grew faster than the population for many years. With a powerhouse such as Wal-Mart increasing its market share, other companies in the same industry might struggle to keep up. Comparing a company's growth rates to the average for the industry can tell you whether the company is a leader or in danger of falling behind.

Success Tip!

For retail companies, same-store or comparable store sales growth is an important predictor of future growth. Same-store sales growth is the internal growth driven by management's efforts, not from the capital-intensive strategy of building more stores.

Guidelines for Interpreting Growth Rates

As a company grows, it often has trouble maintaining its past growth rate. If a company sells $10 million of widgets, selling another $2 million isn't that hard. Home Depot generates annual revenues of $65 billion selling home improvement supplies. At this level, increasing revenues at 15 percent means increasing sales by almost $10 billion, which represents a lot of honey-do projects.

Here are some guidelines for interpreting past growth rates:

- Sky-high growth rates: Don't expect them to continue indefinitely. It's wise to assume a more conservative growth rate for the future. Very few companies can maintain a 20 percent growth rate year after year.

- Signs of slowing growth: Slowing growth is a fact of life. The wise investor realizes that any company will eventually grow at a

VIEWING TRENDS IN HISTORICAL GROWTH RATES

In Investor's Toolkit, the Historical Growth Rate Change Chart plots the past sales and EPS growth for progressively shorter periods of time (from a nine-year period down to a one-year period) so that consistent growth rates plot as a horizontal line. Even small variations in growth over different lengths of time are easily visible on this graph. As illustrated in Figure 7-04, growth rates that drop as you move to the right emphasize slowing growth. To display this graph, click within the Visual Analysis area of Section 1. Then, in the Visual Analysis window that appears, select View Hist. Growth on the menu bar. To see a graph of growth from quarter to quarter use the PERT-A graph, described in Chapter 11.

slower rate, regardless of how fast the growth is now. If a company has already begun to slow down, expect even slower rates to come. In these situations, you must evaluate whether the company's more sedate growth keeps it in the growth company category.

- Steady growth: Companies can grow steadily for many years at moderate rates. For these companies, you can certainly estimate more of the same, but don't expect the growth rate to speed up in the future.

What About EPS that Grow Faster than Sales?

Earnings are what's left after subtracting costs from sales, so it is difficult for a company to grow EPS faster than sales forever. In fact, there are only a few ways for this to occur:

- Stock buybacks: When a company buys back shares of stock, the net income is divided by fewer shares of stock, resulting in higher earnings per share.

A company can buy back shares for only so long—taken to the extreme, it would buy back all the shares and the company would be privately owned.

- Cost cutting: By reducing costs, fewer costs are subtracted from sales, resulting in higher net income and EPS. At some point, when cost cutting moves beyond corporate fat into muscle and vital organs, earnings might suffer instead of improve.

- Improving profit margins: Pre-tax profit margins represent the amount of money a company keeps from each dollar of sales

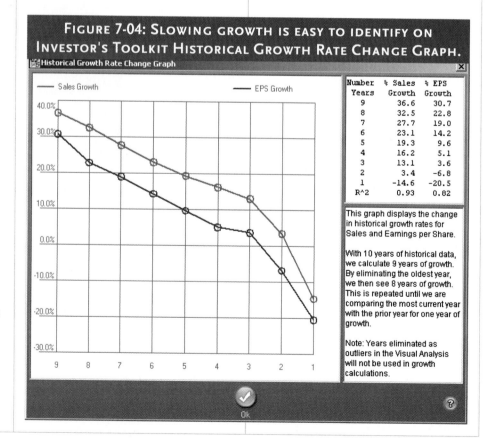

FIGURE 7-04: SLOWING GROWTH IS EASY TO IDENTIFY ON INVESTOR'S TOOLKIT HISTORICAL GROWTH RATE CHANGE GRAPH.

Historical Growth Rate Change Graph

— Sales Growth — EPS Growth

Number Years	% Sales Growth	% EPS Growth
9	36.6	30.7
8	32.5	22.8
7	27.7	19.0
6	23.1	14.2
5	19.3	9.6
4	16.2	5.1
3	13.1	3.6
2	3.4	-6.8
1	-14.6	-20.5
R^2	0.93	0.82

This graph displays the change in historical growth rates for Sales and Earnings per Share.

With 10 years of historical data, we calculate 9 years of growth. By eliminating the oldest year, we then see 8 years of growth. This is repeated until we are comparing the most current year with the prior year for one year of growth.

Note: Years eliminated as outliers in the Visual Analysis will not be used in growth calculations.

Ok

before taxes. Increasing prices brings in more dollars, whereas cutting costs reduces the number of dollars spent. Either approach can increase a company's profit margin, but they can also backfire if not implemented well.

- Reducing dividends: If a company cuts back on dividends, the company retains those earnings, which can be used for future growth. Investors consider cutting dividends as a bad sign, so companies typically use this technique as a last resort.

- Leveraging debt: If a company can generate a higher return than the interest rate it pays on debt, the difference goes into earnings. The same holds true for money raised by selling more shares. In general, increasing debt or issuing shares are not to the shareholders' advantage.

Success Tip!

When the tax rate drops, the money saved in taxes increases EPS. Not only are lower taxes a temporary effect, but a company has only minimal control over the tax rate it pays. Don't depend on a declining tax rate to help EPS growth along.

All of the previous options are temporary tactics, so the conservative approach is to limit EPS growth to no more than sales growth. If you expect a buyback or cost cutting initiative to last for five years or more, you might choose to estimate EPS growth faster than sales. But, remember that you are increasing the risk in your analysis.

The SSG Preferred Procedure

If you're still creating SSGs with pencil, paper, and a handheld calculator, the Preferred Procedure requires more data and several additional calculations. You might not prefer the extra work, but you'll appreciate the improved results it might deliver. As long as you use SSG software, which performs the calculations for you, the Preferred Procedure

offers several advantages with little extra effort. The underlying premise for the Preferred Procedure is that sales are easier to estimate than earnings and are more difficult to manipulate.

The Preferred Procedure enables you to apply judgment to each component that affects EPS: expenses, taxes, preferred dividends, and the number of shares outstanding. In effect, a completed Preferred Procedure, shown in Figure 7-05, represents your expectation for the company's income statement five years in the future. If pre-tax profit margins are decreasing, meaning that costs are increasing, you can specify even higher expenses for the future. If taxes have been decreasing, you can set them back to a higher level to gauge their effect on earnings.

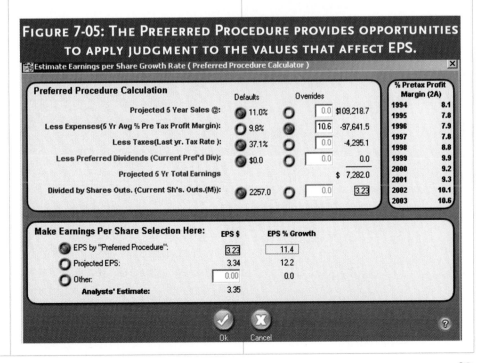

FIGURE 7-05: THE PREFERRED PROCEDURE PROVIDES OPPORTUNITIES TO APPLY JUDGMENT TO THE VALUES THAT AFFECT EPS.

If a company is continually issuing additional shares of stock, you can estimate a higher number of shares for the future.

Even if you decide to leave the components in the Preferred Procedure as they are, simply reviewing the trends in costs, taxes, and other measures is worthwhile. For example, these trends can explain why EPS are growing faster or slower than sales.

The Preferred Procedure doesn't provide easy-to-read graphs of the numbers. Sometimes, the trends are easy to see, for instance when the pre-tax profit numbers bump up a little each year. However, evaluating trends in measures such as costs and taxes includes reviewing annual reports to see where the numbers might head in the future.

The EPS growth rate calculated by the Preferred Procedure is a substitute for a growth trend from Section 1 when a company's earnings are inconsistent or even non-existent. For companies with reasonably well-behaved earnings, the Preferred Procedure EPS growth rate can act as a sanity check on the growth rate you forecast.

Use the following guidelines as you work your way through the Preferred Procedure:

- Pre-tax profit margins: If the margins are increasing, use the average for the last five years or limit the value to last year's margin, as demonstrated in Figure 7-05. If margins are decreasing, use the previous year's margin or less. If management has announced a plan to increase profit margins, you can use management's projected profit margin after researching the feasibility of their plan. On the other hand, if management has admitted to lower profit margins for the future, use their new forecast regardless what the historical trends indicate.

- Tax rate: If the tax rate is increasing, choose a rate higher than the previous year's. If you think that the government is likely to increase or cut rates, adjust the tax rate in the Preferred Procedure accordingly.

- Preferred stock: Although few companies issue preferred stock these days, you must deduct the dividends paid to preferred shareholders if they exist to calculate net profits. Preferred dividends appear in Value Line's Capital Structure box as well as in a company's income statement.

- Shares outstanding: Although it's difficult to estimate the number of shares in the future, consider using a higher number of shares, if the number of shares have been increasing. If the shares are decreasing, check the duration of the buyback before using fewer shares than the previous year. Company buyback programs don't always occur. Don't reduce the shares outstanding just because a company announces a plan to buyback shares.

When the Preferred Procedure corroborates your projected EPS growth rate, you can feel more confident in your estimate. To be conservative, choose the lower of the two projected EPS growth rates. If the result of your Preferred Procedure and your EPS growth projection differ, reevaluate your assumptions to decide which projection is more dependable.

Sustainable Growth

Sustainable growth is another sanity check for the EPS growth rate you select. Sustainable growth, also called implied growth, represents the growth rate a company can produce using only the funds generated by operations—not from selling shares of stock or borrowing money. Growth faster than the sustainable

growth rate could indicate that the company is borrowing money or issuing stock, both of which can adversely affect existing shareholders. It could also indicate increasing profit margins, which are desirable but can't continue indefinitely. Over long timeframes, companies find it difficult to grow faster than the sustainable growth rate, so you can use it to validate the EPS growth rate you choose.

EPS growth that is less than the sustainable growth rate can be due to declining profit margins, share buybacks, paying down debt, or management that doesn't put the company earnings to good use.

The formula for sustainable growth is as follows:

Sustainable growth = ROE * (1 – Dividend payout rate)

Return on equity (ROE) is the return that management produces on shareholders' equity in the company: net income divided by shareholders' equity. When a company pays income out to shareholders as dividends, that money is no longer available to fund company growth. So, the sustainable growth rate is the ROE only for the company's retained earnings. If a company pays no dividends, the sustainable growth rate is equal to ROE.

Lowe's has grown its earnings at approximately 25 percent a year from 1994 through 2003—faster than sales the entire time. Analysts forecast EPS growth at 20 percent. However, sustainable growth tells a different story. For 2003, the numbers look like this:

ROE = 17.7 percent

Dividend payout rate = 4.7 percent

Sustainable growth = .177 * (1 − .047) = 16.8 percent.

That's still an attractive EPS growth rate for a multi-billion dollar company, but significantly less than historical rates or analysts' estimates.

In Toolkit, ROE is EPS divided by book value per share in the second row of Section 2. Stock Analyst refers to ROE as % Earned on Equity. Value Line lists ROE as % Retained to Common Equity. The dividend payout rate is shown in column G in Section 3 of the SSG.

Company Guidance

Quite often, companies announce the growth they expect to generate in the future, in part because the stock market hates surprises. If future growth is liable to be disappointing, companies forewarn analysts and investors ahead of time in the hope that they don't over-react and sell off the stock when the company formally announces earnings. Of course, if the company expects great performance in the future, management likes to toot its horn. Read the annual report or SEC 10-K. (see Chapter 8) for hints about future growth rates. The CEO often mentions them in the Letter to Shareholders.

Don't take the company's word. A CEO can forecast growth, but will the company deliver? Review past reports so see what the CEO proposed to accomplish. Check more recent reports to see if those forecasts came true. What accomplishments is the CEO proposing for the future? Does he or she predict a growth rate? Do the reasons provided support the CEO's prediction?

Stock splits often indicate a company's optimism about future growth. When a company regularly splits its stock, management anticipates ongoing growth and wants to keep the price in a range that is attractive to most investors. (You still should evaluate the company's prospects to see if you agree with their optimism.) This explains why you rarely see share prices greater than $100. One famous exception is Berkshire Hathaway, Warren Buffett's holding company. On May 24, 2004, Berkshire Hathaway's share price was $88,200, because the company does not split its stock. Few investors can afford even one share of Berkshire Hathaway. Paychex' approach is more common. By splitting its stock 8 times between 1992 and 2002, the company kept its stock price under $50 most of the time.

Insider ownership is another indication of management's optimism. Executives and directors buy shares in the company when they expect their investment to perform well. An insider committing a significant percentage of his or her wealth to company stock is a positive signal. Insiders adding to their holdings of company stock is also positive. Insider selling isn't as telling, because insiders might sell for a variety of reasons: to rebalance their portfolios or buy a new house, for example. At Yahoo! Finance *(http:// finance.yahoo.com),* type a ticker symbol in the Enter symbol(s) box, and click Go to open the stock page. Then, click the Insider Transactions link in the navigation bar to view buys, sells, and other insider transactions.

Pulling It All Together

Between researching the company's background and evaluating several methods for forecasting growth, picking a future growth rate might seem like a lot of work. It's not. With time, choosing the best options for forecasting growth based on a company's circumstances

will become second nature. The following estimated growth checklist acts as a final reminder to be conservative:

- Do not estimate a growth rate faster than the historic rate.

- If growth is steady and nothing negative is lurking in the company's business outlook, use the current growth rate.

- Even if EPS growth is faster than sales, limit EPS growth to the sales growth rate.

- If the trend you see is slowing growth, limit your forecast to no more than the average growth rate for the

past several years. Consider a rate that's lower than the previous year's.

- If growth is extremely fast, don't expect that growth rate to continue. For example, you might limit the growth rate to no more than the sustainable growth rate. If EPS growth is slower than the sustainable growth rate, you can use the sustainable rate if the factors affecting EPS are short-lived (share buybacks, debt reduction, etc).

PRICE IN SECTION 1

If you position the price bars in the graph in Section 1 above the EPS trend line, you can see the trends for a company's PE ratio. The distance between the EPS trend line and the price bars shows the relative magnitude of the PE ratio. When investors buy on emotion, the price increases faster than EPS and the distances between the EPS trend line and the price bars grow larger. If investors don't like what they see or the price takes a breather while EPS catch up, the distances between the trend line and the price bars diminish.

- If the graph in Section 1 is erratic or the values in Section 2 are erratic or falling, consider looking for a better company.

- Value Line, IBES, First Call analyst estimates tend to be optimistic but are additional tools you can use to double-check your own estimate. If your estimate is higher than the typically optimistic analyst estimates, it's wise to review your analysis again.

- If anything else bothers you about the company, drop your forecast by another point or move onto another company.

After making it through this checklist, is the growth rate that you have chosen acceptable for the size of company and for your guidelines for your portfolio? If so, you can continue your study.

Scrutinizing Management Quality

In the real estate business, buyers chant "Location, location, location!" For stock investing, the mantra is management. Companies that are well-managed usually deliver consistent growth of sales, pre-tax profit, and earnings per share despite challenges that would twist other companies' growth trends into pretzels. Section 2 of the SSG uses pre-tax profit margin and return on equity to evaluate company management. Ideally, these measures increase steadily over time, although many companies have their businesses so finely tuned that they maintain the percentages year after year.

Pre-tax Profit Margin

The pre-tax profit margin is the percentage of profit that a company retains from sales before paying taxes. A company can increase its profit margin in many ways. No matter which techniques management employs, increasing profit

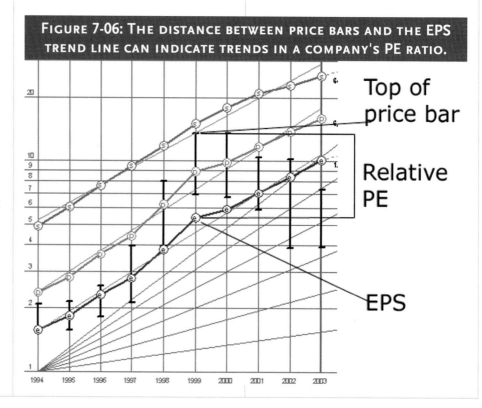

FIGURE 7-06: THE DISTANCE BETWEEN PRICE BARS AND THE EPS TREND LINE CAN INDICATE TRENDS IN A COMPANY'S PE RATIO.

margins is like walking a tightrope. Increasing prices while keeping costs at the same level will increase the profit margin. But, higher prices can drive customers away unless quality is impeccable. Cost cutting can increase profit margin but runs the risk of lower quality, poor service, or inefficient operations. Paying less for supplies, reducing overhead, or increasing productivity also reduces costs. In industries with constant renewal, such as computers and fashion, management must also anticipate and work to minimize obsolete inventory. In every case, strategies don't work forever, so management must continually balance pros and cons.

A steady or consistently increasing trend in profit margin indicates that management effectively balances strategies to increase sales and control costs. If the profit margin is decreasing, see whether costs are out of control or look for an increase in competition. For example, companies with innovative new products often enjoy high profit margins until competition moves into the field, forcing lower prices.

When the pre-tax profit margin drops, the company doesn't keep as much of each dollar it brings in. A company can hide temporary declines in profit margin with cost cutting and layoffs, but lower margins often lead to lower earnings. If pre-tax profit margin trends downward, research the source of the decline to determine whether it is a dangerous long-term trend such as losing market shares to an innovative competitor. If a value is due to a short-term effect, remove the value as an outlier.

Success Tip!

When the tax rate drops, the costs of an acquisition show up in the pre-tax profit margin in Section 2 if you use data that is not normalized. When you see a dip in the numbers in Section 2, see if it is due to an acquisition. If so, you can remove that year as an outlier.

Return on Equity (ROE)

Return on equity is the return that management generates using money from operations. A company can also finance growth by borrowing or selling more shares. However, these strategies are usually bad for shareholders, so higher ROE is the best way to finance growth to benefit shareholders.

Similar to profit margin, an upward trend in return on equity can result from several circumstances. A healthy ROE indicates that management puts the shareholders' investment in the company to good use. On the other hand, if ROE trends downward,

smaller denominator produces a higher ROE. Unfortunately, this says nothing about management's competence.

When a company carries a lot of debt, ROE can look better than it really is because the company is financing growth with debt in addition to shareholders' equity. Some of the net income it produces comes from the debt that the company assumes. For that reason, you shouldn't compare ROE for companies whose levels of debt are significantly different. For companies that use debt, first assure yourself that the company can handle the debt it carries. Then, use return on assets (ROA) to determine whether the company is using debt effectively to grow the business.

Reviewing Management Quality in Section 2

A downward trend in profit margin (section 2A) or return on equity (section 2B) can forewarn of trouble brewing

that eventually surfaces as poorer earnings. If you spot downward trends in either measure or current values that are less than the five-year averages, it's time to do some homework in the company's financial statements (see Chapter 8). Compare values of different categories of costs from year to year. Read management's discussion of the business and the business outlook to see whether the changes are temporary. For example, when the economy slows, companies can't react instantaneously to reduce costs and might not be able to reduce their fixed costs at all. Although the profit margin suffers, all the competitors in the industry are likely to be suffering just as much.

If a company's margins and ROE are declining from values far above the industry average, you might consider lowering your projected EPS growth rate back in Section 1. However, if the company's Section 2 numbers are declining into below-average territory, it might be time to find another investment.

Success Tip!

Erratic numbers in Section 2 don't necessarily indicate poor management. If a company is cyclical, it can have erratic numbers and the management may be the best in the industry.

determine whether the problem is likely to drag down ROE for the long-term. If the source is a short-term issue, simply remove the value as an outlier.

ROE = Net Income / Shareholders' Equity

Buying back shares increases a company's ROE, because the lower number of shares outstanding reduces shareholders' equity and a

However, for a growth company, erratic numbers in Section 2 often indicate problems with company management. As in the other sections of the SSG, you must use your own judgment.

Comparing Section 2 measures to the averages for the industry is important. Some industries are asset and cost intensive such as the grocery industry and profit margins and ROE could be 4 percent or even less. In industries with low margins and ROE, a competitor who identifies a more profitable niche, such as Whole Foods which sells higher markup organic products, obtains a strong advantage. Conversely, other industries use few assets to generate income, so profit margins and ROE could be 25 percent or more. In this case, companies that deliver below-average numbers are in danger of falling so far behind that they can never catch up.

The Importance of P/E Ratios

At the farmers market, one vendor has a basket of shiny red apples, unblemished, the slice proffered juicy and sweet. Another vendor sells small and misshapen nuggets whose flavor merely resembles that of an apple. You would probably be willing to pay more per pound for the first vendor's apples than you would for the second's. The stock market works the same way except that investors pay more per dollar of earnings for higher quality and returns.

PE reflects the optimism or pessimism investors have about a company. High PE ratios mean that investors are paying prices that already take into account future performance, which is known as discounting the future. PEs typically increase because the price increases faster than EPS, which occurs as investors grow more optimistic about the company's prospects.

PEs can decrease in two ways. First, when a company's EPS show signs of deterioration, investors often exit in a hurry.

The price falls even faster than those troubled EPS and the PE falls with it. For high quality companies, the PE can drop when the price stays constant while the EPS continue to grow. Home Depot exhibited this behavior more than once in the past 20 years. Home Depot's EPS grew steadily for years, while the price would skyrocket sending the PE ratio up to the 60s and 70s. Then, the price would plateau for several years, so the PE would gradually decrease to more appropriate values in the 20s or 30s as the earnings grew. With so much talk about efficient markets, you would think that the PE would

Gary begins his portfolio management with proper stock selection via the SSG. He points out that stocks that shouldn't have been purchased only confuse the issues when you get to the PERT Report, PERT-A and other portfolio management tools. Gary uses the PERT Report as a one-line summary of the SSGs for his stocks. Like Rich Beaubien, he uses the SSG to follow stocks in his portfolio to visualize whether sales and EPS are meeting his projections.

GARY SIMMS

remain in a narrow range as the price and EPS grows in parallel. But, a PE that remains constant is one of the rarest occurrences.

Success Tip!

Be sure to use prices and EPS from the same periods of time. NAIC Online Premium Services and Reuters data use a company's fiscal year for both price and EPS. Value Line provides prices for the calendar year but other data for the fiscal year. If you use Value Line data, obtain high and low prices for each fiscal year from online sources or from the company's annual reports.

Projected (or future) PE ratios are almost as important as the growth rates you forecast because risk and reward on the SSG (Sections 4 and 5) use projected PE ratios to calculate potential high and low prices. An overly optimistic high PE ratio results in an optimistic future high price, which makes

the risk look lower and the reward appear higher.

The best investments are those that provide return from both EPS growth and the added kick that increasing PE ratios provide. The PE ratio is the price divided by the EPS. Therefore, if the PE stays the same, you'd expect the price to grow at the same rate as the EPS.

Consider a company that had annual EPS of $1.25 with a price per share of $20. The stock's PE was 16. And suppose that the company grew its earnings at an average annual rate of 15 percent for five years. Table 7-01 shows how the total return you achieve can vary significantly

depending on the direction that the PE ratio takes.

If the PE ratio increases during the five years in this example, the price rises faster than the EPS. As you can see in table 7-01, the return is 20.3 percent even though the EPS grew at only 15 percent. If the PE ratio decreases, the price might still rise, but it does so slower than the EPS growth. The resulting return is lower than the EPS rate of growth. The boost that increasing PE ratios give to your return is one reason investors buy stocks when their PE ratios are below their five-year average PE ratios (relative value less than 100.)

Choosing PE Ratios

Historical P/E ratios are a valuable component for determining the future P/E ratios, but they aren't the sole answer. Unfortunately, many investors don't look further than the five-year average high and low PEs in Section 3 of the SSG for their projected PE ratios. Over long stock market cycles, PEs can move from as low as 5 or 6 to values in the

TABLE 7-01: PE RATIOS AFFECT THE RETURN YOU EARN.			
Example	**Current PE**	**Current Price**	**Return**
PE Stays the Same	16	$40.22	15.0%
PE Increases	20	$50.28	20.3%
PE Decreases	12	$30.17	8.6%

30s. Evaluating where PEs stand in relation to long cycles can help you develop the patience you need to use the changes in PE ratios to your advantage. If you wait until a company's PE is relatively low compared to its historical PEs, you'll improve the returns you achieve on your investments, as Table 7-01 demonstrates. As the long bull market of the 1990s demonstrated, PE ratios even for the past five years can be misleading. Therefore, judgment is essential in choosing PE ratios for the next five years.

Removing outliers from historical PE ratios is the first step in applying judgment in Section 3. If EPS drop one year due to a nonrecurring event, the low EPS inflates the PE ratio for that year. You do not have to eliminate an entire row in Section 3. For example, you might decide to eliminate the high PE for a year, but keep the low PE.

To get a better idea of a typical PE ratio for a company, examine the PE ratios of the company for the past 10 years. For example, the tail of the 1990s bull market pushed PE ratios for many stocks into the 40s and 50s for several years. Using a 5-year average would still inflate the average PE. The PE ratios of the early 90s help identify more realistic PE projections, as shown in Figure 7-07.

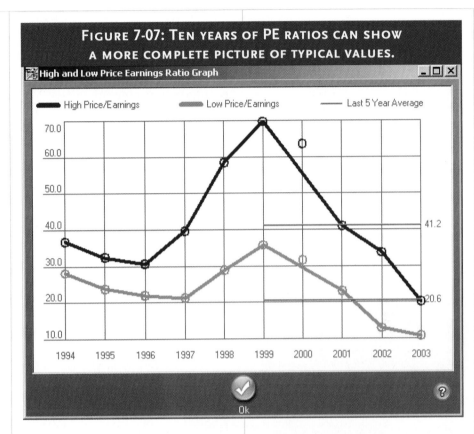

FIGURE 7-07: TEN YEARS OF PE RATIOS CAN SHOW A MORE COMPLETE PICTURE OF TYPICAL VALUES.

You can view 10 years of PE ratios on the PERT-B worksheet or, in *Toolkit,* by clicking either the average high PE box or average low PE box on the back side of an SSG. Value Line includes average annual PE ratios for the past 15 years in the table of data across the top of a stock page.

Use the following checklist to evaluate and choose high and low PE ratios.

- Eliminate outlying high or low PEs that are significantly different from other values. To be conservative, consider eliminating PE ratios only when the result is a lower forecast PE ratio.

- Think twice before eliminating the most recent year's PEs as outliers. They could be the beginning of a trend.

- If the PE ratios have been expanding, limit your forecast to the five-year average PE or at the very most the PE ratio for the most recent year.

- If PEs are declining, use the PE ratio for the most recent year or choose an even lower PE.

- Set your own guidelines for maximum high and low PEs to avoid temptation. Some NAICers limit the high PE to 25 or 30 (read the next section on the PEG ratio to learn the source of this rule).

The PEG Ratio

The PEG ratio is the projected PE ratio divided by the company's projected EPS growth rate. Although the PEG ratio doesn't appear on the SSG, it is useful as a reality check for your projected high PE ratio. Because the PE ratios for high-growth companies tend to stay in the stratosphere, the PEG ratio is also useful for testing the level of euphoria in those sky-high PEs.

Because price tends to increase with earnings, the PE ratio and EPS growth are related. Investors typically pay a higher PE for high growth companies because they expect more earnings from those companies in the future. Experts consider a PEG ratio somewhere between 1.0 and 1.5 as a guideline for fairly valued companies. That means that the PE ratio is 1 to 1.5 times the EPS growth rate. PEG ratios of 1.1 and 1.5 are commonly used as upper limits for fair value. For example, if you forecast EPS growth rate at 10 percent and then choose a forecast high PE ratio of 20, the resulting PEG ratio of 2.0 would highlight how optimistic your projection really is.

The PEG ratio can act as a reminder to reduce your projected high PE if you decide to reduce your forecast for EPS growth. Just as investors pay higher PEs for high growth companies, they expect to pay lower PEs for companies with less growth. For example, if you decide to drop your EPS growth forecast from 18 percent to 14 percent, an upper limit of 1.5 for PEG would drop the high PE ratio limit from 27 to 21.

Judgment for Stocks that Pay Dividends

Section 3 of the SSG also calculates the payout ratio and yield based on the dividends that a company pays. Dividends contribute to your total return, so you must apply judgment to payout ratios and yields in Section 3 to obtain the best picture of the potential return that a company offers. Of course, if a company pays no dividends, you can skip the payout ratio and yield calculations and judgment.

Many investors consider steady dividend increases as a sign of quality and dependability, so companies do their best to maintain or increase the dividends they pay each quarter. Dividends are great if you want current income but they also contribute to the total return that a stock provides. On the down side, dividends consume earnings that the company could use to fund more growth. A company that pays out a lot of earnings as dividends might be saying that it doesn't have that many opportunities for growth and might as well distribute the money to shareholders. On the other hand, a company that pays no dividends can use all its earnings to fund growth, but the safety net that high dividends provide to stock price is gone.

How the Payout Ratio Affects Results

The payout ratio is the percentage of earnings that a company pays out as dividends and is helpful for identifying trends in dividends paid. For example, as long as a company grows its earnings, it can raise

the dollar value of its dividend without increasing the payout ratio. If EPS is $1.00 and the company pays $.03 in dividends, the payout ratio is 3 percent. If EPS increase to $1.50, the 3 percent payout is $.045 in dividends. Use the following checklist to identify outliers in the payout ratio and to determine whether the company has a suitable dividend policy for your investment objectives.

- Increasing payout ratio: When the payout ratio increases, the company is retaining less and less of its earnings to fund growth. Consider whether the company's dividend policy

might hurt its growth potential. Much more than a 33 percent payout ratio means the company retains little to take advantage of growth opportunities.

- Decreasing payout ratio: This can occur if the company increases its dividends at a slower rate than its EPS growth, but it can also occur if the company cuts its dividends. See if the company is continually cutting its dividends to make declining earnings look better.

- Spike in payout ratio: If the payout ratio increases significantly in one year, the company might have maintained its record of paying or increasing dividends despite a bad earnings year. One year that is significantly different might be a candidate for an outlier. However, be cautious when a company continues to distribute more in dividends than the earnings justify. Not only is the dividend likely to be cut, but the money paid out in dividends could hurt future growth.

- Dip in payout ratio: A good earnings year can reduce the payout ratio for that year and is a target for an outlier. Do some research to make sure that the dip isn't the beginning of a trend. For example, Pfizer EPS dropped from $1.54 in 2002 to $.90 in 2003, which increased the dividend payout ratio from 33 percent to 66 percent. However, the 2003 results included the impact of the Pharmacia acquisition. In 2004, EPS was $1.78 and the payout ratio dropped to 38 percent.

Using Yield to Find the Stock Price Safety Net

The yield on a stock is the dividend that the company pays divided by its price. The stock price is like the initial deposit in a savings account and the dividend is the compounded interest you receive on your balance. When a company's dividend provides a significant yield, the share price has some protection if the company hits a rough patch. Many professional money managers pay a great deal of attention to dividend yield data.

Section 4 of the SSG uses the yield in Section 3 to determine the price that the dividend supports. In Section 3, you use the dividend and the price to calculate a yield.

Yield = Dividend / Price

In Section 4, you provide a yield and the annual dividend to calculate a price.

Price = Dividend / Yield

You use the most recent annual dividend paid. But, what yield should you use? To be conservative, you want to find the lowest low price supported by the annual dividend. Because the yield is the denominator in the equation, a higher yield provides a lower price. Therefore, you want to use the highest yield during the last five years, as shown in Figure 7-08.

In Figure 7-08, Merck paid $1.52 in dividends and the high yield is 5.9 percent, the price that the dividend supports is 1.52 / .059, or $25.60. If you had used the low yield (2.4 percent) instead, the price supported by the dividend would be 1.52/.024 or $63.33, which is not a conservative low price.

FIGURE 7-08: THE HIGHEST YIELD PRODUCES A LOWER PRICE.

3 PRICE-EARNINGS HISTORY as an indicator of the future

This shows how stock prices have fluctuated with earnings and dividends. It is a building block for translating earnings into future stock prices.

PRESENT PRICE **28.020** HIGH THIS YEAR **49.330** LOW THIS YEAR **25.600**

Year	A PRICE HIGH	B PRICE LOW	C Earnings Per Share	D Price Earnings Ratio HIGH A ÷ C	E Price Earnings Ratio LOW B ÷ C	F Dividend Per Share	G % Payout F ÷ C X 100	H % High Yield F ÷ B X 100
1 2000	96.7	52.0	2.90	33.3	17.9	1.260	43.4	2.4
2 2001	95.3	56.8	3.14	30.3	18.1	1.380	43.9	2.4
3 2002	64.5	38.5	3.14	20.5	12.3	1.420	45.2	3.7
4 2003	63.5	40.6	2.99	21.2	13.6	1.460	48.8	3.6
5 2004	49.3	25.6	2.61	18.9	9.8	1.520	58.2	5.9
6 TOTAL		213.5		124.2	71.7		239.5	
7 AVERAGE		42.7		24.8	14.3		47.9	

8 AVERAGE PRICE EARNINGS RATIO	**19.5**	9 CURRENT PRICE EARNINGS RATIO	**8.6**

Proj. P/E [8.32] Based on Next 4 qtr. EPS [3.37] Current P/E Based on Last 4 qtr. EPS [3.27]

4 EVALUATING RISK and REWARD over the next 5 years

Assuming one recession and one business boom every 5 years, calculations are made of how high and how low the stock might sell. The upside-downside ratio is the key to evaluating risk and reward.

A HIGH PRICE -- NEXT 5 YEARS
  Avg. High P/E **24.8** **8.0** (3D7 as adj.) X Estimate High Earnings/Share **3.79** = Forecast High Price $ **30.3** (4A1)

B LOW PRICE -- NEXT 5 YEARS
  (a) Avg. Low P/E **14.3** **4.0** (3E7 as adj.) X Estimated Low Earnings/Share **2.61** = $ **10.4**
  (b) Avg. Low Price of Last 5 Years = **42.7** (3B7)
  (c) Recent Severe Market Low Price = **25.6**
  (d) Price Dividend Will Support $\dfrac{\text{Present Divd.}}{\text{High Yield (H)}}$ = $\dfrac{1.520}{0.059}$ = **25.6**

  Selected Estimate Low Price = $ **29.0**

A year with an unrealistically low price can inflate the high yield for that year. If you think a low price is an outlier, such as the result of a market overreaction, eliminate the yield for that year and use the next highest yield in your calculation.

Judging Risk and Reward

Paying too much for a stock whittles away the return you achieve on your investment. Section 4 of the SSG uses several measures to help you determine a reasonable price for a stock. The buy, sell, and hold zones indicate the price points at which a company might be a good investment or a candidate to sell. The relative value is also helpful for identifying overpriced stocks, fairly valued stocks, and those that might have trouble lurking in the wings. The upside-downside ratio measures the price risk of the stock at its current price. A company might offer an attractive total return, but if its potential price drop is too high, the return might not be worth the risk.

High and low prices for the next five years are the foundation for calculating these measures, and, combined with the current price, drive the calculations for total return in Section 5. Overly optimistic prices can make the worst stock look good. Overly pessimistic prices might turn you away from a solid investment.

Forecasting a Future High Price

Price appreciation arises from the growth of EPS and/or an increase in a stock's PE ratio (known as PE expansion.) In Section 4 of the SSG, the forecast high price is calculated as follows:

Forecast high price = Potential high PE ratio * Forecast EPS five years out

You have no control over a company's growth rate. You determined the EPS five years out when you projected an EPS growth rate back in Section 1. (However, if something changed your mind since then, you can always adjust the high EPS in Section 4.) Likewise, the potential high PE ratio for the next five years comes from judgment you applied in the sections "Choosing PE Ratios" and "The PEG Ratio" in this chapter. Remember to use reasonable expectations here, not wishful thinking!

Relative Value

If you want to put PE expansion to work on the stock price, relative value in Section 4 is the place to start. Relative value is PE ratio divided by the five-year average PE and is one way to evaluate whether a stock is "on sale." When relative value is below 1.0, you can study the company's prospects to see if the PE ratio might expand in the future (much like you use the historical EPS growth rates as a starting point for evaluating potential EPS growth in the future.)

Typically, this calculation uses a PE ratio based on the next year's forecast EPS. Some investors use analysts' estimate for EPS, but you can also use the EPS based on the growth rate you forecast. Most of the time, a relative value between .85 and 1.10 is an indication that the stock is fairly valued and has a chance to appreciate from both EPS growth and PE expansion as the PE increases from its five-year average to its average high PE. Relative value greater than 1.10 is a sign that the stock is selling at a premium compared to the past five years. Below .85, the relative value might wave a red flag that the company has problems—investors are buying the stock at a discount.

Success Tip!

Recently, the long bull market of the 1990s and the bear market of the early 2000s has thrown PE ratios and relative value for a loop. First, PE ratios were elevated for several years, which made relative value look overly optimistic. Then, the bear market took prices and PE ratios down so that even rock solid blue-chip companies had relative values that looked like red flags. If you want to evaluate PE ratios over a longer period in Investor's Toolkit, in Section 3, click the high average PE or low average PE box to view a graph of high and low PE ratios for the past 10 years. If you don't use Toolkit, PERT-B also shows these numbers. Looking at PEs over even longer periods of times can reveal where you are in the long cycle.

Forecasting a Future Low Price

Forecasting a potential low price for the next five years requires a bit more judgment than the high price. First, the SSG gives you four options for choosing a low price. If you use *Investor's Toolkit,* you can also bypass those four options to choose a low price with another method that you prefer. In addition, for the option best suited to growth stocks, you must project a low value for EPS and a low PE ratio for the calculation.

Not all companies are alike, but they fall into some major categories: growth stocks, cyclical stocks, turnaround stocks, and stocks that pay significant dividends. Each of the four methods for forecasting a low price is best suited to one of those categories.

Forecasting Low Prices for Growth Stocks

The assumption behind forecasting a low price for a growth stock is that the company's earnings won't be any lower than the EPS for the most recent four quarters. The formula for option (a) low price is:

Low Price (a) = Low PE * Low EPS

All the guidelines for judgment for PE ratios apply to low PEs as well as they do for high PEs. However, the PEG ratio doesn't help define an upper limit for the low PE. Instead, you might limit the low PE to no more than your projected EPS growth rate.

Some investors use the EPS from the last full fiscal year in this equation. Many investors prefer the EPS from the last four quarters (which NAIC suggests for growth companies). The EPS for the last four quarters is particularly useful for companies that are growing quickly, when the increase from the last full fiscal year EPS could be significant.

Some investors also use option (c) as another method for picking low prices for growth stocks.

Forecasting Low Prices for Cyclical and Turnaround Stocks

Companies that are recovering from hard times have probably seen their lowest price over the last few years. Option (b) calculates the average low

price from the last five years for a forecast low, which is useful for these turnaround candidates. If you decide to use option (b), be sure to check the low prices back in Section 3. If any of the low prices seem too high, you can remove them as outliers to reduce the average low price that option (b) calculates.

For cyclical stocks, earnings and price go up and down with the vigor of the economy.

Forecasting Low Price for Dividend Paying Stocks

Option (d) calculates the price that the dividend will support, which is useful for companies that pay significant dividends, as described in the section "Using Yield to Find the Stock Price Safety Net". For example, when a company's yield is competitive with one-year government bonds, the yield provides protection for the stock price. If you choose this option, be sure to remove any outliers in the Yield column in Section 3.

Considering Low Price Options

In addition to the four options shown on the SSG, you can always choose a low price using other methods, such as a recommendation by an analyst's report or using a percentage of the current price. In *Investor's Toolkit*, you can select a low price using the Price Variant Quotient method, which calculates the average ratio of low to high prices for the past five years and multiplies the current high price by that ratio. To use Price Variant Quotient, click the Selected Estimate Low Price box and then press Ctrl-R in the Potential Low Price dialog box.

When the forecast low price is quite close to the current price, it's a good idea to drop your forecast low price even further. Otherwise, you don't have a safety margin to protect you from unforeseen events that can affect the price, such as war, oil prices, bad news from the company itself, or other factors. Upside-downside ratios of 8 or more are often signs that the current price is too close to the forecast low. In this situation, consider using the 52-week low or a low price 20 to 25 percent below the current price. Figure 7-08 shows the low prices produced by the four low price options on the SSG. As you can see in this example, the growth stock option (a) results in a much higher low price than the others, so it is important to match the low price option to the type of stock you are studying. The Other option that appears in *Toolkit 5*, shown in Figure 7-09, is your opportunity to choose a low price different than those offered by the first four methods.

Therefore, option (c) uses the market low price for the company from the most recent down market as a forecast low price. If recent years represent an extended bull market, such as the mid 1990s, the years in Section 3 might not represent any recent down markets. In this case, go back further in time to find the low price for the last down market.

FIGURE 7-09: LOW PRICE OPTIONS FOR PRIORITY HEALTHCARE.

4 Proj. P/E [20.27] Based on Next 4 qtr. EPS [2.47] Current P/E Based on Last 4 qtr. EPS [2.09]
EVALUATING RISK and REWARD over the next 5 years

Assuming one recession and one business boom every 5 years, calculations are made of how high and how low the stock might sell. The upside-downside ratio is the key to evaluating risk and reward.

A HIGH PRICE -- NEXT 5 YEARS

Avg. High P/E **29.4** (3D7 as adj.) X Estimate High Earnings/Share **4.78** = Forecast High Price $ **140.5** (4A1)

B LOW PRICE -- NEXT 5 YEARS

(a) Avg. Low P/E **16.4** (3E7 as adj.) X Estimated Low Earnings/Share **2.09** = $ **34.3**

(b) Avg. Low Price of Last 5 Years = **21.3** (3B7)

(c) Recent Severe Market Low Price = **20.2**

(d) Price Dividend Will Support $\frac{\text{Present Divd.}}{\text{High Yield (H)}} = \frac{0.080}{0.003} = $ **24.1**

Selected Estimate Low Price = $ **24.4** (4B1)

C ZONING

140.5 (4A1) High Forecast Price Minus **24.4** (4B1) Low Forecast Price

(4C2) Lower 1/3 = (4B1) **24.4** to **53.**

(4C3) Middle 1/3 = **53.4** to **111.**

(4C4) Upper 1/3 = **111.5** to **140.**

Present Market Price of **49.980**

D UP-SIDE DOWN-SIDE RATIO (Potential Gain vs. Risk of Loss)

High Price (4A1) **140.5** Minus Present Price **49.980**

Present Price **49.980** Minus Low Price (4B1) **24.4** =

E PRICE TARGET (Note: This shows the potential market price appreciation over t

High Price (4A1) **140.5**

Present Market Price **49.980** = (**2.811**) X 100 = (

Relativ

Judgment - Potential Low Stock Price Selection

Select a Potential Low Stock Price:

- Forecast Low Price — 34.3
- Average Low Price for Last 5 Years — 21.3
- Recent Severe Market Low Price — 20.2
- Price Dividend Will Support — 24.1
- Other — 24.4

Ok   Cancel

5 **5-YEAR POTENTIAL** *This combines price appreciation with dividend yield to get an*

Reward and Risk: The Upside-downside Ratio

The upside-downside ratio is an indication of the risk in the price of a stock. It is the ratio of the potential increase in price during the next five years and the potential decrease in price over the same timeframe. To reduce their risk, most investors look for at least three times as much upside potential to downside loss.

Many investors mistakenly assume that the upside-downside ratio shows the probability of the current price increasing, but it is only a ratio of the estimated increase and decrease from the current price.

Upside-downside ratios below 1.0 are a red flag. Stocks go through cycles of over- and under-value, so stocks won't maintain an upside-downside ratio of 3.0 or better at all times. Solid holdings in your portfolio might carry an upside-downside ratio of 2.0 or even 1.5. But, when the upside-downside ratio drops to 1.0 or less, the risk of loss increases to an unacceptable level compared to the potential return. Quite often, you'll find that the total return is too low as well.

If you accept the original buy, hold, and sell ranges, each of which represents one third of the range between projected high and low price, an upside-downside ratio of 3.0 does not align with the top of the buy range. For this reason, many investors adjust the buy range to represent the bottom 25 percent of the forecast price range, the sell range to the top 25 percent with the hold range the 50 percent in between.

As it turns out, upside-downside ratios that are high (typically 8 or more) are also a red flag. As you divide by a smaller number, a ratio grows larger. Therefore, the closer the current price is to the forecast low price, the higher the upside-downside ratio becomes. When you see an elevated upside-downside ratio, compare the current price to your forecast low price. If the current price is too close to your forecast low, drop your forecast low even lower. As you gain experience, you might decide (after thorough research) that the forecast low price is realistic. In that case, the upside-downside ratio could indicate an incredible opportunity.

The Bottom Line: Total Return

The NAIC methodology strives for a compound annual total return of 15 percent over five years, but that doesn't mean every company must have the potential to provide that level of return. For example, you might accept total return less than 15 percent for high-quality low-risk companies. However, those investments mean that you must then purchase other companies that return **more than** 15 percent. Risk-averse investors sometimes collect these high-quality companies to avoid risk, but the low returns hurt their portfolio. With some patience and perhaps more diligence watching stock prices, you can buy companies with lower growth at prices that provide the potential return you want.

The Components of Total Return

Companies can provide return in two ways: price appreciation and dividends. If a company pays no dividends, its total return is pure price appreciation. For investors interested primarily in income, some types of companies such as real estate investment trusts might offer enough return from dividends that price appreciation isn't an issue. But, by and large, companies produce return through a combination of price appreciation and dividend yield with price appreciation making up the lion's share. For example, EPS growth at Synovus Financial has dropped into single digits so the potential return from price appreciation is quite low. However, the company's average annual yield of 3 percent combined with a purchase on price dip could boost the total return to an acceptable level.

In Section 5 of the SSG, total return is the sum of the compound annual return from price appreciation and dividend yield using the following assumptions:

- Buying at the current price
- Achieving the forecast high price
- Earning the average annual yield from dividends

FIGURE 7-10: REDUCE THE AVERAGE YIELD WHEN THE PAYOUT RATIO IS DECREASING.

	Year	A PRICE HIGH	B PRICE LOW	C Earnings Per Share	D Price Earnings Ratio HIGH A ÷ C	E Price Earnings Ratio LOW B ÷ C	F Dividend Per Share	G % Payout F ÷ C X 100	H % High Yield F ÷ B X 100
1	1999	33.2	21.5	0.90	37.1	24.8	0.062	6.9	0.3
2	2000	33.6	17.1	1.06	31.9	16.2	0.070	6.6	0.4
3	2001	48.9	24.8	1.30	37.6	19.1	0.077	5.9	0.3
4	2002	50.0	32.5	1.85	27.0	17.6	0.085	4.6	0.3
5	2003	60.4	33.4	2.32	26.0	14.4	0.110	4.7	0.3
6	TOTAL		129.3		159.6	67.3		28.7	
7	AVERAGE		25.9		31.9	16.8		5.7	
8	AVERAGE PRICE EARNINGS RATIO	24.3			9 CURRENT PRICE EARNINGS RATIO	21.6			

Proj. P/E [18.44] Based on Next 4 qtr. EPS [2.74]   Current P/E Based on Last 4 qtr. EPS [2.34]

Relative Value: 88.9%   Proj. Relative Value: 75.9%

5 5-YEAR POTENTIAL

This combines price appreciation with dividend yield to get an estimate of total return. It provides a standard for comparing income and growth

Note: Results are expressed as a simple rate; use the table below to convert to a compound rate.

A Present Full Year's Dividend $ 0.120
Present Price of Stock $ 50.490   =   0.002   X 100 =   0.2 (5A)   Present Yield or % Returned on Purchase Price

B AVERAGE YIELD OVER NEXT 5 YEARS
Avg. Earnings Per Share Next 5 Years   3.72   X Avg. % Payout (3G) 5.7 4.7 = 17.5 = 0.3 %
Present Price $ 50.490   (5B)

C ESTIMATED AVERAGE ANNUAL RETURN OVER NEXT FIVE YEARS
5 Year Appreciation Potential (4E) 162.0 / 5   32.4 %
Average Yield (5B)   0.3 %
Average Total Annual Return Over the Next 5 Years (5C)   32.7 %

	P.A.R.	Tot. Ret.
Average Yield	0.2%	0.2%
Annual Appreciation	16.2%	21.2%
% Compd Ann Rate of Ret	16.4%	21.4%

The SSG uses the average earnings for the next five years and average payout ratio from Section 3 to calculate the average yield. In *Toolkit,* the Total Return and Projected Average Returns calculate compound returns including the contribution of dividends. If the payout ratio in Section 3 demonstrates a distinct trend, you might want to adjust the payout ratio value in Section 5, as demonstrated in Figure 7-10. For example, if the payout ratio is decreasing, you can replace the average payout ratio with the payout ratio for the most recent year to reduce the average annual yield and therefore the total return. You can also go back to Section 3 to remove outliers to adjust the average.

Success Tip!

No one forces you to buy a stock at today's current price. If you are in the habit of buying on price dips, you can use limit orders to buy a stock at a specific price. In Investor's Toolkit, *you can find out the total return if you purchase at a specific price. Open the company file and click Data in the menu bar. On the Basic Data tab, enter the buy price you want and click OK. Assuming all your other judgment is already in place, the total return in Section 5 represents the return you achieve buying at your target buy price and selling at your forecast high price.*

Using Projected Average Return

Projected average return is a more conservative estimate of the return you can expect from a stock, and many investors feel it is more attainable. The projected average return assumes that you buy at the current price and earn an average dividend yield, just like total return. However, projected average return assumes that you sell the

stock which achieves a lower forecast price (based on the average of your forecast high and low PE, instead of your high PE.) Since it's less likely that you will sell your stock at its peak, many investors prefer projected average return as a more likely return for an investment. This measure is found in the *Toolkit* software.

Summing Up

Good portfolio management is a combination of getting rid of troublesome stocks without selling too late and holding onto good stocks without selling too soon, and re-evaluating the judgment on your SSGs is an important part of the process.

For example, if the market as a whole is headed down, even your best investments will drop (although usually not as much as more questionable investments.) However, if the economy is doing well and a stock waves red flags, it might be time to find a better place to invest your money. As you review your updated SSGs for the companies you own or look over SSGs for companies you are considering, use this checklist to identify green lights, as well as yellow or red warning flags.

Section 1

- Do insiders own enough of the company stock that their success is aligned with that of the shareholders?

- Is institutional ownership low enough that price volatility isn't likely to make you uncomfortable?

- Is the level of debt reasonable based on the industry and the company's past performance with debt?

- Do sales, earnings, and profit margin historical trends (with outliers eliminated) meet your guidelines for growth based on the company's size?

- Is the historical growth consistent? Is growth for the latest quarter on track with past results and does it meet your future expectations?

- Is the earnings growth trend similar to the sales growth?

- Does your projected growth rate for EPS meet your guideline for growth based on the company's size?

- Does the price trend follow the growth of sales and EPS over time? (Keep in mind that prices fluctuate more than EPS and sales, which means you can take advantage of price dips to improve your return.)

- Are the trends in the Preferred Procedure acceptable (costs, taxes, preferred dividends, number of shares)?

- Is the price volatility at a level you can live with?

Section 2

- Does the pre-tax profit margin remain steady or increase steadily?

- Is the pre-tax profit margin at or above the industry average?

- Has the ROE remained steady or increased steadily?

- Is the ROE at or above the industry average?

- Is a high ROE due to high debt?

Section 3

- Is the current PE ratio at or below the five-year average PE ratio?

- When the current PE ratio is at or below the five-year average PE ratio, is the PE ratio beginning to increase?

- Is the payout ratio at a level that leaves the company funds to finance growth?

Section 4

- Are your forecast high and low PE ratios reasonable?

- Does your forecasted low price have a sufficient safety margin from the current price?

- Is the relative value between .85 and 1.1.? Remember that judgment is needed here.

- Is the upside-downside ratio at least 3.0 to 1?

Section 5

- Do you think the average yield is likely for future yields?

- Does the total return meet your goal for your portfolio based on the level of risk that the company presents?

- When looking at a new stock for potential investment and the total return is low, is the stock worth watching for a price dip?

Analyzing Financial Statements

Where the Money Is

The Stock Selection Guide alone paints a clear picture of a company's financial performance. Often, stocks exhibit unusual characteristics that should stir you to dig a little deeper. With conservative judgment on the SSG, you can evaluate the stock and make a decent decision about its suitability as an investment. But, most stocks have quirks and idiosyncrasies, and even major character flaws. When you're trying to fine-tune your portfolio, a closer inspection can uncover eccentricities that can be the deciding factor for the stock you choose. Financial statements and reports contain all the information you need as long as you know where to look—and the company isn't trying to hide things.

The Art of Accounting

Growth and the Income Statement

Owning and Owing:
the Balance Sheet

It's Hard to Hide the Truth in
the Cash Flow Statement

Separating the Gold from the
Dirt with Financial Ratios

Financial Statements and
Much, Much More

The Fine Art of Accounting

In the previous chapter, you accountants earn a bad rap as geeks who wouldn't dream of leaving the house without pocket protector, an array of superbly sharpened pencils, and a handheld calculator that could find its way to the moon. Although mathematics works the same in accounting as everywhere else, a creative accountant can find ways to categorize a company's money and assets so that the corporation is able to pay less in taxes and present their financial performance in the best possible light.

Accounting Rules and Requirements

That doesn't mean investors are totally in the dark. Three financial statements act as a team to present company performance: the income statement, the balance sheet, and the statement of cash flows. The Financial Accounting Standards Board (FASB) sets the accounting standards that companies follow, known as Generally Accepted Accounting Principles (GAAP). Financial reports presented to anyone outside the company must conform to GAAP.

The Securities and Exchange Commission (SEC) is the watchdog that makes sure that companies comply with the rules regarding financial content, publication frequency, and publication dates for financial reports. Companies must provide quarterly reports, called 10-Qs, within 45 days of the end of the fiscal quarter, although these reports do not have to be audited. Annual reports, called 10-Ks, must be audited by independent third parties and are due within 90 days of the end of the fiscal year.

The 1929 stock market crash and the Great Depression that followed came to pass as much from poor financial reporting as it did from foolhardy investment strategies and cheap "buying on margin" rates. To avert a repeat performance, Congress enacted the Securities Act of 1933 requiring companies to publish financial information in standardized formats. The following year, it enacted the Securities Exchange Act of 1934

CHAPTER EIGHT

to add some structure to the operation of securities markets and brokerage firms. These two congressional acts are the foundation for the information found in modern financial statements and the rules regarding disclosure and frequency of reporting.

Beginners don't have to absorb all the complexities of accounting and financial reports before initiating their first stock study. You can make up for your inexperience by applying conservative judgment to your stock studies. However, understanding more about finance and accounting expands the pool of companies you can study, improves your analyses,

helps you choose a winner when the competition is close, and ultimately should increase your investment success.

The income statement shows a company's performance over a period of time. At its most basic, an income statement includes:

- **Sales (revenues)**—What the company makes selling products or services

- **Expenses (costs)**—What the company spends to run the company and sell products and services

- **Profits**—What is left over after subtracting expenses from sales

- **Earnings per share**— The profits divided by the number of shares outstanding

The balance sheet is a snapshot of the company's finances. At the highest level, a balance sheet includes only three categories:

- **Assets**—What the company owns

- **Liabilities**—What the company owes

- **Shareholders' Equity**— What's left after you subtract liabilities from assets (this is like an individual's net worth)

The statement of cash flows is aptly named; it documents the cash flowing in and out of a company. It starts with the net income from the company's income statement and ends with the cash on the balance sheet. In between, the basic components of cash include:

- **Cash from operating activities**—Cash generated by running the business

- **Cash from investing activities**—Cash made or spent on investments, such as purchasing assets

- **Cash from financing activities**—Cash flowing in or out due to issuing or buying back stock, or from issuing or paying back debt

Fun and Games with Finance

The stock market is a competitive arena and it doesn't handle disappointment well. Some companies would rather stretch the accounting rules to their limits rather than disappoint the market. Unfortunately, there are numerous tricky techniques that can make company results look better than they really are. As long as you know where to look and actually take the time to read the information that companies disclose, usually you can spot these games. Then you can decide whether to adjust your forecasts for the company or look for one that is more forthright for your investment. The following are some of the tactics you might run across.

Revenue Recognition

Revenue and expenses are supposed to appear on the financial statements during the same period, but accounting rules provide some leeway for when a company recognizes revenue. For example, large software projects might recognize revenue based on the percentage of the project duration that has passed. Because many, if not most, software projects take much longer than originally planned; all the revenue could be recognized months before the project expenses finally stop.

A company might go so far as to book sales prematurely—before the revenue would normally be recognized, using the company's revenue recognition policy. The prematurely booked sales improve the current results, but future results look worse—unless the company makes this sort of thing a habit.

Vendor Financing

Companies, such as Cisco and Lucent, have boosted sales by extending liberal payment terms to their customers and even lending the customers money in order to ship products and recognize revenue. If the customers can't pay or decide to return the products, future earnings suffer. One sign of the liberal payment terms technique is accounts receivable that increase faster than sales.

Restructuring Reserve

Companies can write off several years' worth of future restructuring expenses as a one-time charge. By using

this non-recurring write-off, one year's financial results take a hit and then earnings in following years are unaffected by this one-time event. If you use data that doesn't remove the effects of one-time events, the one-time charge shows up as a one-year dip in pre-tax profit and earnings in the SSG Section 1 graph.

In theory, removing these one-time write-offs from a company's results presents a

better picture of the company's ongoing performance. Some companies use these supposedly non-recurring charges time and again to hide the company's poor performance.

Pension Contributions

Companies can change assumptions around their pension plans to shore up earnings. For example, by forecasting a higher investment return, a company can show the pension as over funded and subsequently reduce its contributions. If the projection for the investment return proves to be too high, the company will have to increase its contributions in the future to correct the problem. To protect workers' retirement funds, third parties audit company pension plans, so these games shouldn't get too far out of hand.

Growth and the Income Statement

The income statement documents growth of sales, expenses, and earnings over a period of time. As introduced in the previous section, the income statement begins with sales, then subtracts expenses and other categories of costs to produce the net income at the end. The SSG does a good job of portraying the growth of sales, pre-tax profit,

and earnings per share. But, as soon as something in Section 1 or 2 of the SSG strikes you as odd, the income statement is your starting point for further investigation.

Success Tip!

Accounting principles require that financial reports record revenues and related expenses in the same period, which means some expenses appear in the income statement before the bills are actually paid. By reporting revenues and expenses in this way, the income statement more accurately reflects the company profits. For example, if a company charges the full price for its service up front, it would have to deduct all the corresponding expenses of delivering that service at the same time. Otherwise,

the upfront payment would dramatically increase earnings in the first year, while the cost of providing the service would lower the earnings for length of the contract.

Although income statements often break down revenues and expenses into minute categories, a consolidated statement of earnings provides an overview of the most pertinent information, demonstrated by Home Depot's 2003 report in Figure 8-1.

Sales (net sales, revenues) are the monies generated by selling products and services, selling assets, or earning interest. GAAP rules specify when a company can recognize revenue, which often boils down to when ownership transfers between two parties or when services are complete. Remember, recognizing revenue does not necessarily coincide with when the company is paid.

Cost of goods sold (cost of merchandise sold, cost of sales) is the cost of materials, labor, overhead, and depreciation related to producing the products or services sold. Typically, the cost of goods sold increases along with sales, because the company must produce more products to sell.

FIGURE 8-01: THE CONSOLIDATED STATEMENT OF EARNINGS SHOWS THE MAJOR CATEGORIES OF AN INCOME STATEMENT.

	Fiscal Year Ended[1]		
amounts in millions, except per share data	February 1, 2004	February 2, 2003	February 3, 2002
NET SALES	$64,816	$58,247	$53,553
Cost of Merchandise Sold	44,236	40,139	37,406
GROSS PROFIT	20,580	18,108	16,147
Operating Expenses:			
Selling and Store Operating	12,502	11,180	10,163
Pre-Opening	86	96	117
General and Administrative	1,146	1,002	935
Total Operating Expenses	13,734	12,278	11,215
OPERATING INCOME	6,846	5,830	4,932
Interest Income (Expense):			
Interest and Investment Income	59	79	53
Interest Expense	(62)	(37)	(28)
Interest, net	(3)	42	25
EARNINGS BEFORE PROVISION FOR INCOME TAXES	6,843	5,872	4,957
Provision for Income Taxes	2,539	2,208	1,913
NET EARNINGS	$ 4,304	$ 3,664	$ 3,044
Weighted Average Common Shares	2,283	2,336	2,335
BASIC EARNINGS PER SHARE	$ 1.88	$ 1.57	$ 1.30
Diluted Weighted Average Common Shares	2,289	2,344	2,353
DILUTED EARNINGS PER SHARE	$ 1.88	$ 1.56	$ 1.29

(1) Fiscal years ended February 1, 2004 and February 2, 2003 include 52 weeks. Fiscal year ended February 3, 2002 includes 53 weeks.

Gross profit is the income the company makes after subtracting the cost of goods sold from sales.

Operating costs (operating expenses; S,G,&A expenses) relate to running the business, including selling products and services, marketing and advertising, employee compensation, benefits, travel, R&D, and more. As a company increases its revenues, operating costs will increase. However, good management controls these overhead costs, because they are hard to eliminate quickly if sales drop off.

Although Home Depot's Consolidated Statement of Income doesn't show it, non-cash items such as depreciation and amortization are deducted before calculating the operating income.

Operating income is the income earned after subtracting cost of goods sold and operating costs.

Interest income and interest expense are the monies earned in interest on its investments and the interest a company pays on its debt, respectively.

Earnings before income taxes (EBIT) is income earned after paying all expenses except for income taxes. This is the source of earnings used for pre-tax profit margin in Section 2 of the SSG.

Some money that a company spends can show up as expenses on the income statement, while other money spent ends up on the balance sheet. For example, money spent on a new factory doesn't appear on the income statement. Instead, depreciation appears on the income statement to match the cost of the factory to the revenues generated during the factory's useful life. The money actually spent on the factory appears on the cash flow statement under Cash from Investing Activities and the price paid for the factory appears in the Property, Plant, and Equipment category on the balance sheet.

Likewise, assets and liabilities don't show up on the balance sheet, unless the value or cost is known. For example, land often increases in value over time, but the balance sheet usually shows the land at "cost", not fair market value. Large law suits could threaten a company, but those liabilities won't appear until the awards are announced. When one company purchases another, the purchase price includes the value of these appraised assets and liabilities and the "excess amount" over the net assets. This value appears on the balance sheet as "goodwill".

*When you're ready to tackle the finer points of finance, try the book **How to Read a Financial Report** by John A. Tracy (Wiley & Sons, 1999).*

Income taxes (provision for income taxes) are the monies the company has paid or reserved to pay income taxes.

Net income (net earnings) is income after subtracting all expenses. If the company has discontinued some of its operations, for example closing a factory or selling a business unit, the income statement includes the net income from continuing operations and the net income from discontinued operations. To evaluate a company as an investment, you should use only the net income from continuing operations, because discontinued operations no longer contribute to future growth.

If a company is paying dividends on its preferred stock, the preferred dividends are deducted from the net income before calculating the earnings per share.

Basic number of shares outstanding is the number of shares actually issued at the time of the report.

Basic earnings per share are calculated by dividing the net income by the basic number of shares outstanding.

Diluted number of shares outstanding represent the number of shares outstanding including stocks options and convertible securities likely to be converted into stock.

Diluted earnings per share are calculated by dividing the net income by the diluted number of shares. Issuing stock to management and employees at a discount reduces earnings per share for all shareholders, so you should always evaluate EPS growth using the diluted earnings per share.

Owning and Owing: the Balance Sheet

The balance sheet is a snapshot of what a company owns (assets), what it owes to others (liabilities), and the difference between those two, which is the shareholders' equity in the company. The name, balance sheet, derives from the fact that assets, liabilities, and shareholders' equity must balance at all times. Home Depot's Consolidated Balance Sheet in Figure 8-02 shows the basic components.

amounts in millions	February 1, 2004	February 2, 2003
ASSETS		
Current Assets:		
Cash and Cash Equivalents	$ 2,826	$ 2,188
Short-Term Investments, including current maturities of long-term investments	26	65
Receivables, net	1,097	1,072
Merchandise Inventories	9,076	8,338
Other Current Assets	303	254
Total Current Assets	13,328	11,917
Property and Equipment, at cost:		
Land	6,397	5,560
Buildings	10,920	9,197
Furniture, Fixtures and Equipment	5,163	4,074
Leasehold Improvements	942	872
Construction in Progress	820	724
Capital Leases	352	306
	24,594	20,733
Less Accumulated Depreciation and Amortization	4,531	3,565
Net Property and Equipment	20,063	17,168
Notes Receivable	84	107
Cost in Excess of the Fair Value of Net Assets Acquired, net of accumulated amortization of $54 at February 1, 2004 and $50 at February 2, 2003	833	575
Other Assets	129	244
Total Assets	$34,437	$30,011
LIABILITIES AND STOCKHOLDERS' EQUITY		
Current Liabilities:		
Accounts Payable	$ 5,159	$ 4,560
Accrued Salaries and Related Expenses	801	809
Sales Taxes Payable	419	307
Deferred Revenue	1,281	998
Income Taxes Payable	175	227
Current Installments of Long-Term Debt	509	7
Other Accrued Expenses	1,210	1,127
Total Current Liabilities	9,554	8,035
Long-Term Debt, excluding current installments	856	1,321
Other Long-Term Liabilities	653	491
Deferred Income Taxes	967	362
STOCKHOLDERS' EQUITY		
Common Stock, par value $0.05; authorized: 10,000 shares, issued and outstanding 2,373 shares at February 1, 2004 and 2,362 shares at February 2, 2003	119	118
Paid-In Capital	6,184	5,858
Retained Earnings	19,680	15,971
Accumulated Other Comprehensive Income (Loss)	90	(82)
Unearned Compensation	(76)	(63)
Treasury Stock, at cost, 116 shares at February 1, 2004 and 69 shares at February 2, 2003	(3,590)	(2,000)
Total Stockholders' Equity	22,407	19,802
Total Liabilities and Stockholders' Equity	$34,437	$30,011

Assets

Assets are the things that a company owns, but the balance sheet separates assets into several categories. Current assets include cash or other assets that the company can quickly convert into cash, such as short-term investments, the money owed to the company (called receivables), and inventory. The property and equipment category includes other assets that help generate revenue, but aren't readily converted to cash. Property and equipment includes land, buildings, equipment, and leases for capital assets.

The rest of the entries in the assets section of a balance sheet represent long-term assets that don't fall under property and equipment. For example, Home Depot shows the cost it has paid over fair value of acquired companies' assets as good will in this category.

Liabilities

Liabilities are the company's financial obligations to others. Liabilities are categorized into current and long-term obligations. Current liabilities are the financial obligations that will be due within the next 12 months such as unpaid expenses and the upcoming payments on long-term debts. Long-term liabilities are the financial obligations from 12 months on. These include the rest of the payments on long-term debt, estimates of future expenses such as pensions, and money received for products or services not yet delivered.

Shareholders' Equity

Shareholders' equity (shown as stockholders' equity on Home Depot's balance sheet) is the value that remains after you subtract liabilities from assets. It has nothing to do with what most shareholders paid to buy their shares in the company. Shareholders' equity might be easier to grasp if you think about the equity in your house. When you purchase your home, it becomes one of your assets—valued at the purchase price you paid. Your liability is the mortgage you assume to buy the house and your equity is your down payment. As time passes, your home increases in value and the balance on your mortgage drops. Your equity increases.

Financial analysts consider shareholders' equity to be the value that management produces. Management raises capital in order to purchase assets that they then use to generate income. If management finds a way to increase the value of assets while reducing the level of liabilities, shareholders' equity increases.

WHEN ACCOUNTING GETS COMPLICATED

The balance sheet isn't always a realistic portrait. Because the balance sheet doesn't show the fair market value of assets and liabilities, some items can be dramatically over- or under-stated. Although land usually increases in value over time, that price appreciation isn't apparent on a financial statement until the company sells the land and its value is quantified. The value of a brand name doesn't appear on a balance sheet either. Likewise, the potential payouts for lawsuits, such as those in the tobacco industry, don't appear as liabilities in the balance sheet until there is a legal obligation to pay. Footnotes to the financial statements often give clues about pending lawsuits.

Hidden assets and liabilities do affect the stock price. If a company owns significant assets that don't appear on the balance statement, investors might pay more for the stock than earnings alone would justify. Finding undervalued assets is a great way to find good investments—it was a favorite strategy for Benjamin Graham. Conversely, if the PE ratio makes the stock look like a bargain, liabilities not seen on the balance sheet could be the culprit. You can learn about these hidden elements by reading the fine print (especially the footnotes) in annual reports and SEC filings.

Some companies place overly optimistic values on some of their assets. When WorldCom filed bankruptcy, nearly half of its assets were goodwill—the price that Worldcom paid above fair value for assets. Financial analysts questioned that number and the company eventually eliminated its goodwill altogether—$45 billion of assets up in smoke, down the drain, but gone nonetheless. To prevent this kind of surprise, you can stick to evaluating a company strictly with assets that have quantifiable value by using tangible book value. Standard and Poor's stock reports show tangible book value explicitly. Other data providers use tangible book value but don't label it as such.

explanation, the potential for hanky-panky is present. In addition, the rules that require revenues and related expenses in the same time-frame have disconnected company earnings from the cash generated by a business. As a result, cash flow has become the preferred measure of corporate financial health.

Cash flow is easy to understand if you start with a more personal example. Your personal balance sheet might look fantastic—$4 million in assets, including your Lake Tahoe home, Ferrari, and retirement plan; and $2 million in liabilities for your house mortgage and car loan, resulting in $2 million in net worth. However, if you just lost your job and you don't have any cash stashed in savings to make your loan payments, you have a cash flow problem.

It's Hard to Hide the Truth in the Cash Flow Statement

The Cash Flow Statement as it looks today has been a required financial statement only since 1988. Because of the idiosyncrasies of balance sheets and income statements, values on a balance sheet can change based on transactions that don't show up on the income statement for the corresponding period. When numbers can change without

How the Cash Flow Statement Works

Companies need cash just like you do. The cash flow statement is like a good detective—it follows the trail of cash flowing in and out of a company. The cash flow statement starts with net income from the income statement, as illustrated in Figure 8-03. Then, it categorizes every monetary transaction as operations, investing, or financing. After adding and subtracting all the cash transactions, the cash flow statement ends with the cash shown on the balance sheet, so it acts as the bridge

FIGURE 8-03: A CASH FLOW STATEMENT CATEGORIZES EVERY CASH TRANSACTION AS AN OPERATING, INVESTING, OR FINANCING ACTIVITY.

	Fiscal Year Ended[1]		
amounts in millions	February 1, 2004	February 2, 2003	February 3, 2002
CASH FLOWS FROM OPERATIONS:			
Net Earnings	$ 4,304	$ 3,664	$ 3,044
Reconciliation of Net Earnings to Net Cash Provided by Operations:			
Depreciation and Amortization	1,076	903	764
Decrease (Increase) in Receivables, net	25	(38)	(119)
Increase in Merchandise Inventories	(693)	(1,592)	(166)
Increase in Accounts Payable and Accrued Liabilities	790	1,394	1,878
Increase in Deferred Revenue	279	147	200
(Decrease) Increase in Income Taxes Payable	(27)	83	272
Increase (Decrease) in Deferred Income Taxes	605	173	(6)
Other	186	68	96
Net Cash Provided by Operations	6,545	4,802	5,963
CASH FLOWS FROM INVESTING ACTIVITIES:			
Capital Expenditures, net of $47, $49 and $5 of non-cash capital expenditures in fiscal 2003, 2002 and 2001, respectively	(3,508)	(2,749)	(3,393)
Purchase of Assets from Off-Balance Sheet Financing Arrangement	(598)	–	–
Payments for Businesses Acquired, net	(215)	(235)	(190)
Proceeds from Sales of Businesses, net	–	22	64
Proceeds from Sales of Property and Equipment	265	105	126
Purchases of Investments	(159)	(583)	(85)
Proceeds from Maturities of Investments	219	506	25
Other	–	–	(13)
Net Cash Used in Investing Activities	(3,996)	(2,934)	(3,466)
CASH FLOWS FROM FINANCING ACTIVITIES:			
Repayments of Commercial Paper Obligations, net	–	–	(754)
Proceeds from Long-Term Debt	–	1	532
Repayments of Long-Term Debt	(9)	–	–
Repurchase of Common Stock	(1,554)	(2,000)	–
Proceeds from Sale of Common Stock, net	227	326	445
Cash Dividends Paid to Stockholders	(595)	(492)	(396)
Net Cash Used in Financing Activities	(1,931)	(2,165)	(173)
Effect of Exchange Rate Changes on Cash and Cash Equivalents	20	8	(14)
Increase (Decrease) in Cash and Cash Equivalents	638	(289)	2,310
Cash and Cash Equivalents at Beginning of Year	2,188	2,477	167
Cash and Cash Equivalents at End of Year	$ 2,826	$ 2,188	$ 2,477

between the income statement and the balance sheet.

Cash comes from three different sources:

- **Cash from operating activities (cash from operations)** is cash a business generates or spends. If cash from operating activities is positive, the company generates cash by running the business and can sustain itself. If cash from operating activities is negative, the company is spending more cash to run the company than it brings in and that's not good.

- **Cash from investing activities** includes the money used to buy or sell assets and investments. Companies that sell products need factories to build more products if they want to increase sales. Companies that sell services might need office buildings and equipment to house the additional employees needed to deliver more services.

- **Cash from financing activities** is cash coming from outside sources: borrowed from banks or investors or capital raised by issuing more shares. If financing helps a company grow, great. Young companies don't often generate enough cash from operations to fund

explosive growth, so financing activities (usually issuing shares) are the only option. Using cash from financing activities to cover the cost of operating the business is a huge red flag.

Success Tip!

On an income statement, the gain or loss from selling an asset temporarily increases or reduces the company's earnings. On a cash flow statement, the cash from operating activities is unaffected by the outcome of a sale.

What to Look For in Cash Flow

Some investors become intimidated by the terminology: asset accounts, equity accounts, depreciation, sources and uses of cash, free cash flow, and so on. Certainly, it helps to understand what's going on in the cash flow statement, but you can spot red flags or green lights by answering a few basic questions.

Did cash increase or decrease during the period?

If cash decreases, check the trend for the last few years. If cash has been decreasing for several years, the company might have to borrow money or issue more stock, which will eventually hurt the values of your shares. Read the management discussion in the annual report or call investor

UNDERSTANDING CASH FLOWS IN AND OUT

Depending on the type of account in question, an increase might represent a cash flow in (a source of cash) or a cash flow out (a use of cash). It's easy to decipher a cash flow by asking whether the company has more money to put to work.

Operating activities: If inventories increase, the company has more money tied up in inventory and less to use, so the amount on the cash flow statement is negative. If accounts payable increases, the company has put off paying bills and has that money to use, so the amount on the cash flow statement is positive. Conversely, if accounts receivable increases, customers owe the company more money, so the amount on the cash flow statement is negative. On the income statement, depreciation is deducted to calculate net income, but no cash actually flows out of the company. Since the cash flow statement starts with net income, depreciation is added back in under cash from operating activities. As you can see in the Cash Flows from Operations Section of Figure 8-03, Home Depot added back over $1 billion dollars of depreciation and amortization.

Financing activities: If a company sells an asset, it receives money, so the entry on the cash flow statement is positive. If the company buys a building or purchases an investment, it has less cash, so the entry on the cash flow statement is negative. In Figure 8-03, Home Depot purchased over $3.5 billion in assets.

Financing activities: When a company issues stock or borrows money, it receives cash, so the entries on the cash flow statement are positive. If the company pays back debt or repurchases shares, it has less cash so the entry on the cash flow statement is negative. In Figure 8-03, Home Depot spent $1.5 billion repurchasing shares.

relations to learn why cash is decreasing. Conversely, increasing cash is good. For example, Home Depot increased cash in 2003 and the amount of cash has remained reasonably stable for the past three years; both good signs.

Success Tip!

Companies often park cash in current marketable securities, which appear on the balance sheet. Compare the sum of these securities and actual cash to the sum for the previous year. If the total has decreased, the company

sold short-term securities to raise cash and an explanation is in order.

Is cash flow from operations negative?

Companies often use financing activities initially to jump start their growth. Without financing, the company can grow only as fast as the cash it generates from operations. Eventually, companies have to grow up and run their businesses on cash generated from operations. If cash flow from operations is negative, look for receivables and inventory that are increasing significantly faster than sales. This is often a sign of poorly selling or poor quality products. Customers aren't buying the products, or they aren't paying for them. Home Depot produces boatloads of cash from operations—more than $6 billion in 2003. No worries there!

Are net income on the income statement and cash from operating activities close in value?

When net income and cash from operating activities are similar, the company's earnings are primarily from operations, a sign that the business can sustain itself. Home Depot's cash from operation activities is much higher than net income. Even though the values aren't that close the company has money to spare to invest or apply to buying back shares or reducing debt.

Are net income and cash from operations growing at a similar rate?

If cash from operations grows more slowly than net income, the source of earnings is gradually changing from operations to financing or investing, which reduces the quality of the earnings and the sustainability of the business.

Is the company selling assets to raise cash?

Assets are often the underlying source of growth for a company, so selling assets is a bad way to raise cash. Read management discussion and notes in the annual report to find out what the company sold. You might want to reduce your growth forecasts. In addition, the sale might boost earnings in that year, so that year could be an outlier. Selling assets also can indicate that a company has used up its credit line, so check for excessive levels of debt. Conversely, asset purchases can lead to better growth in the future. As you might expect, Home Depot is using much of the cash from operations to purchase assets; in 2003, the company spent $3.5 billion on capital expenditures.

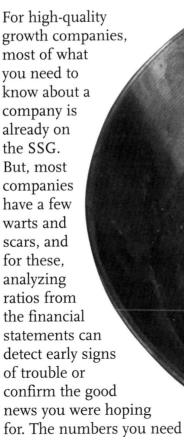

Success Tip!

Home Depot's cash flow statement shows that the company used cash from operating activities to buy back shares in 2002 and 2003. Share buybacks increase the EPS by reducing the number of shares outstanding. Home Depot's sales growth has been steadily slowing. The share buybacks helped boost the company's EPS growth to keep it from dropping into the single digits.

Separating the Gold from the Dirt with Financial Ratios

For high-quality growth companies, most of what you need to know about a company is already on the SSG. But, most companies have a few warts and scars, and for these, analyzing ratios from the financial statements can detect early signs of trouble or confirm the good news you were hoping for. The numbers you need come from the income

statement, balance sheet, and cash flow statement. Studying financial ratios is a career for many, so it's certainly worthy of a lifetime avocation. Here's an introduction to financial ratios you can employ to improve your stock studies, stock challenges, and portfolio management decisions.

Evaluating Profitability

A company can sell all the gizmos it wants, but it has to make a decent profit to grow. You're already familiar with a few profitability ratios from Section 2 of the SSG: pre-tax profit margin and ROE (see Chapter 7). Chapter 7 also described another profitability ratio you can use to evaluate performance: sustainable growth. The following profitability ratios can improve

your analysis of profitability regardless how a company generates earnings.

Return on Assets

ROE compares net income to shareholders' equity, so a company that uses debt as a source of capital should produce a higher ROE than companies with little or no debt. Since capital is often spent to purchase assets, return on assets (ROA) can help you evaluate a company's use of capital.

Return on assets = Net income / Total assets

Home Depot 2003
ROA = $4,304 / $34,437 = 12.5%

Remember, net income appears near the bottom of an income statement, In the Home Depot income statement shown in Figure 8-01, the label for net income is Net Earnings, $4.3 billion for the 2003 fiscal year ending February 1, 2004. To find total assets, turn to the balance sheet. In Figure 8-02, Home Depot's

Total Assets are over $34 billion for fiscal year 2003.

Trends in ROA are important as they are for ROE. Because business models vary from industry to industry, compare a company's ROA to its competitors or to the industry average. Many investors look for ROA of at least 7 percent. For example, using results from MSN Money *(http://money.msn.com)*, Home Depot's ROA looks good; it is greater than 7 percent; it is trending up; and it is higher than the industry average.

- Five-year average ROA = 12.3%

- Industry average ROA = 11.5%

Return on Invested Capital

Return on invested capital (ROIC) is the return earned on all the long term capital the company has at its disposal: shareholders' equity and long-term debt. If a company uses both types of capital, ROIC presents a more realistic portrait of management effectiveness. The formula is as follows:

Return on invested capital = Net income / (Shareholders' equity + Long-term debt)

Because ROIC includes more capital than shareholders' equity, this return will be lower than ROE. Companies should use capital to their advantage, regardless of the source of the money, so you should apply the same guidelines to ROIC that you do for ROE; look for company returns above industry averages, with steady or increasing trends. Here is a comparison of 2003 ROE and ROIC for Home Depot, which uses both shareholders' equity and debt.

- Net income = $4,307 million from the bottom of the income statement (Figure 8-01)

- Shareholders' equity = $22,407 million from the bottom of the balance sheet (Figure 8-02)

- Long-term debt = $856 million in the Liabilities and Stockholders' Equity section of the balance sheet in Figure 8-02

- ROE = 4,307 / 22,407 = 19.2 %

- ROIC = 4,307 / (22,407+ 856) = 18.5 %

Free Cash Flow

Free cash flow is the unfettered cash that the company can use any way it wants: acquire companies, invest in new opportunities, pay down debt, pay additional dividends, or buy back shares. Free cash flow is cash generated from operations minus dividends paid and the money spent on property, plant, and equipment.

Free cash flow = Net cash from operating activities – Capital expenditures – Dividends

Home Depot's free cash flow = $6,545 – $3,508 – $595 = $2,442 (Numbers shown in Figure 8-03)

For the net cash from operating activities, look at the total for the first section of the Statement of Cash flows. In Figure 8-03, Home Depot labels this as Net Cash Provided by Operations. Capital expenditures typically appear at the top of the second section of the Statement of Cash Flows, also shown in Figure 8-03. Dividends show up in the third section of the Statement of Cash Flows.

In Figure 8-03, Home Depot labels dividends as Cash Dividends Paid to Stockholders.

Negative free cash flow isn't always a bad thing. Young companies often reinvest all their cash into growing the company. Established companies should generate positive free cash flow.

Of course, if you want to compare one company's free cash flow with another, the magnitude of dollar values is a problem. Just as the SSG uses pre-tax profit margin, you can use the free cash flow margin to compare free cash flow between companies. Ideally, comparing these margins

For Free cash flow margin, find the number of Sales at the top of the income statement. In Figure 8-01, Home Depot's Income Statement labels sales as Net Sales.

Home Depot's free cash flow margin is relatively low, in part from the billions that the company is sinking into new stores and refurbishing existing stores. This is exacerbated by the cannibalization of same store sales that some new stores produce on existing stores. Then again, when a company generates $6 billion in cash, it has to do something with it!

Debt and Liquidity

Some companies and industries use little or no debt, while others have learned to live quite happily with very high levels of debt. For example, industries that generate revenue using few assets, such as software companies or Internet retailers, typically use very little debt. Industries that require expensive equipment or facilities, such as utilities, often carry very high levels of debt. Because debt can be a problem if sales slow, debt and liquidity ratios show whether a company is healthy enough to survive some bad times.

The debt to equity ratio (also called leverage) shows how much of the company's capital comes from borrowing versus internally generated earnings and equity offerings. A companion ratio, debt as a percentage of total capitalization, is one of the measures in the header of the SSG, and is described in detail in Chapter 7. The debt to equity ratio is known as leverage because borrowing money can sometimes help a company do more than it could with only the money it generates from operation—just as a crowbar can help you move a rock that you wouldn't dream of trying to move with your bare hands.

Leverage isn't the only important measure on a balance sheet. Liquidity is a measure of how quickly and easily assets can be converted to cash, whether it's for paying bills or making long-term investments to grow the business. Management should focus on running the business instead of worrying about where to find cash to pay the bills.

within an industry is the best method of analysis. Read the Management Discussion and Analysis section of the annual report carefully to see if this makes sense.

Free cash flow margin = Free cash flow / Sales

Free cash flow margin = $2,442 / $64,816 = 3.76%

Current Ratio

The current ratio is a measure of whether a company has sufficient short-term assets to pay off its short-term liabilities. If it doesn't, it might have to sell long-term assets that help generate sales to pay for short-term obligations. And that is the beginning of a downward spiral.

Current ratio = Current assets / Current liabilities

Current ratio = $13,328 / $9,554 = 1.39

In Figure 8-02, Home Depot's balance sheet, look for Total Current Assets and Total Current Liabilities.

A current ratio of at least 2 to 1 is a general benchmark, although you should compare a company's current ratio to the industry average. Some companies, such as Home Depot and Wal-mart, operate mainly on a cash basis and have tuned their operations to maintain low levels of inventories and accounts receivable. These companies sometimes sell their inventory before they pay their suppliers, which is like getting an interest-free loan. Home Depot's low current ratio is a sign of highly efficient operations, not a pending liquidity crunch.

SuccessTip!

If the current ratio is too high, the company is keeping money in short-term investments that could be used more productively elsewhere in the operation.

Quick Ratio

The quick ratio is a tougher measure of a company's liquidity. While the current ratio uses total current assets, the quick ratio uses only cash or assets that can be quickly converted into cash.

A quick ratio of at least 1.0 is a rule of thumb benchmark, but once again, companies that turn over inventory quickly might show a lower ratio. For example, Home Depot's quick ratio is less than 0.5.

Quick ratio = (Cash and cash equivalents + Short-term investments + Accounts receivable) / Current liabilities

Home Depot's Quick Ratio = (2,826 + 26+ 1,097) / 9,554 = .41

All these measures are on the balance sheet. In Figure 8-02, Home Depot labels these measures Cash and Cash Equivalents (the first line under the Current Assets heading,) Short-Term Investments (the second line under the Current Assets heading,) Receivables, net (the third line under the Current

Assets heading,) and Total Current Liabilities (the first subtotal underneath Liabilities and Stockholders' Equity.

Interest Coverage

When a company raises capital with debt, interest coverage measures how easily the company can pay the next twelve months worth of interest from profits. An interest coverage ratio greater than 5 means that the company is unlikely to default on its loans and bonds. Interest coverage less than 1.5 is a red flag that the company barely generates enough cash to cover its interest payments.

Interest coverage = (Pre-tax profit + Interest expense) / Interest expense

Home Depot's interest coverage = ($6,843 + $62) / $62 = 111

These numbers come from the income statement. For example, in Figure 8-01, Home Depot labels pre-tax profit as Earnings Before Provision for Income Taxes. Interest Expense shows up as Interest Expense underneath the Operating Income heading. Because Home Depot lists interest expense within an income section, the number for interest expense is negative.

Home Depot's interest coverage clearly exceeds the minimum guideline, showing the company can comfortably carry its debt.

Efficiency of Operations

Operational efficiency means that management generates a significant level of profit from the company assets at their disposal. Investors use turnover ratios and other related measures to evaluate how efficiently management runs the company.

Inventory turnover

Inventory turnover measures how many times a company replaces its inventory over a period of time. Higher numbers are preferable, because they indicate that inventory is moving from warehouse to customer with regularity. If inventory turnover is low or declining, inventory could be obsolete or out-of-date. When worse comes to worst, a company might write-off inventory against income if it can't even give the inventory away.

Inventory turnover = Cost of goods sold / Inventory

Inventory turnover = $44,236 / $9,076 = 4.8

Cost of Goods Sold appears on the income statement, whereas Inventory is an asset and shows up on the balance sheet. In Figure 8-01, Home Depot's

income statement, the cost of goods sold is called Cost of Merchandise Sold. In Figure 8-02, Home Depot's balance sheet, inventory is labeled Merchandise Inventories.

Many industries must deal with short-lived products: clothing fashions change quickly, technology renders previous products obsolete, and food spoils. Companies today often use business processes and computer technology to minimize inventory. For example, Dell builds computers to order and ships them immediately to the customers. Other companies arrange for parts and materials to be delivered from suppliers "just in time".

Cost of goods sold comes from an income statement (Figure 8-01) and represents the amount the company spent to produce its inventory during the period that the income statement covers. Inventory comes from the balance sheet and represents the value of inventory at the end of the period.

There's no set guideline for inventory turnover. However, an increasing trend shows the company is making the operation more efficient. In addition, comparing inventory turnover to the industry average is helpful. Home Depot's inventory turnover is about par for the industry.

Receivables Turnover

The faster a company receives payment from its customers, the easier it is to pay bills and put the money to work earning more money. Receivables turnover measures the number of times in a period that the company converts accounts receivable into cash. Because timeliness is critical when collecting money, the average receivables used are from the previous two quarters instead of the last two years.

Receivables turnover = Sales / Average accounts receivable (previous two quarters)

Average receivables = ($1,097 + $1,432)/2 = $1,264.5

Receivables turnover = $64,816 / $1,264.5 = 51.25

Turn to the income statement for the number for sales (Figure 8-01 for Home Depot.) You can find accounts receivable for the previous two quarters by looking at the balance sheet published in the company's quarterly report or SEC 10-Q. In this example, $1,097 is accounts receivable from the fourth quarter of 2003, shown in the balance sheet in Figure 8-02. $1,432 is the accounts receivable published in the balance sheet for the third quarter and published in the 10-Q report for the period ending December 2, 2003. Home Depot refers to accounts receivable as "Receivables, net."

Accounts receivable increase as sales increase, because higher sales means customers owe the company more money. As long as customers continue to pay promptly, the receivables turnover won't be affected. But, if accounts receivables increase without a corresponding increase in sales, there's a problem. When a company can't collect its accounts receivables, cash flow suffers. In addition, collection problems might indicate quality problems, product obsolescence, or overly aggressive shipments to customers to boost sales.

As you would expect from a company that turns inventory over quickly, Home Depot is also very effective at collecting receivables. Companies in low profit margin industries, such as grocery stores, typically produce receivables turnover ratios higher than 50. For example, according to the MSN Money web site, the average receivables turnover ratio for the grocery industry is 44.4. Auto manufacturers on the other hand average 1.9!

Days Sales Outstanding

Days sales outstanding is another way to depict the efficiency of collecting receivables. This measure calculates the number of days

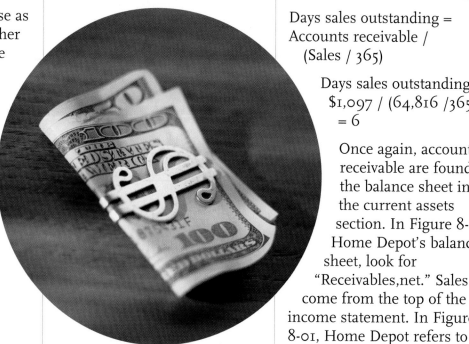

it takes for a company to collect its accounts receivable. Every dollar of sales must come into the company through accounts receivable. By dividing the most recent accounts receivable by the sales per day, you obtain the number of days it takes to collect accounts receivable.

Days sales outstanding = Accounts receivable / (Sales / 365)

Days sales outstanding = $1,097 / (64,816 /365) = 6

Once again, accounts receivable are found on the balance sheet in the current assets section. In Figure 8-02, Home Depot's balance sheet, look for "Receivables,net." Sales come from the top of the income statement. In Figure 8-01, Home Depot refers to sales as Net Sales.

Values below 60 are good. Once again, Home Depot's cash-based business and high volume show up in days sales outstanding. The company requires only six days to collect its accounts receivable.

Asset Turnover Ratio

The asset turnover ratio measures how many dollars in sales a company generates for

COMPARING INVENTORY AND RECEIVABLES TO SALES

Inventories and receivables increase as sales increase, because the company must stock more products to fulfill more orders and receives more money from those orders. Inventories and receivables also increase when products fall out of favor. Compare the percentage change in inventory and receivables to the percentage change in sales. If inventories increase faster than sales, competition or pricing are often to blame. Receivables increasing faster than sales might show that customers aren't satisfied with the products they bought.

each dollar of assets it owns, so higher asset turnover ratios are better. If a company is highly effective at using assets to generate sales, it can survive on low profit margins, an essential trait in highly competitive environments. The asset turnover ratio is the total sales for a period divided by the average assets for that same period.

Asset turnover ratio = Total sales / Average assets

The asset turnover ratio uses the average assets for a period: the average of the beginning and ending value for total assets. Because a company generates sales over the entire period, the average assets figure is a better representation of the assets the company had to work with. For example, if a company continually purchases assets, the lower asset value at the beginning would make the asset turnover ratio look better than it is, while the higher asset value at the end would make it look worse.

As you would expect, Home Depot is very effective at generating sales from its assets. Most companies in low profit margin industries such as grocery stores and discount stores show asset turnover ratios of 2.0 or higher.

Average assets (balance sheet in Figure 8-02) = ($34,437 + $30,011) / 2 = $32,224

Home Depot's asset turnover ratio = $64,816 / $32,224 = 2.01

Financial Statements and Much, Much More

With an SSG and a bunch of financial ratios at hand, you might think there's nothing more to know about a company. But, some analysis and judgment about a company is more qualitative than quantitative. You need to know what really makes the company tick, and what could affect its fortunes in the future. Getting a sense of whether company management is optimistic about the future is helpful as well. For this sort of information, you can turn to the rest of the sections in published financial reports.

The SEC requires companies to disclose financial data for each fiscal quarter and fiscal year. The quarterly report (10-Q) and the annual report (10-K) include the information that the SEC requires: financial performance, an explanation of business operations, and information about management and management compensation. The reports also describe opportunities, problems, and risks that the company faces as well as information about the industry in which the company operates.

Companies also produce quarterly reports and annual reports for their shareholders. These reports duplicate a lot of the ground covered by the 10-Q and the 10-K, but they take more of a marketing slant—in some cases the fluff factor is quite high. You can tell a lot about a company simply by the nature of its annual report. Some are forthright, easy to read, and upfront about issues, not to mention printed on frugal recyclable paper. Others pack in the pictures on shiny and colorful page, but sidle around sticky points in the company performance.

The Crucial Elements of a Financial Report

Some sections of an annual report are more fluffy than others. For example, the corporate profile in an annual report often includes lots of pictures of impressive buildings, equipment, and personnel, as well as heart-warming stories about the company's philanthropic activities. On the more useful side, the corporate profile often discusses business strategies, the company's structure, and might explain more complicated technology or products. You can obtain much of this information without the warm and fuzzy presentation from the 10-K

report or by heading straight for the Management Discussion and Analysis section of the annual report.

Letter to Shareholders

The letter to shareholders is the president or CEO's chance to communicate to the company's owners— its shareholders. The letter to shareholders often reflects the CEO's personality and philosophy, so its tone and language can be as informative as the words themselves. How a CEO talks about problems is significant. If the CEO bypasses the tough issues, beware. If explanations of problems seem defensive or unrealistic, inspect the other sections of the report more closely or look for a company that is more willing to communicate.

CHECKING UP ON THE BOARD OF DIRECTORS

Similar to the U.S. government, the governing of a company is a matter of checks and balances. The shareholders elect a board of directors to represent their interests in the company. The board of directors defines company policies, appoints the CEO and other top executives to run the company, and makes other overarching decisions. If directors are also employees of the company, they report to the CEO, and the conflict of interest is readily apparent.

Even independent directors might not be as autonomous as you might think. Directors can belong to an old-boys network, in which directors appoint each other to CEO positions. Annual reports and proxy statements provide information about the people running a company. As a shareholder, be sure to vote for independent directors whom you trust to represent your interests. If a proposed director has a poor record running another company, don't give him or her a chance to produce poor performance at the company you own.

The 2003 Chairman's Letter for Home Depot (the annual report is available online at *http://ir.homedepot.com/down loads/HD_2003_AR.pdf*) brags about the company's history of growth and strong financial condition—with good reason. The company grew 20 to 25 percent a year for almost 20 years and carries a debt to equity ratio of only 4 percent. The chairman talks about the capital recently invested in the company and the hiring and training efforts for personnel. These are important initiatives, but the chairman doesn't actually admit that they are in response to sales and customer service problems in recent years. The chairman talks about being positioned for future growth, but doesn't offer a specific growth rate forecast. However, the Management Discussion section does provide some growth rate forecasts.

When a CEO makes projections about the future, consider whether they seem reasonable and feasible in the company's upcoming competitive environment. For example, forecasting double-digit growth in the face of increasing competition and interest rates should raise a red flag. Make a point of comparing past projections to actual results to see how good the CEO's predictions are.

Auditors report

Auditors' reports almost always follow a standard format that first describes the company and then the auditor's responsibility preparing and reviewing company financials. Auditors don't recommend companies as investments or estimate company value. You must read between the lines for signs of problems. If you see any variation from the standard format, read the qualification that the auditors provide. If the auditors' report includes notes, read them.

Management Discussion and Analysis

You can learn a great deal about how a company operates by reading the Management Discussion and Analysis section of the annual report. Management often discusses its strategies and initiatives for the future, which can be very helpful when you are trying to forecast future growth. For example, in Home Depot's 2003 annual report, management forecasts sales growth between 9 and 12 percent for 2004 based on same store sales increases between 3 and 6 percent, and the addition of 175 new stores.

operations, any impact from competition or monetary factors (inflation or exchange rates), how the company utilized capital resources, and the company's liquidity. For example, Home Depot explained how some new Home Depot stores took sales away from other Home Depot stores, which reduced same store sales by about 4 percent. However, projected impact of this cannibalization is 2 percent for 2004.

Success Tip!

The Management Discussion and Analysis section sometimes appears under other names. Look through the table of contents for headings such as Financial Review.

When companies contain multiple business units, you might find financial performance broken down by business unit, geographic regions, or product lines. By understanding which parts of the company are the most

productive, you can decide how a planned divestiture might affect the business. For example, if a company is ditching a poor performer, growth might increase in the future.

The section on liquidity and capital resources explains how the company uses its money. If you have questions about company assets, debt, or unusual results in financial ratios such as ROE or ROA, read this section carefully. You can learn exactly what the company invested in or what types of debt it assumed.

Depending on the company, Management Discussion and Analysis might also include accounting policy changes, risk management strategies, foreign currency exchange issues, or legal proceedings. For example, a company with significant business overseas might discuss the potential affect of currency exchange rates on future results. If a company faces lawsuits, it might discuss its projection of the impact.

If you're looking for an explanation of questionable financial results, this is one place to look. Management should explain why values are changing (You can see for yourself that values are changing, but you usually need management's help to understand why.) The topics that management presents vary from company to company, but this section usually explains the results of company

OBTAINING FINANCIAL REPORTS AND SEC FILINGS

With the advent of online investing, financial reports and SEC filings are easy to obtain online. In fact, the reports are so easy to access, you can save trees and space on your bookshelf by reading the reports online and saving a bookmark to the report in your Web browser for future reference. In addition, you can use the Search feature in your Web browser to find the information you want quickly. On the Web, look for an Investor Relations link on the company's Web site. For example, on Home Depot's Web site (www.homedepot.com), click Investor Relations in the navigation bar, then click Financial Reports. You can access or download annual reports as far back as 1982 and SEC filings go back to 1994.

You can search for SEC filings in the SEC's EDGAR database (www.sec.gov/cgi-bin/srch-edgar/). Free Edgar (www.freeedgar.com) enables you to search for filings by company name, ticker symbols, SIC code (which stands for Standard Industry Classification) or location, after you register (no charge).

To snag multiple annual reports at once, use the Annual Report Service Web site (www.annualreportservice.com). It won't win any awards for best Web site design and it offers annual reports for only 4,500 companies, but you can download online versions of annual reports and 10-Ks or request copies to be mailed.

Notes to Financial Statements

You've already read about the financial statements that a company publishes. The notes to financial statements explain the details behind the financial statements. For example, a company might explain when it recognizes revenue, how it depreciates assets, the accounting policies it uses, or exceptions to the statements. This section is often the toughest read, but it also a favorite repository for information that management wants to keep quiet.

Selling Stocks

Such Sweet Sorrow

Some investors can't bear to part with a stock they've come to know and love—it's like betraying a friend. Others can't stomach the idea of cozying up to a strange stock. But buying stocks can be thrilling. Based on the number of books and advisory services that focus on buying, most investors enjoy the hunt for good stocks, the satisfaction of adding to a

portfolio, and the anticipation of great results. Selling seems sad whether you're parting with a stock because it's doing poorly or because it's done too well. Get over it. Selling stocks to prevent losses or increase gains is as important to portfolio performance as buying.

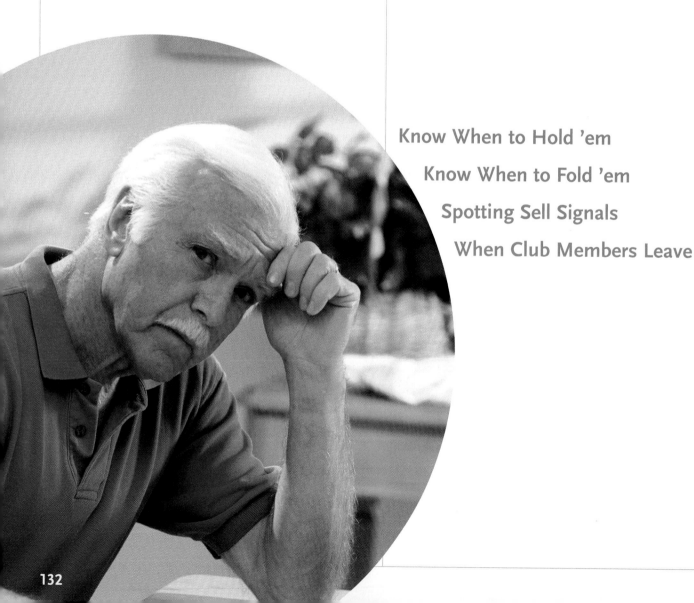

Know When to Hold 'em

Know When to Fold 'em

Spotting Sell Signals

When Club Members Leave

Know When to Hold 'em

Warren Buffett has been quoted as saying the best time to sell is NEVER. He makes a point of buying only the best quality companies and then is content to ride out any market volatility those companies might experience. Selling is a challenge, because you have to make two good choices instead of one. You must sell the right stock for the right reasons and then replace it with a better one—one with less risk, higher potential returns, or higher quality. If you don't have to sell, why go through all that effort? The better your buy decision, the less likely you'll have to sell.

The Wrong Reasons for Selling

If you sell too quickly, the regular selling and buying will require excessive effort and could produce below par portfolio returns to boot. Before you sell a stock, run through the following list to make sure you aren't selling for the wrong reasons.

- **You think you should be doing something.** Holding onto stocks and mutual funds when they are doing what they are supposed to is as significant to portfolio management as buying or selling. Your regular review of your holdings (see Chapter 10), the updates you make to your SSGs (see Chapter 7), and review of mutual fund Trend Reports (see Chapter 14) are your portfolio management actions.

- **The stock hasn't done anything.** For all the talk of an efficient stock market, the fact is that stock price does not move in lockstep with company value, as the graph for Lowe's demonstrates in Figure 9-01. You purchase for the long term. If the company is growing and no red flags are waving, be patient and give your investment some time to prove itself. The stock price eventually catches up if the company's EPS are increasing. Remember, your regular portfolio reviews include an inspection of company fundamentals, so you'll know whether the stock is still a buy or has become a target to sell. Although

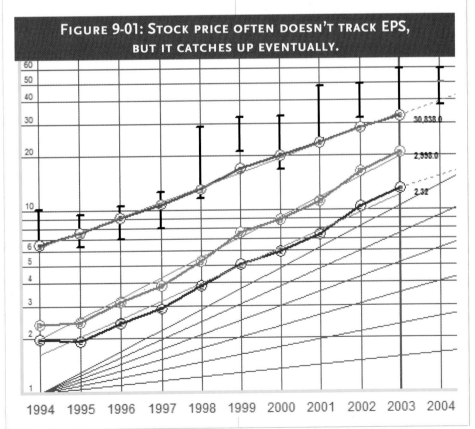

FIGURE 9-01: STOCK PRICE OFTEN DOESN'T TRACK EPS, BUT IT CATCHES UP EVENTUALLY.

Lowe's price went up and down between 1998 and 2000, its high price hovered between $29 and $33 from 1998 to 2000, while EPS kept growing. In 2001, the high price jumped to $48.88. Because EPS continued to grow, the high PE ratio in 2001 was lower than the high PE in 1998.

Success Tip!

When you invest in equity mutual funds, the underlying investments are still individual stocks. Patience and regular review are just as important in your mutual fund investments, although your criteria for selling are a little different (see Chapter 14).

- **The price has dropped.** Prices drop for an amazing number of mostly wrong reasons. News about inflation, oil prices, war, the low number of jobs created, and other large-scale factors can drive stock prices down market-wide. Yes, these things can affect the economy, which in turn can adversely affect stocks, but the price drops are often temporary and out of proportion to the risk. Bad news about one company can drive the prices of its competitors down even though the news has nothing to do with them.

Even if a company issues bad news, the price drop that follows might be larger than the problem warrants. Research whether the price drop was caused by a problem in the company or a market-wide weakness.

If the market has affected all stocks, the price drop could be an opportunity to buy, not sell. If the company has a problem, review your stock study with the problem in mind and adjust your growth forecasts if necessary. Then, you can decide whether the price drop is warranted and whether you should sell.

For example, Lincare Holdings dropped in 2003 due to concerns about future government reimbursements for healthcare services. However, Lincare has operated successfully under these conditions for many years and has increased its growth by acquiring smaller companies that can't handle the government requirements. The price drop from a high of $43 to $28 offset the potential affect on future growth and presented what many investors considered an opportunity to buy the stock.

- **The price has gone up a little.** Selling to lock in a small profit means that you sell your winners and hang onto your losers. Wait, that doesn't sound right. If you haven't noticed already, price has very little to do with selling. If the stock's fundamentals still look good and its potential return meets your objectives, hold onto the company.

- **An analyst downgrades a stock.** One analyst might downgrade a stock, while five other analysts upgrade it. Use your own judgment to determine a stock's potential. If your analysis contradicts most of the analysts' opinions, revisit your research. However, if you are comfortable with your analysis, sell only when you see signs of deterioration and poor prospects for the future.

- **Insiders are selling stock.** Insiders sell for many reasons that have nothing to do with low expectations of the stock. Insiders need to diversify their portfolios like the rest of us, or they might sell to satisfy SEC requirements or because they need the cash for some other reason. Major insider selling could indicate problems on the horizon, so research is in order if you see a lot of insider sales.

(Yahoo! Finance includes an Insider Transactions link in each stock page navigation bar.) On the other hand, insider buying is a good sign because insiders usually buy because they see their stock as an excellent investment.

Success Tip!

*Out of the small selection of books on selling, **When to Sell** by Justin Mamis (Fraser Publishing Co., 1999) comes highly recommended by investors regardless of the investment methodology they use.*

The Wrong Reasons for Holding

Then there are the folks who don't sell fast enough. These investors hold onto investments that should go.

- **You've grown attached to your investment.** For whatever reason, you have fond feelings for your investment—maybe it's the cache of owning it or you've held it so long that you feel you owe it loyalty. Kidnap victims sometimes grow attached to their kidnappers, but that doesn't mean it's right. Your investment doesn't care what you do. Sell the stock if it isn't working out.

- **You don't want to admit you made a mistake.** Financial professionals specify sell criteria before they buy.

When you decide to purchase a stock, decide what conditions would make you sell. For example, if you purchased a stock because it offered potential 20 percent EPS growth, you might consider a drop to projected EPS growth of 12 percent as a mistake. Learn to admit your mistakes and prevent a small loss from growing into a bigger one. Conduct a post-mortem review to identify where you went wrong so you're less likely to repeat your error in the future.

- **You hate to lose money.** Losing money on an investment over a short period of time is often no more than market volatility, but losing money on a stock that you've owned for several years might mean that you made a mistake (see the previous wrong reason). But, waiting 10 years for a stock to recover to the price at which you purchased it is a much bigger mistake. If you haven't done so already, update your SSG on the stock and, if you see signs of deteriorating fundamentals and your research points to poor prospects for the future, sell the stock at a loss and reinvest your money in a stock with better prospects. Suppose a stock you own dropped from $10,000 to $5,000. After you recover from shock, you re-evaluate the stock and project its annual total return at 10 percent. At that rate, it will take about seven years for the stock to recover to $10,000. Although the price drop might be the symptom that catches your attention, the 10 percent growth rate is a drag on your future portfolio performance. If you reinvest the $5,000 in a better company with a projected annual total return of 15 percent, you can have over $13,000 at the end of seven years.

Success Tip!

If you have a stock that has declined in price and it doesn't look like it's coming back, you can sell it and use the loss to offset any capital gains in your portfolio.

Know When to Fold 'em

Now that you know when to hold onto your investments, it's time to learn when to let them go. Selling is inevitable unless you plan to work until you drop. At some point, you should sell some stocks and enjoy some of the money you've earned from investing. Other good reasons to sell fall into two categories: protecting your portfolio from losses and improving your portfolio's characteristics.

- **Another company offers equal or better returns with less downside risk.** The one problem with truly spectacular winners is that they usually end up spectacularly overpriced. Then, these winners offer little additional upside potential, but a great deal of downside risk. (They probably mess up your portfolio diversification, too.) You don't want to sell your winners too quickly and you certainly don't want to start chasing fractionally better returns. However, when the valuation measures on the SSG all scream sell, other less risky companies might be worth considering as replacements.

- **A company of equal or higher quality offers better potential returns.** Potential returns can be low for several reasons: the stock price is grossly overvalued; a low-risk blue-chip company, which you inherited from your aunt, grows slowly and doesn't offer much chance for price appreciation; or, in a moment of weakness, you paid too much for a stock. To improve your portfolio return, look for replacements for the stocks

OVERCOMING THE TAX BITE

As you study stocks and review your portfolio, you're bound to run across stocks that look interesting. If you invest in a taxable account and have to sell one stock to buy another, commissions and taxes are a factor in your decision. When you pay taxes on the capital gains from the proceeds of the sale, you have less money to invest in the new stock. A new purchase in a taxable account might have to increase by 5 to 40 percent (in simple price appreciation) just to cover the costs of selling. Chapter 10 explains how to use the stock challenge tree when commissions and taxes are a factor.

with the lowest total annual return. It's never a good idea to reduce the quality of the stocks you own, so make sure that replacements at least match the quality of your current holdings.

- **You need the money.** Most people invest to achieve financial goals (see Chapter 3). When

your financial goals require funding, you have to sell your investments. There's nothing wrong with selling stocks to access your money. Just make sure you sell the right stocks, which is explained in the rest of this chapter.

- **Company fundamentals or business outlook are deteriorating.** Companies can lose their edge: the management team could reach the limits of their ability or new management could take the wrong road; external factors such as competition, new technology, or government regulation could put a permanent dent in a company's prospects. Regardless of the reason, when fundamentals deteriorate, the price usually follows. Read the section "Spotting Sell Signals" in this chapter

Carefully study stock positions greater than 5% to 10% of the total portfolio.

Factors that Influence Selling

Chapter 7 took an in-depth look at evaluating stocks with the SSG—and with good reason. The SSG is the foundation for your opinion of a stock; you can use it to decide whether to buy a stock, but you can also use it to decide whether to sell. The factors that influence your decision to sell are simply the opposite of the factors that influence you to buy. Table 9-01 compares the green lights and red flags that you can see on an SSG.

One sell signal doesn't mean you should sell, but it's a warning to look at the company more closely. If you haven't already done so, dissect the annual report and evaluate financial ratios for signs of trouble (see Chapter 8). Keep a watchful eye on the company when quarterly data becomes available. If several additional sell signals appear, it's time to

to learn how to sell before the stock price drops too far. You still need to keep up with company news to learn about management changes and external influences on company performance.

- **Your portfolio diversification is out of whack.** Unless you have so much spare cash that you can rebalance your portfolio by depositing more money for additional purchases, maintaining diversification might require some selling (See Chapter 2). Your winners can take over your portfolio, which, in turn, might raise the risk to unacceptable levels. An ideal portfolio holds approximately 15 to 25 stocks in at least 10 different (unrelated) industries.

BRIAN LEWIS

For Brian Lewis, portfolio management comprises three choices regardless how you choose to monitor your stocks:

- Buy shares of a stock
- Sell some or all shares of a stock
- Do nothing

Brian uses "sweet 16 plus or minus 4" as a guideline for the right number of stocks. Although he warns that too many stocks lead to insufficient knowledge of the companies you own, he considers five stocks to be the bare minimum for diversification—and then only if they are large, high-quality companies. He belongs to the camp that believes that sector diversification is more important than size diversification as long as the overall portfolio growth and total return meets your objectives.

Brian recommends acting quickly on your sell decisions once you've made them. For example, don't wait until the day you need the proceeds of a sale, because the stock market is volatile and your stock may hit a rough patch. If you made a mistake when you purchased a company or its fundamentals have deteriorated, sell immediately and don't pay any attention to the price you originally paid.

Brian doesn't rush to sell stocks just because they are overvalued. He also is slow to sell when one stock or sector represents too large a percentage of a portfolio. He prefers to maintain balance.

TABLE 9-01: BUY AND SELL FACTORS ON THE SSG

SSG Section	Buy Factors	Sell Factors
Section 1	Sales, pre-tax profit margins, and EPS growth increasing steadily at an acceptable rate.	Growth slows to an unacceptable rate.
Section 1	Growth is consistent.	Growth is erratic.
Section 1	Sales and EPS grow at similar rates.	EPS grows much slower or faster than sales.
Section 1	The most recent quarter is equal or better than the historical and projected growth rates.	The most recent quarter is significantly less than the historical and projected growth rates.
Section 2	Profit margin or ROE are stable or trend steadily upward.	Profit margin or ROE trend downward.
Section 2	Profit margin and ROE are above the industry average.	Profit margin and ROE are significantly below the industry average.
Section 3	The payout ratio is stable or increasing slightly and is low enough to leave earnings to fund growth. The payout ratio can decrease if it is due to increasing earnings and stable dividends.	The payout ratio is decreasing due to dividend cuts. Also, the dividend payout is increasing faster than earnings, thus lowering the future EPS growth rate.
Section 4	The relative value is roughly between .85 and 1.1.	The relative value is significantly more than 1.1. The relative value is less than .85 due to company problems.
Section 4	The upside-downside ratio is between 3 to 1 or better.	The upside-downside ratio is less than 1.
Section 5	The total return meets or exceeds your target return.	The total return and/or the projected average return is significantly less than your target rate.

move on to another stock. Chapter 10 describes how to use PERT to spot both defensive and offensive sell signals.

Reviewing pre-tax profit margin trends when quarterly data comes out can provide early warning of deterioration in growth. When the pre-tax profit margin drops, the company keeps less of each dollar it brings in. Unless it reacts to control costs in some way, earnings will drop, which leads inexorably to a drop in price. By spotting the downward trend in profit margin, you might be able to sell before the price plummets. The PERT-A graph described in Chapter 11 makes it easy to spot trends in sales, EPS, and pre-tax profit margin. Remember that one quarter's results do not necessarily represent a trend.

Sell Signals that Aren't on the SSG

OK, so not all the sell signals are on the SSG. Other sell signals can become apparent if you read the quarterly and annual reports that the company publishes (SEC filings or the glossy versions) and keep an eye on company news.

- **An adverse management change has occurred.** Management is the key to ongoing performance, so any management change for the worse is a huge red flag. If new executives take over who have a record of poor performance at another company, beware. Individual investors might have trouble spotting these adverse changes so consider what professional analysts say about company management. Even if the executives are unknown quantities, keep an eye on the trends in pre-tax profit margin and ROE in Section 2 for signs of deterioration.

- **The customer base is shrinking.** If major customers go elsewhere, a company has problems somewhere in the organization: costs, quality, old technology, competition, or poor service all could be to blame. In addition, if a company depends on one major customer for a significant part of its business, the risk for the future is high.

- **Competition is tough.** Every successful product attracts competition and with that, product prices usually drop. If a company has only one product, the declining price shows up immediately in declining pre-tax profit margins and the dominos start to fall. Good management builds a diversified product line and funds strong research and development programs to continually introduce new products with higher margins to offset the older commodity products.

- **The product pipeline is deteriorating.** Products have a lifecycle. Early on, competition is low and margins are high. As the product ages, competition increases, improved versions appear, and profit margins get squeezed. Companies can maintain a steady profit margin by keeping the product line balanced between new and older products. If this product mix begins to tip toward older less profitable products or important products fall out of favor or become obsolete due to new technology, profit margins are in danger of dropping dramatically. Similar to a one-customer company, a one-product company is a high risk.

- **Funding for research and development is decreasing.** R&D is critical in many industries such as healthcare and information technology. Cutting costs by reducing the money spent on R&D drastically affects a company's ability to stay competitive. If R&D funding grows slower than sales, the product pipeline could deteriorate.

- **The financial results shows problems or worse—signs of manipulation.** Problems on the income statement are obvious in Section 1 of the SSG. To spot problems on the balance sheet and cash flow statement, you must evaluate a number of ratios (see chapter 8). For example, if accounts receivable and/or inventory are increasing, the company might have problems with product quality or obsolescence. If these measures are increasing faster than sales, the company is extending easier credit terms to bolster sales. If debt is increasing or is excessively high, the company might not generate enough money to operate.

- **The price drops below your estimated low on the SSG for no apparent reason.** Your estimated low on the SSG should be a conservative estimate based on what you know about the company. If the price drops below that number, other investors might know something distressing about the company that you don't. Research the company more carefully. If you can't find a problem, you might consider selling to be safe.

Chapter 15 discusses how to handle special situations such as mergers, major acquisitions, tender offers, IPOs, and more.

Managing Stock Portfolios with PERT

Use PERT and PMG to Perk Up Your Portfolio

Many individual investors and investment club members seem to get stuck on the buy side. After spending their efforts learning how to use the SSG to buy stocks, they don't move on to checking whether they should continue to hold the stocks they've bought. You're going to do better. As soon as you purchase your first stock, you must add portfolio review to your regimen of stock analysis and buying.

The SSG shows many of the signs of deterioration or overvaluation you must look for, but you need a convenient way to review all the stocks in your portfolio. NAIC PERT reports and PMG focus on fundamental and price performance, so you can work your way down from high-level defense and offense to detailed examination of the stocks that need attention.

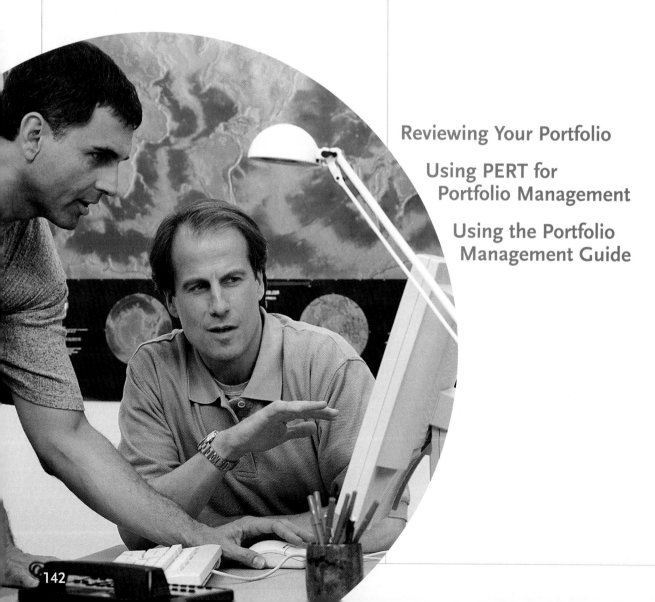

Reviewing Your Portfolio

Using PERT for
Portfolio Management

Using the Portfolio
Management Guide

Reviewing Your Portfolio

One of the issues that might hold you back is not knowing what to review in a portfolio. But, as you learned in Chapter 9, reasons to sell are often the opposite of the reasons you buy, so portfolio review doesn't require you to learn new concepts. Portfolio review is little more than checking your stocks for buy and sell factors, and then deciding whether to sell any stocks you own or choosing which stocks to buy with your cash on hand. The second snag for portfolio review is trying to keep all the information from your SSGs in front of you as you look for deterioration or overly high stock prices. Most of the information you need for portfolio review data is available on the SSG, but covering your desk with an SSG for every stock is not the most effective way to analyze buy, hold, and sell factors. Fortunately, NAIC PERT reports summarize the information about all the stocks in a portfolio, so you can more easily evaluate the portfolio as a whole. *Investor's Toolkit 5* makes it even easier to find stocks that require defensive or offensive attention before you drill down into the details.

Tools for Portfolio Review

NAIC offers a number of reports and forms that help with portfolio review. PERT forms and reports present the information needed to make buy, hold, and sell recommendations. Here's a quick introduction to NAIC's portfolio review tools.

- **PERT Report**—A good place to start for both defense and offense for an entire portfolio. For defense, it includes growth rates for the most recent quarter for sales, EPS, and pre-tax profit, and EPS growth rate for the trailing twelve months. For offense, it provides numerous valuation measures such as PE ratio, relative value, PEG ratio, upside-downside ratio, and total return.

- **Portfolio Trend Report**—For many investors, the next step in defense after the PERT Report when stocks show signs of deterioration. This report includes the

RICH BEAUBIEN

Rich Beaubien has been teaching NAIC methodology for 15 years and tries to simplify the portfolio management process for his students.

He doesn't want portfolio management to be a second full-time job, and believes it doesn't have to be. Unlike many NAICers, Rich claims that selling is no easier or harder than buying, because sell signals are simply the inverse of buy signals.

Just as Ralph Seger teaches, Rich believes that the SSG is the key to buy and sell signals, but he goes one step further. He doesn't use the Portfolio Management Guide, the PERT Report, or the PERT-A Report. Instead, Rich maintains two SSGs for each holding in his portfolio. The first is the original SSG with the original judgments that led to his buy decision, but with quarterly data added. Approximately four weeks after the end of each quarter, Rich collects the quarterly reports for his holdings, updates the second SSG for each company, and compares the original projected trend line for a company to its quarterly data graph, as shown in Figure 10-01.

Total return is the driving force behind Rich's portfolio decisions. He sorts all the newly updated SSGs by the five-year total returns

in Section 5 of the SSGs. His goal for total portfolio return is at least 15 percent, so companies with less than 12 percent returns are potential sell candidates. For Rich, there are only three out and out reasons to sell:

1. **Cash:** plain and simple, he needs cash.

2. **Bad news:** the fundamentals for a company are unfavorable

3. **Good news:** the stock has become overvalued.

Everything else is a "signal," such as stalled growth, declining profit margins, management fumbles, low upside-downside ratios, low total returns, or relative value

over 150. Any company sporting any signal is a candidate to be sold. With three or more signals, a company is probably a dog. Rich evaluates the remaining companies with the lowest potential becoming a target for replacement with quality candidates of greater potential. If SSGs show buy signals, he considers additional purchases.

This approach takes three to four hours plus a few more hours over the course of a quarter to search for candidates to improve the portfolio, and has improved this average return. His turnover rate is between 10 and 20 percent of his holdings each year.

FIGURE 10-01: COMPARING THE PROJECTION LINE WITH QUARTERLY DATA QUICKLY SHOWS ANY SIGN OF DETERIORATION.

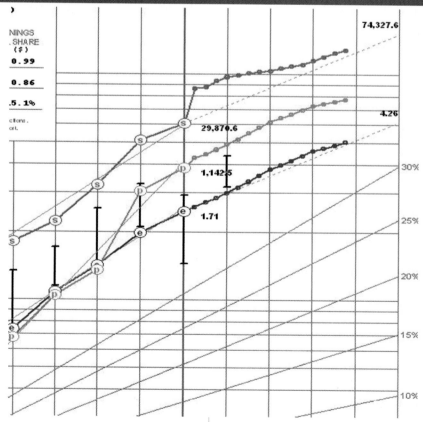

quarterly growth of sales, EPS, and pre-tax profit for the most recent two quarters, and the EPS growth for two consecutive trailing twelve month periods for every stock in the portfolio. If a stock shows a disturbing trend for two quarters, drill down even further to find out if this is a long-term problem.

- **PERT Worksheet-A**—If you spot downward trends in the Portfolio Trend Report, this table drills down into the longer term trends for one stock. It provides

quarterly and trailing twelve month growth rates for the past five years, so you can see whether the downward trends have lasted more than two quarters.

- **PERT-A Graph**—A visual analysis of the quarterly and trailing twelve month growth rates shown in a PERT Worksheet-A. Spotting the magnitude of trends is often easier on the graph than in the PERT Worksheet-A.

- **PERT Worksheet-B**—This worksheet calculates the

five-year averages for high, low, and average PE ratios. In addition, this worksheet shows trends in the percent payout and high yield, and calculates the five-year average percent payout for several years.

- **Portfolio Summary**— A report that focuses on offense. This report includes valuation measures such as PE ratio, total return, relative value, upside-downside ratio, the current price, and the buy below and sell above prices. It also includes the percentage that each stock comprises in the portfolio, so you can see whether purchasing a stock would disrupt your portfolio diversification.

Helpful Portfolio Review Features in *Investor's Toolkit 5*

Investor's Toolkit 5 introduced features to facilitate portfolio management defense and offense. Not a substitute for the NAIC portfolio review forms, *Investor's Toolkit 5* reminds you to update the necessary data and pinpoints the companies likely to require your attention. *Investor's Toolkit 5* features include:

- **Requires Attention Reminders**—On the *Investor's Toolkit 5* home page shown in Figure 10-02, the Requires

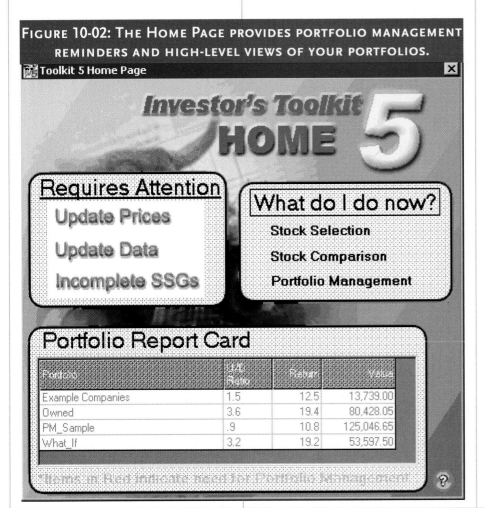

FIGURE 10-02: THE HOME PAGE PROVIDES PORTFOLIO MANAGEMENT REMINDERS AND HIGH-LEVEL VIEWS OF YOUR PORTFOLIOS.

Toolkit 5 Home Page

Investor's Toolkit HOME 5

Requires Attention
Update Prices
Update Data
Incomplete SSGs

What do I do now?
Stock Selection
Stock Comparison
Portfolio Management

Portfolio Report Card

Portfolio	1/4 Ratio	Return	Value
Example Companies	1.5	12.5	13,739.00
Owned	3.6	19.4	80,428.05
PM_Sample	.9	10.8	125,046.65
What_If	3.2	19.2	53,597.50

Items in Red indicate need for Portfolio Management

Attention section notifies you when stock data and prices require updates. It also warns you if you have SSGs that are not complete. To check for deterioration or overvaluation, you must have an up-to-date SSG including the most recent quarterly data as well as the current price.

- **The Portfolio Report Card—** On the *Investor's Toolkit 5* home page, the Portfolio Report Card shows aggregate values for each portfolio you maintain in the application. The Report Card shows the aggregate upside-downside ratio, total return, and market value for all stocks in a portfolio. If any stocks in the portfolio require attention, the portfolio appears in red.

- **Portfolio Overview—** When you double-click a portfolio within the Portfolio Report Card, the Portfolio Overview dialog box appears for that portfolio, as shown in Figure 10-03. This view includes additional aggregate values for your portfolio and highlights valuation measures such as total return, relative value, and upside-downside ratio for each stock in the portfolio.

- **Alerts—** When you click the Alerts button in the upper right corner of the Portfolio Overview dialog box, the view changes to show stocks requiring defensive or offensive action. If any companies include adverse trends in sales, EPS, or pre-tax profit growth, they appear in the Defense section. The expected growth rates appear side by side with the actual growth rates. Any stocks that fall short on return or drop below your target

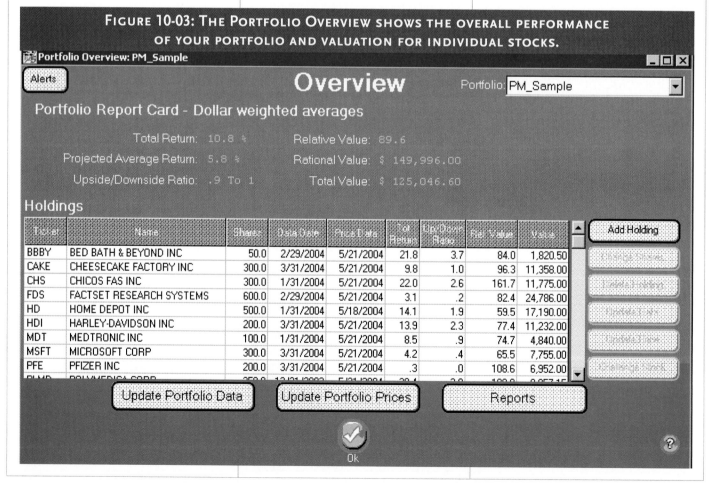

FIGURE 10-03: THE PORTFOLIO OVERVIEW SHOWS THE OVERALL PERFORMANCE OF YOUR PORTFOLIO AND VALUATION FOR INDIVIDUAL STOCKS.

upside-downside ratio appear in the Offense section. The Offense section shows the relative value, upside-downside ratio, and total return compared to your target return.

Using PERT for Portfolio Management

NAIC offers numerous forms and reports that help with your portfolio management tasks, but the plethora of options makes it hard to figure out which report to use when. Each report contains a different collection of measures but several measures appear on more than one report. In addition, some reports work primarily for offensive portfolio management: actions you can take to replace existing stocks with better ones. Other reports provide assistance with defense and offense. Whether you produce your PERT reports manually or use NAIC software, this section describes when to use each PERT report in your portfolio management process.

Success Tip!

Before you look at any of the PERT reports or graphs, double-check that all your SSGs are up to date with the most recent quarterly data, the most recent price, and any judgment changes you feel are necessary based on the newest quarterly performance

or news. Investor's Toolkit 5 checks the dates for the stock prices and quarterly data for the companies in your Toolkit database. If any information is out of date, the Requires Attention section of the Investor's Toolkit home page displays reminders to update prices, update data, and complete SSGs.

Playing Defense with PERT

Playing defense means selling companies with deteriorating fundamentals. Ideally, you'd spot a problem before the stock market catches on and massacres the stock price, but that isn't a realistic goal. However, when you play defense and find signs of deterioration, you can decide to sell a stock instead of holding on to it, watching the price languish and hoping that it comes back.

Although deterioration also pops up in ratios from financial statements, the early warning sign of deterioration in NAIC portfolio management is a downward trend in pre-tax profit growth, with downward trends in sales and EPS growth

confirming the problem. Therefore, the key measures for spotting signs of deterioration are:

- Sales, pre-tax profit, and EPS growth for the most recent two quarters

- EPS growth for the last 12 months

- Your projected sales and EPS growth rates

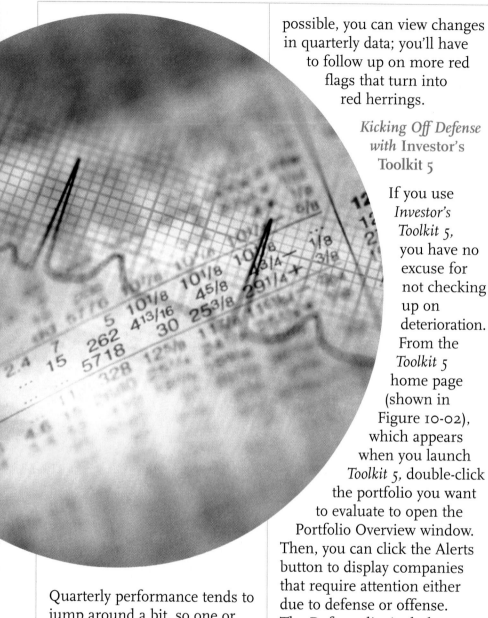

possible, you can view changes in quarterly data; you'll have to follow up on more red flags that turn into red herrings.

Kicking Off Defense with Investor's Toolkit 5

If you use *Investor's Toolkit 5*, you have no excuse for not checking up on deterioration. From the *Toolkit 5* home page (shown in Figure 10-02), which appears when you launch *Toolkit 5*, double-click the portfolio you want to evaluate to open the Portfolio Overview window. Then, you can click the Alerts button to display companies that require attention either due to defense or offense. The Defense list includes companies whose recent growth rates fall short of the growth rates that you projected in Section 1 of your SSG.

The Defense list displays your projected sales and EPS growth rates next to the actual recent growth rates in the % Change Sales, % Change PTP, and % Change EPS columns. Depending on whether you

want more immediate feedback or smoother trends, click the Quarterly or Trailing 12 Mos option buttons respectively. For example, if you forecast EPS growth at 15 percent, but the EPS growth for the trailing four quarters was only 12 percent, *Toolkit 5* changes the trailing EPS growth percentage to red to emphasize the shortfall.

Success Tip!

Seeing red in the Defense list doesn't always indicate a problem. If you forecast EPS growth at 15 percent, and the most recent EPS growth came in at 14.9 percent, Toolkit 5 still shows the growth rate in red. When you look over the numbers that are red, you can choose to ignore those that are only a few tenths of a percent below your forecasts.

The Defense list also contains % Diff columns, which indicate the percentage difference between your projected performance and actual performance. You can sort the Defense results by any column to list the companies from best to worst or vice versa. If you have more than one rotten apple, start your defense on the worst one—the company whose sales or EPS growth fall the farthest from your expectations.

Quarterly performance tends to jump around a bit, so one or two bad quarters don't automatically flag a trend, but they do warn you to do some research. In several places, PERT provides both quarterly results and trailing 12-month results. Trailing 12-month values tend to smooth out short term perturbations, so trends are easier to spot. However, if you want to see downward trends as early as

Finding Deterioration on the Portfolio Trend Report

Because trends are the most important factor in defense, if you use *Investor's Toolkit,* the Portfolio Trend Report is a good place to start. If the most recent quarterly performance raises a red flag, you can immediately check the previous quarterly performance for signs of an undesirable trend. Chapter 6 describes the defensive steps for stocks. Here's how to follow those steps with the Portfolio Trend Report:

1. Display the Portfolio Trend Report.

2. Sort the companies in the report for the percent change in pre-tax profit to look for the earliest warning of future declines in EPS. In *Investor's Toolkit 5,* choose % Chg. PTP in the Sort On: drop-down list.

3. Compare the most recent values for quarterly sales, quarterly pre-tax profit, quarterly EPS, and trailing 12-month EPS to your estimated EPS growth rate. If the most recent quarterly growth rates are below your estimated EPS growth rate, *Toolkit* emphasizes those shortfalls with red highlighting. Flag the company for defensive homework. For example, in Figure 10-04, the red highlighting shows that several companies fall short

in the most recent quarter compared to the forecast EPS growth. However, Bisys Group is the most serious because its pre-tax profit and EPS growth is negative.

4. If the performance in the most recent quarter doesn't meet your expectations, look at the performance for the previous quarter. Place more emphasis on companies that have not met your expectations for two quarters in a row. When below expectation performance gets worse from one quarter to the next, place those companies at the top of your defense list. For example, Bisys Group, Polymedica,

Medtronic, and Pfizer show two quarters of below par performance, although not in every fundamental measure. Bisys Group is the only one that underperforms in every category. In addition, Bisys' quarterly EPS went from −25 percent to a whopping −66.67 percent.

5. Even if recent quarterly performance meets your expectations, check for declining growth rates from quarter to quarter. For example, in Figure 10-04, Bed Bath and Beyond met expectations in every fundamental measure.

FIGURE 10-04: COMPARE RECENT PERFORMANCE TO YOUR EXPECTATIONS TO LOOK FOR PROBLEMS. AS LONG AS RECENT GROWTH RATES ARE HIGHER THAN YOUR FORECASTS, *TOOLKIT* DOESN'T APPLY ANY RED HIGHLIGHTING. HOWEVER, IF THE MOST RECENT QUARTER PRODUCED SLOWER GROWTH THAN THE QUARTER BEFORE AS EXHIBITED BY BED BATH AND BEYOND, YOU MIGHT ADD YOUR OWN RED FLAG.

TICKER	COMPANY NAME / Size	PERCENT CHANGE				EST. E/S GROWTH
		QTR. SALES	QTR. PTP	QTR. EPS	12 Mo. EPS	
BSG	BISYS GROUP INC	11.2%	-71.5%	-66.67%	-30.69%	17.0%
	Medium	13.0%	-25.8%	-25.00%	-12.87%	
PLMD	POLYMEDICA CORP	18.4%	3.4%	1.20%	8.33%	20.0%
	Medium	19.6%	30.9%	27.03%	13.27%	
MDT	MEDTRONIC INC	14.7%	11.2%	14.29%	15.56%	15.0%
	Large	14.4%	14.2%	14.71%	16.15%	
HDI	HARLEY-DAVIDSON INC	5.2%	11.6%	11.48%	21.33%	15.0%
	Large	13.0%	22.8%	22.45%	31.75%	
FDS	FACTSET RESEARCH SYSTEMS INC	11.4%	14.2%	22.86%	21.71%	10.0%
	Small	12.2%	17.9%	18.18%	22.13%	
SNV	SYNOVUS FINANCIAL CP	10.6%	16.5%	13.33%	5.56%	10.0%
	Medium	2.8%	2.7%	-2.86%	4.03%	
CAKE	CHEESECAKE FACTORY INC	27.6%	30.6%	28.00%	16.50%	16.6%
	Medium	23.0%	14.1%	15.38%	14.14%	
PFE	PFIZER INC	46.8%	31.9%	-2.44%	-41.77%	12.0%
	Large	51.8%	-25.7%	-51.06%	-40.38%	
BBBY	BED BATH & BEYOND INC	23.7%	37.0%	34.29%	31.00%	20.0%
	Large	25.5%	33.8%	32.00%	27.96%	

Below expectations and getting worse

Slowing growth requires watching

However, quarterly sales growth fell from 25.5 percent to 23.7 percent. Unless the company can boost sales again or permanently reduce costs, EPS are likely to decline in the future. Add companies with slowing growth to a watch list. If the growth continues to slow, you might want to adjust your projected growth rates on your SSG.

6. For each company that shows worrisome deterioration, drill down into its longer term performance by looking at its PERT-A Worksheet and the PERT-A graph. (See the next section "Drilling Down with PERT Worksheet-A".)

Success Tip!

In Investor's Toolkit 5, sort the Portfolio Trend Report by the % of Portfolio criterion. Click Sort Z-A in the toolbar to show companies from the largest percentage of your portfolio to the smallest.

Drilling Down with PERT Worksheet-A and PERT-A Graph

The PERT Worksheet-A shows the percent change in sales, pre-tax profit, and EPS for the last several years. The left side of the table shows growth quarter by quarter and the right side compares growth over trailing 12-month periods.

When a stock shows up on the Portfolio Trend Report with poor recent performance, you should dig deeper into its history on the PERT Worksheet-A or the PERT-A Graph.

1. Going straight to the PERT-A Graph is a quick way to spot trends in growth rates quarter by quarter. If you use NAIC software, it's easy to scan the trends for sales, pre-tax profits, pre-tax profit margins, and EPS, both for quarterly and trailing 12-month periods.

For example, in the Bisys Group PERT-A Graph shown in Figure 10-05, pre-tax

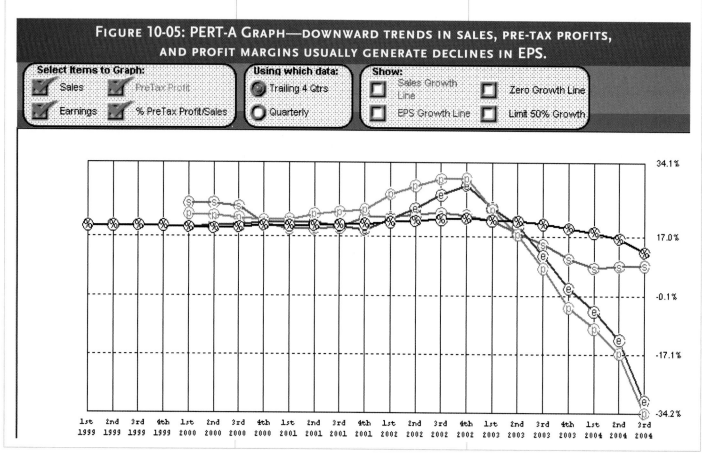

FIGURE 10-05: PERT-A GRAPH—DOWNWARD TRENDS IN SALES, PRE-TAX PROFITS, AND PROFIT MARGINS USUALLY GENERATE DECLINES IN EPS.

FIGURE 10-06: PERT WORKSHEET-A—LOOK FOR DOWNWARD TRENDS IN SALES AND PRE-TAX PROFITS AS EARLY WARNING SIGNS FOR DECLINING EPS.

PERIOD	EPS $	EPS % CHANGE	PRE-TAX PROFIT $MIL	PRE-TAX PROFIT % SALES	PRE-TAX PROFIT % CHANGE	SALES $MIL	SALES % CHANGE	INCOME TAX RATE	EPS $	PRE-TAX PROFIT $MIL	PRE-TAX PROFIT % SALES	SALES MIL	INCOME TAX $MIL	INCOME TAX % RATE	% CHANGE EPS	% CHANGE PRE-TAX PROFIT	% CHANGE SALES
09/97								40.2						40.0			
12/97	0.09		16.69	18.3		91.43		39.8						40.0			
03/98	0.12		22.22	22.5		98.95		39.6						39.9			
06/98	0.14		25.09	24.0		104.50		39.8						39.9			
09/98	0.09		16.34	16.0		101.92		55.1	0.44	80.34	20.2	396.8	35.0	43.6			
12/98	0.11	19.6	20.35	18.2	21.9	111.96	22.5	39.8	0.46	84.00	20.1	417.3	36.6	43.6			
03/99	0.15	18.9	27.33	22.5	23.0	121.30	22.6	40.1	0.48	89.11	20.3	439.7	38.9	43.7			
06/99	0.17	19.6	31.17	22.7	24.2	137.49	31.6	40.0	0.51	95.19	20.1	472.7	41.6	43.7			
09/99	0.11	22.2	20.47	15.5	25.3	132.31	29.8	39.5	0.53	99.33	19.7	503.1	39.6	39.8	19.9	23.6	26.8
12/99	0.13	20.9	24.51	17.8	20.4	138.04	23.3	38.8	0.55	103.48	19.6	529.2	41.0	39.6	20.2	23.2	26.8
03/00	0.18	20.7	33.03	22.7	20.9	145.66	20.1	39.2	0.58	109.18	19.7	553.5	43.0	39.4	20.7	22.5	25.9
06/00	0.20	21.2	38.03	24.5	22.0	155.39	13.0	39.4	0.62	116.04	20.3	571.4	45.5	39.2	21.2	21.9	20.9
09/00	0.14	22.7	25.59	15.9	25.0	161.44	22.0	38.5	0.64	121.16	20.2	600.5	47.2	39.0	21.3	22.0	19.4
12/00	0.16	20.3	31.24	18.6	27.5	168.30	21.9	38.8	0.67	127.89	20.3	630.8	49.8	39.0	21.2	23.6	19.2
03/01	0.21	17.1	40.75	23.0	23.4	177.36	21.8	39.3	0.70	135.61	20.5	662.5	52.9	39.0	20.1	24.2	19.7
06/01	0.24	17.5	47.36	24.3	24.5	194.65	25.3	39.4	0.74	144.94	20.7	701.8	56.5	39.0	18.9	24.9	22.8
09/01	0.19	37.0	37.40	19.0	46.2	196.53	21.7	39.2	0.79	156.75	21.3	736.8	61.4	39.2	22.1	29.4	22.7
12/01	0.22	34.4	43.16	20.6	38.1	209.91	24.7	38.8	0.84	168.67	21.7	778.5	66.1	39.2	25.4	31.9	23.4
03/02	0.27	31.7	53.62	24.3	31.6	220.54	24.3	37.5	0.91	181.54	22.1	821.6	70.3	38.7	29.3	33.9	24.0
06/02	0.30	27.7	60.14	25.2	27.0	238.73	22.6	37.9	0.97	194.32	22.4	865.7	74.5	38.3	32.0	34.1	23.4
09/02	0.20	8.1	38.93	17.1	4.1	227.34	15.7	37.0	0.99	195.85	21.8	896.5	74.0	37.8	25.5	24.9	21.7
12/02	0.24	11.6	45.97	19.7	6.5	233.11	11.1	36.8	1.01	198.65	21.6	919.7	74.1	37.3	20.2	17.8	18.1
03/03	0.27	0.0	50.79	20.8	-5.3	244.78	11.0	35.8	1.01	195.83	20.7	944.0	72.2	36.9	11.6	7.9	14.9
06/03	0.28	-6.7	51.69	20.4	-14.1	253.19	6.1	34.3	0.99	187.37	19.6	958.4	67.4	36.0	2.1	-3.6	10.7
09/03	0.15	-25.0	28.60	12.0	-26.5	237.38	4.4	36.3	0.94	177.05	18.3	968.5	63.4	35.8	-4.6	-9.6	8.0
12/03	0.18	-25.0	34.10	12.9	-25.8	263.33	13.0	36.6	0.88	165.18	16.5	998.7	59.0	35.7	-12.9	-16.9	8.6
03/04	0.09	-66.7	14.46	5.3	-71.5	272.30	11.2	24.4	0.70	128.84	12.6	1,026.2	42.4	32.9	-30.7	-34.2	8.7
06/04								38.2						33.9			
A	B	C	D	E	F	G	H	I	J	K	L	M	N	O	P	Q	R	S	T

profits and EPS began to increase in 2002, but when sales growth started to slow in late 2002, pre-tax profit and EPS growth went from bad to worse. In addition, as sales growth declined, the pre-tax profit margin started to decline as well.

2. You can also scan the values for percent change in trailing 12-month sales (Column T) in the company's PERT Worksheet-A (Figure 10-06). Because sales appear at the top of the income statement, sales growth is harder to manipulate. Downward trends in sales often lead the way for declines in pre-tax profit and EPS.

Success Tip!

When trailing 12-month growth rates change significantly, be sure to check the quarterly growth on the left side of the worksheet. A particularly good or bad quarter could throw off the 12-month numbers.

3. Watch for downward trends in percent change in trailing 12-month pre-tax profit (Column S). If pre-tax profit

grows more slowly than sales, the profit margins get squeezed, which leads to lower earnings.

Success Tip!

Although pre-tax profit margins might be declining, compare the current pre-tax profit margin to the industry average. If the company's margins are still above average, cut it some slack. My company may end up taking market share from competitors that are in even deeper trouble. I usually go right to the ratio comparison chart at http://www.reuters.com *(found by clicking Education within the Stocks section of the menu) to compare my company with its industry and sector. A company most likely will discuss a decline in margins in quarterly conference calls and in the Management's Discussion and Analysis section of its 10-Q. Falling pre-tax margins should alert us to the need for more investigation.*

4. Check for a drop in percent change in trailing 12-month EPS (Column R). By the time the declines reach EPS, the stock price is probably already headed down. Add the company to your high-priority defense list so you can decide whether to sell before the price drops even further.

5. Next, check the trends in pre-tax profits as a percentage of sales (Column N), also called profit margin. Increasing levels of competition typically lead to steadily decreasing pre-tax profit margins, as prices drop to match competing products. When the pre-tax profit margin drops, the company keeps less of each dollar it brings in. Unless it reacts to control costs in some way, earnings will drop, which leads inexorably to a drop in price. In Figure 10-06, the pre-tax profit margins in Column N began to decline right after sales. Companies can't make drastic cuts in some costs, so falling sales often impact profit margins.

6. Look for unusual quarterly results on the left side of PERT Worksheet-A. One quarter being compared to a particularly good quarter the previous year can generate a lower or even negative growth rate. If you use data that includes the effects of non-recurring events (see Chapter 7), quarterly results can be thrown off. Read the quarterly report to see if an acquisition, divestiture, or other one-time event affected the quarter.

Remember that several factors can affect EPS. For example, a share buyback program or decreasing tax rates can make EPS grow faster than sales for a time.

With deteriorating fundamentals, you don't get much time to decide whether to sell before the price really tanks. But, investors who focus on stocks for the long term might struggle making decisions based on a few quarters' performance. When you notice a change in an overall trend, consider it a warning, not a call to drastic action. Put the company under the microscope; read quarterly reports, analysts' reports, company press releases, and news headlines. Dig deeper into the company's financial ratios in search of explanations (see Chapter 8). Listen to the company's quarterly conference call. Call the company's investor relations department and ask questions about things you've uncovered that bother you or that you don't understand. If the price has already dropped because of poor fundamentals, use the signs of deterioration as a reminder that the company is suffering from a long-term problem. Instead of waiting for the stock to recover, sell the stock and then look for a better place for your money.

Playing Offense with PERT

Playing offense requires more criteria than defense. In defense, when fundamentals deteriorate, it's mostly given that the price will follow. For offense, you have to make sure that you aren't sacrificing growth or quality and you also have to evaluate price-related measures, so you can improve your returns. Offense is about looking for even stronger companies than the ones you already own.

You purchase a stock not only for its growth and quality, but also the return that it can provide. A stock doing well is fun to see, but a stock that does too well can result in a future with too much risk and little additional return. At that point, looking for stocks of equal or better quality but higher potential future returns is in order. The warning signs that a stock's price has gone too high include:

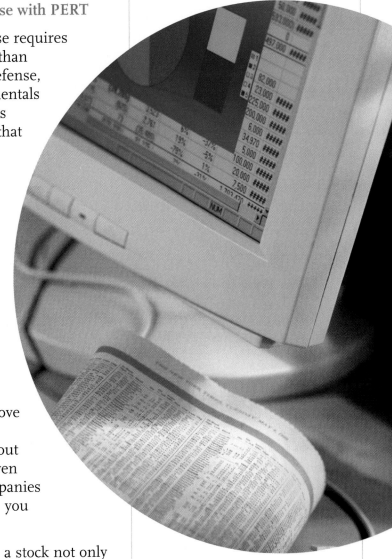

- Relative value that is greater than 150 percent. (The current PE is 150 percent of the five-year historical average PE ratio. Some investors consider a relative value higher than 110 as a red flag.)

- Upside-downside ratio that is less than 1.0 to 1

- Total return that is below your target for the size of the company

One of these warning signs is just that: a warning. Watch the stock carefully, but don't rush to sell your winners. Sometimes, stocks get ahead of themselves and have to take a breather before continuing their upward journey. (Look at the SSG for Home Depot from 1998 to 2000 to see an example of a company that became overpriced. At that point, you'd study the company in more depth to see whether you thought the future prospects warranted holding onto the stock. When you see two or more signs of overvaluation, consider looking for a stock to replace your current holding. The goal is to find a stock of equal or better quality with higher potential returns and less risk.

Chapter 6 outlined the steps to take playing offense with stocks. Here are the nuts and bolts of that process.

Kicking Off Offense with Investor's Toolkit 5

Click the Alerts button in the Portfolio Overview window in *Investor's Toolkit 5* to display companies that you might want to replace to improve your portfolio. The Offense list shows companies that don't

meet the target return or upside-downside ratio that you set. However, the companies on this list do meet or exceed the growth rates you forecast.

In Toolkit 5, set your target return and upside-downside ratio by clicking Preferences and then clicking the Threshold tab. In the "Upside/Down side below" box, type the upside-downside value that flags a company for possible replacement. For example,

many investors consider an upside-downside ratio less than 1 to 1 as a red flag for possible replacement.

In the Total Return Below box, type the return that flags a company you might consider selling. For example, although you might decide that a company must provide a potential average annual total return of 15 percent before you buy, you might not want to flag a company for possible replacement unless its potential total return drops below 10 percent. Type the total return that you want to use to flag a company for possible replacement.

The Offense list shows the relative value, upside-downside ratio, and total return for companies that fall short of the return target you set for your portfolio. You can specify the target for your portfolio, but that doesn't mean every company has to meet that target every day that you own it.

FIGURE 10-07: THE *TOOLKIT 5* OFFENSE LIST SHOWS VALUATION MEASURES FOR COMPANIES THAT DON'T MEET YOUR RETURN OBJECTIVES.

Offense

Ticker	Name	Relative Value	U/D	Total Return	Target Return	Action
CAKE	CHEESECAKE FACTORY INC	104.6	.7	8.0	15.0	
FDS	FACTSET RESEARCH SYSTEMS	93.7	.0	.5	15.0	
HDI	HARLEY-DAVIDSON INC	84.5	1.7	11.9	15.0	
HD	HOME DEPOT INC	61.8	1.7	13.2	15.0	
MDT	MEDTRONIC INC	76.9	.8	8.0	15.0	
MSFT	MICROSOFT CORP	69.6	.2	3.0	15.0	

FIGURE 10-08: CHECK VALUATION MEASURES TO FIND STOCKS THAT ARE SIGNIFICANTLY OVERVALUED.

PORTFOLIO SUMMARY

NAME: 05/17/04

TICKER	COMPANY NAME	DATE	PRICE	P/E	TOT RET	REL VAL	U / D	BUY BLW	SELL ABV	% Port REC
PFE	PFIZER INC	06/15/04	35.16	38.2	.06	109.8	0.0	16.1	26.6	5.17%
FDS	FACTSET RESEARCH S	06/15/04	46.92	29.9	.51	93.7	0.0	25.7	39.5	20.70%
MSFT	MICROSOFT CORP	06/15/04	27.49	30.5	2.97	69.6	0.2	17.3	26.6	6.07%
CAKE	CHEESECAKE FACTORY	06/15/04	41.11	34.3	7.96	104.6	0.7	25.9	48.8	9.07%
MDT	MEDTRONIC INC	06/15/04	49.69	31.9	7.97	76.9	0.8	35.2	58.7	3.65%
BSG	BISYS GROUP INC	06/15/04	13.50	19.3	7.30	79.4	1.0	10.7	16.4	0.99%
SNV	SYNOVUS FINANCIAL	06/15/04	25.39	19.1	10.58	83.0	1.2	20.8	31.7	13.07%
HDI	HARLEY-DAVIDSON IN	06/15/04	61.20	23.9	11.93	84.5	1.7	52.7	88.0	9.00%
HD	HOME DEPOT INC	06/15/04	35.78	19.1	13.20	61.8	1.7	30.3	53.2	13.16%
BBBY	BED BATH & BEYOND	06/15/04	38.01	29.0	14.56	99.3	2.0	33.5	61.2	1.40%
CHS	CHICOS FAS INC	06/15/04	43.80	37.8	19.38	180.9	2.1	37.0	83.1	9.66%
PLMD	POLYMEDICA CORP	06/15/04	31.27	17.8	18.13	118.7	2.9	30.9	57.4	8.05%

For example, in Figure 10-07, Home Depot doesn't meet the 15 percent target return for the portfolio, but it's 13.2 percent return is sufficient for a giant-cap company.

Spotting Overvalued Companies with the Portfolio Summary

The Portfolio Summary in *Toolkit 5* is the one NAIC report that is totally dedicated to offense, but it lists every company in your portfolio. Therefore, you must be sure to first eliminate the companies with deteriorating fundamentals. Why? In a pure valuation view, the dogs in your portfolio often are the most attractively priced; that's because no one wants them! When you play offense, you look for stocks that are overpriced and are candidates for replacement.

The portfolio dogs aren't a problem for that. But when you start looking for stocks to use as replacements, you have to look for companies with quality, growth, and good value.

The Portfolio Summary, shown in Figure 10-08 is perfect for identifying a short list of companies you want to replace.

1. Look for excessive risk represented by below par upside-downside ratios. When the upside-downside ratio drops below 1.0, the risk from a price drop is more than the reward from price increases.

In Figure 10-08, several of the stocks possess upside-downside ratios less than 1.0 and several more are between 1.0 and 2.0. In this situation, focus on the stocks with the lowest upside-downside ratios and the highest percentage in the portfolio. For example, Factset Research has an upside-downside ratio of 0 and represents 20 percent of the portfolio.

An upside-downside ratio of 0 occurs when the current price is greater than your forecast high price for the next five years. You should be able to make a huge improvement in future portfolio performance by replacing this major holding which has a poor outlook.

2. Check the total return, which represents the forecast return from potential price appreciation from the current price to your projected high price plus the yield from dividends. Although you might set a goal for the return of your entire portfolio, the goal for each company can differ. For large high-quality companies, you might not worry until the forecast return drops below 5 percent or perhaps the going rate for CDs. For more risky high-growth companies, you should think about replacing the stock when the forecast return drops below 10 percent.

3. Look at relative value greater than 150, which means that the current PE is 150 percent of the average adjusted PE for the past five years. When the current PE is significantly above the average PE, the chance of PE expansion is limited. In fact, the PE is more likely to contract back to the average, meaning the price will grow more slowly than the EPS growth rate would indicate.

Success Tip!

Relative value is the least important of the valuation measures. Relative value is easily thrown off by aberrations in the last five years. For example, Factset Research carried PEs in the 40s and 50s for the past five years when it grew quickly. Although its current PE is much lower than the average for the last five years, it is still too high for the company's current growth rate. In addition, if you do not eliminate outliers in Section 3 of your SSG or adjust the calculated average PEs to values you consider reasonable, the relative value on the Portfolio Summary and other PERT reports will not be helpful to your analysis.

When a stock fails two or all three of the valuation tests, even with an optimistic SSG, consider replacing the stock. If your portfolio diversification

SELL YOUR WINNERS SLOWLY

Great management is hard to find at any price, so you should be cautious about selling high-quality companies even when they appear to be significantly overvalued. Most investors, including Warren Buffett, prefer to never sell. Unfortunately, most investors aren't as adept as Mr. Buffett at choosing stocks to buy. No matter how good you are at choosing stocks to buy, the business concept of continuous improvement applies to portfolios as well.

NAIC recommends being conservative when studying stocks to increase your chance of success. This leads to conservative SSGs and conservative sell prices. One way to prevent selling too soon is to prepare a second updated SSG—a more optimistic one— before deciding to sell. Use relevant information, remove outliers, and follow common sense; just be a bit more optimistic. For example, if the company CEO forecasts 17 percent growth, but you reduced your forecast of growth because of signs of slowing in the recent past, consider going with the CEO's forecast. Likewise, if the market has been paying high PEs for the company, don't apply an arbitrary limit to your forecast high PE. For example, if the high PE stayed in the low 30s while the company grew at 20 percent, consider using the average high PE in the low 30s as long as the company is still growing at 20 percent.

is out of balance, you can improve your portfolio return and reduce risk from over allocations.

Using PERT to Find a Challenger

Because a replacement company should offer a better return with equal or higher quality, you need to consider company growth as well as return. The PERT report includes all the information you need to choose a stock from your existing portfolio. Companies that you consider as potential replacements should pass your quality and growth tests: sales and earnings growing consistently with stable or increasing pre-tax profit margin and return on equity.

Success Tip!

The PERT report shows only the companies in your portfolio. If you want to look for new companies that could fit your criteria for a replacement, you can use the Smart Challenger in Toolkit to look at companies in your Stock Library. Chapter 12 explains how to use stock screens to look for candidates.

1. Look for companies that offer equal or higher growth rates for trailing 12 month EPS (Column O). Check the most recent quarterly growth rates for sales, pre-tax profit, and EPS in Column H, J, and M.

2. When you are considering replacing a stock with one from the same industry, look for higher values for pre-tax profit margin (pre-tax profit as a percentage of sales in Column L). You can't compare pre-tax profit margin between industries. If you want to replace a stock with a company from another industry, be sure to look for replacements that offer above-industry-average profit margins.

The Value Line industry page includes industry averages, such as profit margin. You can also find industry averages on many financial Web sites.

3. Look for better upside-downside ratios. Whether you are replacing a stock with one you already own or plan to invest in a new company for your portfolio, the 3 to 1 guideline for upside-downside ratio helps reduce the risk in your portfolio.

4. Look for higher growth rates for percent compound annual rate of return (Column Z). If your overall portfolio return has fallen below your target, you should focus on companies that provide higher future returns, even if that means accepting a little additional risk.

appreciation from both the company's growth and the increasing PE ratio. Remember that the PERT report calculates relative value based on the average PEs in Section 4 of your SSGs, and is not the same relative value that you see on the SSG. If you do not remove outliers or adjust your average PEs, relative value is not meaningful.

Using Investor's Toolkit 5 *to Find Replacements*

Regardless of the reason for looking for a replacement, your task is to find a company of equal or better quality whose stock offers a better potential return. *Investor's Toolkit 5* includes several new features that make it easy to spot companies to replace as well as identify companies to consider as replacements.

- **Alerts** in *Investor's Toolkit 5* show you the companies in your portfolio that need attention for defensive or offensive reasons. To see which companies need

attention, click the Alerts button in the *Toolkit* Overview window.

- The **Smart Challenge** displays all the companies in your *Toolkit* database sorted by total return in descending order and highlights the company you selected. The Smart Challenge list displays columns for a variety of quality measures so you can scan for companies of equal or better quality.

For the Smart Challenge to be effective, every company in the Smart Challenge list must have an updated SSG.

- The **Challenger** (originally known as the Challenge Tree developed by George Nicholson) compares the overvalued company to a contender you select from the Smart Challenge list to see whether the replacement makes sense.

Finding Potential Replacements with the Smart Challenge

Because the Smart Challenge sorts the companies in your database by total return, every company listed before the one that is highlighted provides a better potential return. The Challenge list includes columns for industry, quality rating, total return, revenue and EPS growth rates, pre-tax profit margin and pre-tax profit margin trend.

5. Look for lower PEG ratios (P/E as % of growth rate in Column W); approximately 110 or less is desirable.

6. Look for relative value (Column R) of 100 or less. When relative value is below 100, the current PE is less than the five-year average PE, which means that the company offers the potential for the PE to expand. And, when the PE expands, you often receive price

FIGURE 10-09: THE SMART CHALLENGER SHOWS QUALITY MEASURES FOR COMPANIES SORTED IN ORDER OF TOTAL RETURN.

Challenge: HOME DEPOT INC

Ticker	Name	Industry	Quality	Tot Return	Sales Growth	EPS Growth	Profit Margin	Trend PTP	Sales R^2	EPS R^2
SNV-O	SYNOVUS FINANCIAL CP Orig	Regional Banks	A+	25.7%	15.9	15.6	23.5	UP	0.98	1.00
PFE-O	PFIZER INC Orig	Pharmaceuticals	A+	24.9%	19.4	23.9	31.5	UP	0.94	0.96
EMC	EMC CORPORATION	Computer Storage &	B+	24.5%	19.7	9.3	12.7	DOWN	0.78	0.09
PHCC	PRIORITY HLTHCARE CP -CL B	Health Care Distributors		22.3%	37.7	36.5	6.6	DOWN	1.00	0.96
CHS	CHICOS FAS INC	Apparel Retail		22.0%	36.4	57.7	18.7	UP	0.95	0.91
BBBY	BED BATH & BEYOND INC	Specialty Stores		21.8%	29.5	31.7	12.7	UP	0.99	1.00
LOW	LOWES COS	Home Improvement Retail	A+	21.4%	20.4	25.1	7.9	UP	1.00	0.98
SGP	Schering-Plough	Pharmaceuticals		21.2%	11.9	16.5	30.2	UP	0.97	0.99
INTC	INTEL CORPORATION	Electronics-Semiconductors	A	20.5%	25.1	31.9	39.7	UP	0.95	0.94
PLMD	POLYMEDICA CORP	Health Care Supplies		20.4%	41.6	79.8	17.7	EVEN	0.96	0.69
ORLY	O REILLY AUTOMOTIVE INC	Specialty Stores	B+	19.8%	30.1	21.7	9.9	UP	0.97	1.00
KV B	KV Pharmaceutical			19.6%	26.2	27.8	24.4	DOWN	0.98	0.68
FISV	FISERV INC	Data Processing &	B+	19.1%	20.1	56.0	17.6	DOWN	1.00	0.39
ACS	Affiliated Computer	data processing	IAS	18.5%	39.6	25.7	9.9	UP	0.96	1.00
ICUI	ICU MEDICAL, INCORPORATED	Health Care (Med	B+	18.5%	25.2	20.0	30.6	UP	0.99	0.81
MRK	MERCK & CO	Pharmaceuticals	A+	18.4%	19.0	14.4	26.9	DOWN	0.99	0.97
SDS	SUNGARD DATA SYSTEMS INC	IT Consulting & Services	B+	18.0%	24.3	20.3	21.0	EVEN	0.99	0.87
ESRX-O	Express Scripts Inc. Orig	Pharmacy benefits manager	B+	17.4%	77.8	37.2	4.2	DOWN	0.98	0.99
MRK	Merck	Pharmaceuticals		16.7%	19.4	13.8	26.0	DOWN	0.99	0.99
CSCO	CISCO SYSTEMS, INC.	Communications Equipment	B+	16.5%	37.3	14.8	21.1	UP	0.89	0.24
COF	CAPITAL ONE FINL CORP	Consumer Finance		15.3%	40.6	27.4	15.3	UP	1.00	0.97
RMD	RESMED INC	Health Care Equipment	B+	15.2%	38.2	37.4	27.2	DOWN	0.99	0.98
DGX	QUEST DIAGNOSTICS INC	Health Care Distrib & Svcs		15.0%	29.3	67.3	6.9	UP	0.80	0.84
FDC	FIRST DATA CORP	Data Processing	B+	14.9%	17.1	15.9	20.9	DOWN	0.75	0.98
HD_O	Home Depot Orig	Retail Building		14.9%	32.3	29.3	7.8	EVEN	1.00	0.99
HD	HOME DEPOT INC	Home Improvement Retail	A+	14.1%	20.9	24.0	9.8	UP	0.98	0.99
HDI	HARLEY-DAVIDSON INC	Motorcycle Manufacturers	A	13.9%	15.8	25.3	19.4	UP	0.97	0.99
ADVP	ADVANCEPCS	Health Care Services		13.9%	110.5	93.2	1.7	EVEN	0.98	0.86

Ok   Cancel

1. To initiate the Smart Challenger, select a company in the Offense list in the *Toolkit* Overview window and click the Challenge button.

2. Enter the number of shares, the price you paid, your capital gain tax rate, and the commission information. When you click OK, the Challenge list appears.

3. Start at the top of the list and scan for better quality measures, as illustrated in Figure 10-09: a higher quality rating, higher pre-tax profit margins, better trends in pre-tax profit margins, and more consistent sales and EPS (based on the statistical measure R-squared, which indicates how closely historical data matches a straight line).

4. If you want a company in a particular industry, scan down the list for that industry and then evaluate the quality measures for the companies you find.

Particularly for investments held in taxable accounts, capital gains and commissions affect your return. The Challenge takes these costs into account and shows you how long it takes to break even with your proposed transaction.

When you find a company that you want to use as a challenger, double-click it to open the individual Challenge dialog box. Key growth and quality values from your SSGs appear in the table on the left, as well as information about your transaction costs. The top half of the Challenger table compares growth and quality measures for the two companies. Sales and EPS growth, sales and EPS consistency come from Section 1 of your SSGs. Profit margin, ROE, and their trends come from Section 2. The Quality Source/Rating is one of the fields you enter in the Basic data for each company.

The lower half of the Challenger table calculates the capital gains on the sale of your existing stock based on the number of shares you own and the average price you paid for them. Using your capital gains tax rate and brokerage commissions, the Challenger calculates the amount of money left to invest in the new stock. Using your forecast of annual total return for each stock, the table shows the estimated after-tax value of each stock at the end of each of the next five years. The after-tax values represent the projected gross value of each stock minus the tax liability associated with selling the appreciated stock.

The graph on the right side of the Challenge window provides a visual comparison of the potential future after-tax value of the two stocks. As shown in Figure 10-10, if the

FIGURE 10-10: LOOK FOR A CHALLENGER THAT REPAYS YOUR SALES COSTS QUICKLY.

Challenge for: HD - HOME DEPOT INC

Parameters   Company List   Print   Help

Ticker:	HD	LOW
Company:	HOME DEPOT INC	LOWES COS
Hist Sales Growth:	20.9	20.4
Hist EPS Growth:	24.0	25.1
Sales R-Squared:	98.3	99.8
EPS R-Squared:	98.9	98.4
5-Year Profit Margin:	9.8	7.9
5-Year Avg. ROE:	17.9	15.9
Profit Margin Trend:	UP	UP
ROE Trend:	UP	UP
Quality Source/Rating:	S&P/A+	S&P/A+
Current Price:	34.38	50.49
Gross Proceeds:	17,190.00	
Brokerage on Sale:	25.00	
Net On Sale:	17,165.00	
Capital Gain/Loss:	4,665.00	
Shares of Challenger:		340.0
Tax on Gain/Loss:		699.75
Brokerage on Purchase:		25.00
Starting Investment:	17,190.00	16,440.25
After Tax Value End Year 1	18,522.5	19,409.6
After Tax Value End Year 2	20,874.1	23,045.6
After Tax Value End Year 3	23,557.4	27,460.7
After Tax Value End Year 4	26,619.3	32,821.8
After Tax Value End Year 5	30,113.0	39,331.7
Total Return:	14.1	21.4

Ticker: HD   LOW
Company: HOME DEPOT I   LOWES COS
Start Invest.: 17,190.00   16,440.25
Total Return: 14.1 %   21.4 %

39,332

16,440

Yr 0   Yr 1   Yr 2   Yr 3   Yr 4   Yr 5

From the sale of your 500 shares of HD at 34.4 and after paying your discount broker $25, you would gross $17,190 for a capital gain of $4,665 with which you could purchase 340 shares of LOW at 50.5 a share. After paying a tax of $700 on the gain and $25 to your broker for the trade, you would start with $16,440

Close

challenger's line crosses above the incumbent's in the first few years, the challenger is likely to be a suitable replacement in your portfolio.

Using the Portfolio Management Guide

The original purpose of the Portfolio Management Guide (PMG) was to update a stock's status as a buy, hold, or sell each month based on the updated price for that month. The graph on the back of the Portfolio Management Guide shows the historical trends in stock price and PE ratio along with the current buy and sell prices and the forecast high and low PE ratios. In the NAIC investment methodology, price always takes second place to growth and quality, so the Portfolio Management Guide is only useful for companies that show no signs of deterioration in fundamentals.

If you use NAIC software, you can obtain the information you need about price and PE ratios from the PERT report or the PERT Summary Report.

Sell Signals on the PMG

The Portfolio Management Guide uses two criteria to highlight potential candidates for selling: the relative value is greater than 150 percent and the current price is in the sell zone. You can obtain better readings of the valuation of

your stocks on the PERT Report and the PERT Summary report.

For relative value, the PERT Report and the PERT Summary Report both show relative value for all the companies in your portfolio. The current price being in the sell zone isn't the most influential of sell signals for overvalued companies. The upside-downside ratio dropping below 1.0 to 1 indicates that the company is becoming overvalued. Potential total return or projected average return less than your target for the size of the company ties the current price more directly to your portfolio goals. Both of these measures appear on the PERT Report and the PERT Summary Report along with relative value.

Success Tip!

Remember, you must first update the SSG for the company before you consider selling. If the fundamentals that made you buy the stock are still present and the stock is not ridiculously overpriced, consider waiting to sell. Alternatively, you could sell a portion of your shares.

Buy Signs on the PMG

The Portfolio Management Guide also uses two criteria to identify stocks that might warrant additional purchase: the relative value is less than 100 percent and the current price is in the buy zone. As you did for sell signs, you can go to the PERT Report or the PERT Summary Report to see relative value for all of the stocks in your portfolio. Instead of the price in the buy zone, you can look for an upside-downside ratio above 3.0 (when you divide the price range using 25-50-25 percent) and a total return or projected average return that meets or exceeds your target.

The Benefits of the PMG Graph

The back of the PMG graphs the price and PE ratio for a

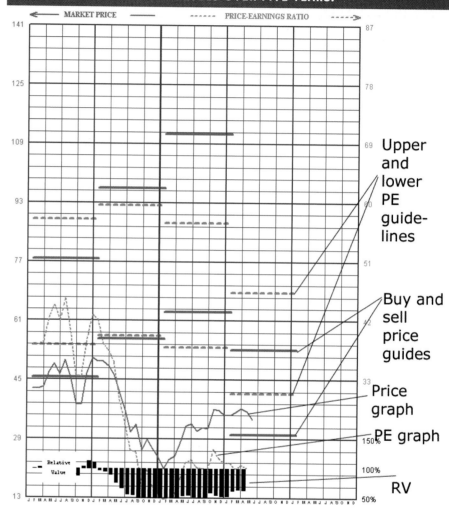

FIGURE 10-11: THE PMG GRAPH SHOWS PRICE AND PE LEVELS OVER FIVE YEARS.

Upper and lower PE guidelines

Buy and sell price guides

Price graph

PE graph

RV

stock for the last five years. For each year, the graph includes horizontal lines for price and PE ratio limits: the price and PE ratio above which you should consider selling and the price and PE ratio below which you might consider buying. You can view the PMG graph to see if the price and/or PE ratio indicate a buy or sell. You can also view the price and PE on the PERT Report or the PERT Summary Report.

However, the PMG graph offers an additional benefit by showing the variation in price and PE ratio during the course of each year; it acts as a gentle reminder of the reasons for patience and the guidelines for relative value; you can see that most stocks drop into the buy zone from time to time and you usually see that stocks that sell at high PEs drop back to more reasonable levels, as shown in Figure 10-11.

FIGURE 10-12: THE FRONT OF THE PMG REQUIRES INPUT FROM SEVERAL SOURCES TO CALCULATE PRICE AND PE GUIDELINES.

1 PRICE EARNINGS ZONES — Refer to Section 3, columns D and E, Line 7, of your Stock Selection Guide study of this company for the information in columns 2 and 3 below.

1 YEAR	2 Average Price Earnings Ratios for Previous Five Years — High	3 Low	4 Sum of Cols. 2 and 3	5 Column 4 Divided by 2 Low PE Guide Line	6 Column 5 Multiplied by 1½ High PE Guide Line
2000	46.2	26.3	72.5	36.3	54.4
2001	49.7	27.0	76.6	38.3	57.5
2002	52.2	27.3	79.5	39.7	59.6
2003	50.7	25.2	75.9	37.9	56.9
2004	41.2	20.6	61.8	30.9	46.4

2 PRICE ZONES — See Section 4C of Stock Selection Guide. 1 below is top of Buy Zone. 2 Below is bottom of Sell Zone

YEAR	1. Consider Buying Below	2. Consider Selling Above
2000	39.6	66.1
2001	45.7	77.7
2002	56.1	97.0
2003	63.4	111.7
2004	30.3	53.2

3 CUMULATIVE EARNINGS AND CURRENT PRICE-EARNINGS RATIO COMPUTATIONS

1 3 Months Ending	2 Earnings per Share	3 Total Earnings for last 4 Quarters	4 Date	5 Price	6 P/E Ratio at Time of Meeting	7 Date	8 Price	9 P/E Ratio at Time of Meeting	10 Date	11 Price	12 P/E Ratio at Time of Meeting
04/99	0.21		05/99	37.71		06/99	42.96		07/99	42.54	
07/99	0.31		08/99	41.00		09/99	45.75		10/99	50.50	
10/99	0.25		11/99	52.79		12/99	68.75		01/00	56.63	
01/00	0.25	1.02	02/00	57.81	56.8	03/00	64.50	63.4	04/00	56.50	55.6
04/00	0.27	1.07	05/00	48.81	45.4	06/00	49.94	46.5	07/00	51.75	48.2
07/00	0.36	1.13	08/00	48.06	42.6	09/00	53.06	47.1	10/00	43.00	38.2
10/00	0.28	1.16	11/00	39.19	33.8	12/00	45.69	39.4	01/01	48.20	41.6
01/01	0.20	1.11	02/01	42.50	38.3	03/01	43.10	38.8	04/01	47.10	42.4
04/01	0.27	1.11	05/01	49.29	44.4	06/01	46.55	41.9	07/01	50.37	45.4
07/01	0.39	1.14	08/01	45.95	40.3	09/01	36.37	33.7	10/01	38.23	33.5
10/01	0.33	1.19	11/01	46.65	39.2	12/01	51.01	42.9	01/02	50.09	42.1
01/02	0.31	1.30	02/02	50.00	38.5	03/02	48.61	37.4	04/02	46.37	35.7
04/02	0.36	1.39	05/02	41.69	30.0	06/02	36.73	26.4	07/02	30.88	22.2
07/02	0.50	1.50	08/02	32.93	22.0	09/02	26.10	17.4	10/02	28.86	19.3
10/02	0.40	1.57	11/02	26.40	16.8	12/02	24.02	15.3	01/03	20.90	13.3
01/03	0.30	1.56	02/03	23.45	15.0	03/03	24.36	15.6	04/03	28.13	18.0
04/03	0.39	1.59	05/03	32.49	20.4	06/03	33.12	20.8	07/03	31.20	19.6
07/03	0.56	1.65	08/03	32.16	19.5	09/03	31.85	19.3	10/03	37.07	22.5
10/03	0.50	1.75	11/03	36.76	21.0	12/03	35.49	20.3	01/04	35.47	20.3
01/04	0.42	1.87	02/04	36.31	19.4	03/04	37.36	20.0	04/04	36.49	19.5
04/04			05/04	34.36		06/04			07/04		
07/04			08/04			09/04			10/04		
10/04			11/04			12/04			01/05		
01/05			02/05			03/05			04/05		

Callouts: Current high and low PE guidelines · Current buy and sell price guides · PE based on price and TTM EPS · Monthly price · Quarterly EPS · TTM EPS

to update the cumulative EPS and monthly prices.

Success Tip!

Stock splits do not affect the PE ratios on the PMG, because both stock price and EPS are split. However, you must adjust the prices on the PMG to reflect the split.

Price Earnings Zones and Price Zones

Section 1 of the PMG calculates the PE ratios that flag potential buy and sells.

- **Year**—Column 1 shows the last five years.
- **Average High PE Ratio**—Column 2 contains the five-year average high PE ratios from Section 3 of the SSG.

In some cases, the PMG graph might not follow the norm. Prices and PE ratios might remain depressed or extraordinarily high. When this occurs, the PMG guidelines aren't enough. You must research the company and the economic environment (see Chapter 7).

PMG without NAIC Software

You must gather data from several places including your SSG, sources for quarterly EPS, and monthly price quotes to complete the front of the PMG, shown in Figure 10-12.

When you first purchase a stock, you don't fill in any values on the PMG. At year end you fill in the information for the past year in Sections 1 & 2. For example, in Figure 10-11, after the first year of ownership the PMG would show PE and price guidelines only for 1999 based on the original SSG. Each year that you own the stock, you use the updated values from your SSG to add to the price and PE guidelines and you continue

EPS and Price Data

Section 3 is a record of quarterly EPS, monthly prices, and the resulting PE ratios. The first three columns relate to EPS. The remaining columns use the quarterly EPS from column 3 with the monthly prices to calculate a PE ratio for each month of the following quarter.

- **3 Months Ending—**Column 1 lists the end dates for each fiscal quarter.

- **Earnings per Share—** Column 2 contains the quarterly earnings per share.

- **Total Earnings for Last Four Quarters—**Once you have four quarters of information filled in, Column 3 represents the cumulative earnings for the most recent four quarters. For each row, add the EPS in Column 2 in the same row to the three previous quarterly values.

- **Date—**Columns 4, 7, and 10 contain the dates when you obtain price quotes for each month for the quarter shown in Column 1. Use the same date each month or pick a day of the week, such as the fourth Friday of each month. For investment clubs, a date a few days before the meeting is ideal.

- **Price—**Columns 5, 8, and 11 show the price on the price quote date.

If you do not eliminate outliers in Section 3 of the SSG, the average high PE in the PMG won't produce an appropriate high PE guideline in the PMG.

- **Average Low PE Ratio—** Column 3 contains the five-year average low PE ratios from Section 3 of the SSG. You must eliminate outlying PE ratios in your SSG to eliminate inappropriate low PE guidelines in the PMG.

- **Five-year Average PE Ratio—** Column 4 is the sum of the average high and low PEs in that year (used to calculate the average PE).

- **Low PE Guideline—** Column 5 calculates the average PE ratio for that year, which you can use as the PE ratio below which you might consider purchasing more in that year.

- **High PE Guideline—** Column 6 calculates the PE ratio that is 150 percent of the average for that year, (corresponding to a relative value of 150 percent.) This is the PE ratio above which you might consider selling in that year.

In Section 2 of the PMG, the top of the buy zone and the bottom of the sell zone come directly from your SSG.

- **P/E Ratio at Time of Meeting**—Columns 6, 9, and 12 calculated the PE ratio using the price in Columns 5, 8, and 11 respectively and the cumulative EPS in Column 3.

Completing the PMG Graph Manually

The back of the Portfolio Management Guide is a graph of price and PE performance, but it also includes indicators for buy and sell zones. The scale for price is in the left margin and is indicated with the label Market Price and an arrow pointing left at the top of the form. The PE scale is in the right margin with a corresponding label and arrow at the top of the form. If you use NAIC software, price and price guidelines are green, whereas PE and PE guidelines are red. The last five calendar years and the letter for each month appear along the bottom of the graph.

1. Assign price values in the left margin for each of the nine major horizontal lines on the PMG graph. Check the price range for the next five years on your SSG. Assign a price slightly below your forecast low price to the bottom grid line. The nine major divisions mean that you can assign eight price intervals. Select a number of dollars for major interval so that your forecast high price ends up near the top of the graph. For example, if your forecast low is 24 and your forecast high is 110, start with 20 at the bottom of the graph. If each major interval represents $12, the top of the graph will represent $116.

To calculate the interval to use, subtract the low price from the high price and then divide by 8. For example, (110 − 20) ÷8 = 11.25. Round the result up to the next whole dollar or $12.

2. Repeat the approach in step 1 to assign PE ratio values along the right margin to the same major horizontal grid lines.

3. Using the high and low PE guidelines in Section 1 of the PMG, draw horizontal lines on the graph. Each horizontal guideline is good for one year so you draw each guideline from the first month of the fiscal year to the last, as shown in Figure 10-12. Keep in mind that the scale at the bottom of the graph shows calendar years, not fiscal years.

4. Finally, plot the price and PE for each month on the graph.

What Makes NAIC Portfolio Tools Tick?

A Tour of the PERT Worksheets and Reports

Each PERT report and worksheet is a treasure trove of information—sometimes it can be a little intimidating to sort through the columns looking for the information you want. On top of that, if you prepare these reports and worksheets manually, knowing where to find the information for all those columns is a challenge in itself. When you break each report and worksheet down, you'll find that creating and analyzing them isn't so bad after all. If you want to get right to portfolio review with PERT, go to the section "Using PERT for Portfolio Management."

Updating Stock Data

PERT Worksheet-A

PERT-A Graph

PERT Worksheet-B

Growth and Price on the PERT Report

Portfolio Trend Report

Portfolio Summary

Updating Stock Data

Because NAIC portfolio management tools use information from the SSG, you must update your SSGs with recent quarterly data and the current stock price before you evaluate your portfolio. Otherwise, you might come to the wrong conclusions about your stocks. To use PERT reports to analyze stocks, you need the following data:

- Quarterly sales (dollars) for the last five years including the most recent quarter

- Pre-tax profits (dollars) for the last five years including the most recent quarter

- Quarterly EPS (dollars) for the last five years including the most recent quarter

- Taxes paid (dollars) for the last five years including the most recent quarter

- Stock price for each month for the last five years including the most recent month

This task isn't as intimidating as it might appear at first. You collect quarterly data and monthly prices over time, so you don't have to gather all this information at once. In addition, the PERT-A report

is the only one that uses all of this data.

If you use NAIC software, NAIC Online Premium Services data include 20 quarters of sales, pre-tax profit, EPS, and tax data. When you download an SSG file from OPS, the quarterly data is entered for you automatically. You can also automate price updates by downloading them from the Internet or by importing a price file.

FIGURE 11-01: THE PERT WORKSHEET-A IS THE REPOSITORY FOR A STOCK'S QUARTERLY AND TTM (TRAILING TWELVE MONTHS) PERFORMANCE. THE ENLARGED IMAGE SHOWS THE LAST THREE COLUMNS OF THE HOME DEPOT PERT WORKSHEET A, WHICH HELPS YOU SPOT TRENDS.

PERT Worksheet-A

Company: HOME DEPOT INC (HD)

PERIOD	EPS $	EPS $	EPS %CHANGE	PRE-TAX PROFIT $MIL	PRE-TAX %SALES	PRE-TAX %CHANGE	SALES $MIL	SALES %CHANGE	INCOME TAX RATE	EPS $	PRE-TAX PROFIT $MIL	PRE-TAX %SALES	SALES MIL	INCOME TAX $MIL	INCOME TAX %RATE	%CHANGE EPS	%CHANGE PRE-TAX PROFIT	%CHANGE SALES
04/99		0.21		805.00	9.0		8,952.00		38.1						38.2			
07/99		0.31		1,118.00	10.7		10,431.00		35.9						37.6			
10/99		0.25		942.00	9.5		9,877.00		38.7						37.7			
01/00		0.25		939.00	10.2		9,174.00		37.4	1.02	3,804.00	9.9	38,434.0	1,426.7	37.5			
04/00		0.27	26.8	1,027.00	9.2	27.6	11,112.00	24.1	38.1	1.07	4,026.00	9.9	40,594.0	1,510.4	37.5			
07/00		0.36	17.3	1,369.00	10.8	22.5	12,619.00	21.0	38.2	1.13	4,277.00	10.0	42,782.0	1,629.1	38.1			
10/00		0.28	13.4	1,062.00	9.2	12.7	11,544.00	16.9	38.0	1.16	4,397.00	9.9	44,449.0	1,667.1	37.9			
01/01		0.20	-20.0	759.00	7.3	-19.2	10,463.00	14.1	38.1	1.11	4,217.00	9.2	45,738.0	1,605.6	38.1	9.1	10.9	19.0
04/01		0.27	0.0	1,030.00	8.4	0.3	12,200.00	9.8	38.5	1.11	4,220.00	9.0	46,826.0	1,610.6	38.2	3.4	4.8	15.4
07/01		0.39	8.3	1,504.00	10.3	9.9	14,576.00	15.5	38.9	1.14	4,355.00	8.9	48,783.0	1,670.7	38.4	1.2	1.8	14.0
10/01		0.33	17.9	1,267.00	9.5	19.3	13,289.00	15.1	38.7	1.19	4,560.00	9.0	50,528.0	1,757.9	38.6	2.6	3.7	13.7
01/02		0.31	55.0	1,201.00	8.9	58.2	13,488.00	28.9	39.1	1.30	5,002.00	9.3	53,553.0	1,941.9	38.8	17.1	18.6	17.1
04/02		0.36	33.3	1,372.00	9.6	33.2	14,282.00	17.1	37.9	1.39	5,344.00	9.6	55,635.0	2,067.5	38.7	25.2	26.6	18.8
07/02		0.50	28.2	1,894.00	11.6	25.9	16,277.00	11.7	37.6	1.50	5,734.00	10.0	57,336.0	2,199.6	38.4	31.6	31.7	17.5
10/02		0.40	21.2	1,507.00	10.4	18.9	14,475.00	8.9	37.8	1.57	5,974.00	10.2	58,522.0	2,277.7	38.1	31.9	31.0	15.8
01/03		0.30	-3.2	1,099.00	8.3	-8.5	13,213.00	-2.0	37.0	1.56	5,872.00	10.1	58,247.0	2,207.1	37.6	20.0	17.4	8.8
04/03		0.39	8.3	1,442.00	9.5	5.1	15,104.00	5.8	37.9	1.59	5,942.00	10.1	59,069.0	2,232.3	37.6	14.4	11.2	6.2
07/03		0.56	12.0	2,065.00	11.5	9.0	17,989.00	10.5	37.6	1.65	6,113.00	10.1	60,781.0	2,295.9	37.6	10.0	6.6	6.0
10/03		0.50	25.0	1,823.00	11.0	21.0	16,598.00	14.7	37.3	1.75	6,429.00	10.2	62,904.0	2,405.9	37.4	11.5	7.6	7.5
01/04		0.42	40.0	1,513.00	10.0	37.7	15,125.00	14.5	37.0	1.87	6,843.00	10.6	64,816.0	2,561.1	37.4	19.9	16.5	11.3
A	B	C	D	E	F	G	H	I	J	K L	M	N	O	P		Q	R	S T

PERT Worksheet-A

The PERT Worksheet-A, illustrated in Figure 11-01, shows quarterly and trailing 12-month data for sales, pre-tax profit, and EPS, so you can evaluate year-over-year percentage changes. The left side of the PERT Worksheet-A focuses on the changes from quarter to the same quarter the previous year. The right side of the worksheet evaluates the percentage changes in trailing 12-month values.

If you prepare the PERT Worksheet-A by hand, enter the following data:

- **Column A**—The fiscal quarter.

- **Column C**—Diluted quarterly EPS in dollars from the bottom of the quarterly income statement

- **Column E**—Quarterly re-tax profit in millions of dollars from the income statement

- **Column H**—Quarterly sales in millions of dollars from the beginning of the income statement

The results in the remaining columns of the worksheet use the values in these four columns. By hand, this initial data entry and the subsequent calculations take some time. After that, you update this worksheet with the most recent quarterly data once every three months.

Tracking Quarterly Stock Measures with PERT Worksheet-A

Columns A through J include the quarterly data and percentage changes from one quarter to the same quarter a year ago. Here's how to find or calculate the values in each column:

- **Period**—Column A is the ending date for the fiscal quarter documented in the row of the worksheet.

- **EPS**—On the paper form, columns B and C are provided for recording quarterly EPS. The second column is used for reentering the quarterly EPS if the company performs a stock split and the EPS values change. For example, if the EPS in a row is $1.00 and the stock splits 2 for 1, use the extra column to replace the $1.00 with an updated value of $.50. If you use NAIC software, you only see one column because the software processes stock split calculations for you.

- **EPS % Change**—Column D represents the percentage change in EPS between each quarter and the same quarter of the previous fiscal year. For example, in the row for a 04/00 quarter, calculate the percentage change between the 04/00 EPS and the 04/99 EPS.

Success Tip!

To calculate a percentage change, use the following formula:

% Change = (Current Qtr Value / Last Year's Qtr Value) − 1

- **Pre-tax Profit**—Column E shows quarterly pre-tax profit in millions of dollars. Pre-tax profits are not shown per share, so stock splits have no effect on these numbers.

- **Pre-tax Profit % Sales**— Column F is the percentage of pre-tax profit to sales, otherwise known as the pre-tax profit margin. Divide the pre-tax profit value in Column E by the sales in Column H.

Success Tip!

Downward trends in pre-tax profit margin are early warning signals for potential declines in EPS, so this is a key column on the worksheet. The annual pre-tax profit column (column N) is another key column for portfolio review.

- **Pre-tax Profit Margin % Change**— Column G represents the percentage change in pre-tax profit between one quarter and the same quarter of the previous fiscal year.

- **Sales**—Column H shows quarterly sales in millions of dollars.

- **Sales % Change**—Column I represents the percentage change in sales between one quarter and the same quarter of the previous fiscal year.

- **Income Tax Rate**—To calculate this by hand, divide the taxes on the quarterly income statement by pre-tax profit.

Tracking Trailing 12-Month Values with PERT Worksheet-A

Columns K through T perform similar calculations to those on the quarterly side. However, trailing 12-month values smooth out variations that can appear from quarter to quarter. Here's how to find or calculate the values in each column:

- **EPS $**—Columns K and L represent the total EPS for the past four quarters. As with quarterly EPS, there are two columns to enter updated post stock-split EPS values. Add up the most recent four quarters of EPS in Column B or C. For example, in Figure 11-01,

EPS $ for the 01/04 quarter includes EPS from 04/03 through 01/04 (.39 + .56 + .50 + .42 = $1.87).

- **Pre-tax Profit**—Column M shows the trailing 12-month pre-tax profit in millions of dollars. Add up the most recent four quarters of pre-tax profit from Column E.

- **Pre-tax Profit % Sales**—Column N is the percentage of trailing 12-month pre-tax profit to trailing 12-month sales (Column M divided by Column O).

- **Sales**—Column O shows the trailing 12-months sales in millions of dollars. Add up the most recent four

quarters of sales from Column H.

- **Income Tax**—Column P is the income tax paid over the last four quarters. To obtain this value, add up the taxes paid for the most recent four quarters.

- **Income Tax Rate**—This is the average income tax rate for the last four quarters. To calculate this, divide the income tax paid by the pre-tax profit (Column P divided by Column M.)

- **% Change: EPS, Pre-tax Profit, Sales**—Columns R, S, and T show the percentage change over trailing 12-month periods for EPS, pre-tax profit, and sales. By placing these values side by side, you can look for trends in pre-tax profit and sales that might lead to problems with EPS. Because these percentages are based on trailing 12-month values, drops in pre-tax profit don't show up as quickly. On the other hand, trailing 12-month values smooth out the effect of one bad quarter.

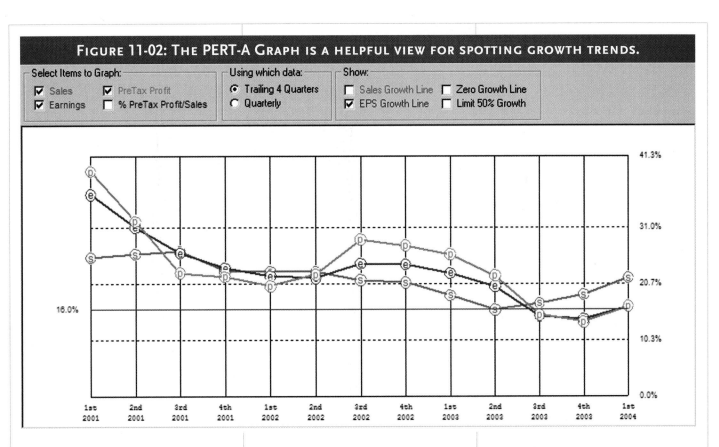

FIGURE 11-02: THE PERT-A GRAPH IS A HELPFUL VIEW FOR SPOTTING GROWTH TRENDS.

PERT-A Graph

If you are using NAIC software and OPS data, the PERT-A Graph is an easier approach for spotting growth trends than the PERT Worksheet-A, as demonstrated in Figure 11-02. Because a given growth rate appears as a horizontal line in this graph, slowing growth shows up easily as a line that falls as it moves from left to right. Similarly, when the lines move upward as they move to the right, you can spot signs of increasing growth rates. If you see slowing growth on this graph, you might decide to lower your forecasts for a stock's future growth rates.

FIGURE 11-03: THE PERT WORKSHEET-B CALCULATES FIVE-YEAR AVERAGE PE RATIOS AND DIVIDEND PAYOUT TRENDS.

NATIONAL ASSOCIATION OF INVESTORS CORPORATION
NAIC
INVESTMENT EDUCATION FOR INDIVIDUALS AND CLUBS SINCE 1951

PERT Worksheet-B

Company HOME DEPOT INC   Symbol HD

YEAR	EPS	PRICE RANGE HIGH	PRICE RANGE LOW	P/E RATIO HIGH	P/E RATIO LOW	5 YR AVG P/E RATIO HIGH	5 YR AVG P/E RATIO AVG	5 YR AVG P/E RATIO LOW	DIV/ SHARE	% PAYOUT THIS YEAR	% PAYOUT 5 YR AVG	% HIGH YIELD
1994	0.29	10.8	8.3	36.8	28.2				.033	11.3		.4
1995	0.34	11.1	8.1	32.5	23.8				.042	12.3		.5
1996	0.43	13.2	9.4	30.7	21.9				.051	11.8		.5
1997	0.52	20.5	11.0	39.7	21.3				.063	12.2		.6
1998	0.71	41.3	20.4	58.5	28.9	39.6	32.2	24.8	.077	10.9	11.7	.4
1999	1.00	69.8	35.8	69.8	35.8	46.2	36.3	26.3	.113	11.3	11.7	.3
2000	1.10	70.0	34.7	63.6	31.5	52.5	40.2	27.9	.160	14.5	12.2	.5
2001	1.31	53.7	30.3	41.0	23.1	54.5	41.3	28.1	.170	13.0	12.4	.6
2002	1.56	52.6	20.1	33.7	12.9	53.3	39.9	26.4	.210	13.5	12.6	1.0
2003	1.88	37.9	20.2	20.2	10.7	45.7	34.2	22.8	.260	13.8	13.2	1.3
A	B	C	D	E	F	G	H	I	J	K	L	M

PERT Worksheet-B

The PERT Worksheet-B, illustrated in Figure 11-03, is a support worksheet for calculating the five-year averages for high, low, and average PE ratios. If a stock pays dividends, you also enter those dividends on PERT Worksheet-B and calculate the percent payout, the five-year average percent payout, and the high yield for the stock.

If you prepare the PERT Worksheet-B by hand, each year, enter the following data:

- **Column A**—The fiscal year.

- **Column B**—The EPS for the fiscal year.

- **Column C**—The high price during the fiscal year.

- **Column D**—The low price during the fiscal year.

- **Column J**—The dividends paid per share during the fiscal year.

Calculating Average PEs on PERT Worksheet-B

Columns E through I contain PE ratios for the last 10 years. If you are concerned that the five-year average PE does not provide a true picture of a stock's typical PE, you can scan the high and low PE ratios for the last 10 years. For example, in Figure 11-03, Home Depot's high PE ratio was in the 60s in 1999 and 2000, and this elevated the five-year average PE ratios for the company.

- **P/E Ratio High**—Column E is the high PE ratio based on the high price and the EPS for the fiscal year. Divide the high price in Column C by the EPS in Column B.

- **P/E Ratio Low**— Column F is the low PE ratio based on the low price and the EPS for the fiscal year. Divide the low price in Column D by the EPS in Column B.

- **5 Yr Avg P/E Ratio High**—Column G is the average of the high PE ratios in Column E for the preceding five years. For example, in Figure 11-03, the five-year average high PE for 2003 uses the high PE ratios for 1999 through 2003. (69.8 + 63.6 + 41.0 + 33.7 + 20.2) / 5 = 45.7

- **5 Yr Avg P/E Ratio Average**—Column H is the average of the five-year average high and low PEs in Column G and I.

- **5 Yr Avg P/E Ratio Low**—Column I is the average of the low PE ratios in Column F for the preceding five years.

Calculating Payout Trends on PERT Worksheet-B

If a stock pays no dividends, Columns J through M are unnecessary. However, with cash dividends, you can use these columns to look for undesirable trends in dividend payouts.

- **% Payout This Year**— Column K is the percent payout for the fiscal year calculated by dividing the dividend per share in Column J by the EPS in Column B. This column is good for spotting payout trends.

- **% Payout 5-Yr Avg**— Column L is the average payout for the preceding five years. Calculate the average using the same method for the five-year

average PE ratios in Columns G and I.

- **% High Yield**—Column M is the highest yield provided by the dividend during the fiscal year, calculated by dividing the dividend per share in Column J by the low price in Column D.

Growth and Price on the PERT Report

With updated quarterly data and SSG judgment in place, the PERT Report provides a comprehensive look at the growth and value measures for every company in a portfolio, as shown in Figure 11-04. The data and key measures shown in the PERT report come from SSGs. Even if you use *Investor's*

Toolkit to produce your portfolio reports, it's important to understand the calculations behind the columns. Use the following guide to find the information you need:

- **Div**—Column B contains the annual dividend for the most recent fiscal year, shown as the numerator in Section 4B option d of the stock SSG.

- **Company**—Column C shows the name of the company from the SSG.

- **% Yld**—Column D shows the current yield, which is the dividend in Column B divided by the current price in Column Q. The current yield is also the first calculation in Section 5 of the SSG.

FIGURE 11-04: THE PERT REPORT SHOWS GROWTH PERFORMANCE AND VALUATION MEASURES FOR ALL THE STOCKS IN A PORTFOLIO.

NATIONAL ASSOCIATION OF INVESTORS CORPORATION

NAIC INVESTMENT EDUCATION FOR INDIVIDUALS AND CLUBS SINCE 1951

PERT

Portfolio Evaluation Review Technique

Date _____ 05/16/2004

Page: 1 of 1
Portfolio: PM_Sample
Prepared using The NAIC Investor's Toolkit

DIV	COMPANY	% YLD	EST EPS	EPS QTR END	EPS $	EPS % CHG	SALES MILL $	SALES % CHG	PRE-TAX PROFIT MILL $	PRE-TAX PROFIT % SALES	PRE-TAX PROFIT % CHG	TRAILING 12 MOS EPS $	TRAILING 12 MOS EPS % CHG	CUR P/E	PRICE	RV	5 YR AVE P/E RATIO HI AVGLOW	EST GROWTH RATE EPS	P/E AS % OF GROWTH RATE	US/ DS	% COMPD ANNUAL RATE OF RETURN	EST FIVE YEARS LOW PRICE	EST FIVE YEARS HIGH PRICE
0.00	BED BATH & BEYOND INC	0.0	1.57	02/04 02/03	0.47 0.35	34.3%	1,297.9 1,049.3	18.1% 16.3% 37.0%	234.6 171.2	23.7%	1.31 1.00 31.0%			24.4	38.43 06/15/04	73.9	30.0 22.5 15.0	20.0	122.2	3.2	20.5	19.6	97.8
0.00	CHICOS FAS INC	0.0	1.45	01/04 01/03	0.29 0.17	70.6%	215.5 138.3	19.2% 17.5% 70.4%	41.4 24.3	55.8%	1.16 0.77 50.6%			30.3	43.98 06/15/04	145.1	30.0 21.0 12.0	25.0	121.3	2.1	19.3	13.9	106.2
0.60	POLYMEDICA CORP	1.9	2.11	12/03 12/02	0.42 0.42	1.2%	106.5 89.9	16.8% 19.3% 18.4%	17.9 17.3	3.4%	1.76 1.62 8.3%			15.0	31.53 06/15/04	99.8	18.0 14.0 10.0	20.0	74.9	2.8	19.4	17.6	70.6
0.28	HOME DEPOT INC	0.8	2.08	01/04 01/03	0.42 0.30	40.0%	15,125.0 13,213.0	10.0% 8.3% 14.5%	1,513.0 1,099.0	37.7%	1.87 1.56 19.9%			17.3	35.96 06/15/04	55.9	20.0 15.0 10.0	11.4	151.3	1.7	13.2	18.8	64.6
0.32	HARLEY-DAVIDSON INC	0.5	2.94	03/04 03/03	0.68 0.61	11.5%	1,246.2 1,184.5	25.5% 24.0% 5.2%	317.2 284.3	11.6%	2.56 2.11 21.3%			20.8	61.10 06/15/04	73.3	21.0 17.5 14.0	15.0	138.4	1.7	12.1	35.0	105.6
0.69	SYNOVUS FINANCIAL CP	2.7	1.46	03/04 03/03	0.34 0.30	13.3%	646.8 585.0	26.4% 25.0% 10.6%	170.8 146.5	16.5%	1.33 1.26 5.6%			17.5	25.54 06/15/04	75.9	18.0 15.0 12.0	10.0	174.6	1.1	10.5	15.4	37.1
0.29	MEDTRONIC INC	0.6	1.79	01/04 01/03	0.40 0.35	14.3%	2,193.8 1,912.5	31.0% 32.0% 14.7%	679.8 611.1	11.2%	1.56 1.35 15.6%			27.8	49.79 06/15/04	66.9	25.0 20.0 15.0	15.0	185.0	0.8	7.8	23.4	70.5
0.00	CHEESECAKE FACTORY INC	0.0	1.40	03/04 03/03	0.32 0.25	28.0%	220.5 172.9	11.6% 11.4% 27.6%	19.7	30.6%	1.20 1.03 16.5%			29.4	41.19 06/15/04	89.8	25.0 18.5 12.0	16.6	177.4	0.7	7.9	14.4	60.3
0.16	MICROSOFT CORP	0.6	.99	03/04 03/03	0.29 0.20	45.0%	9,175.0 7,835.0	52.4% 40.8% 17.1%	4,804.0 3,197.0	50.3%	0.90 0.71 26.8%			27.8	27.49 06/15/04	63.4	20.0 17.0 14.0	10.0	277.7	0.2	3.1	12.6	31.2
0.24	FACTSET RESEARCH SYSTEMS INC	0.5	1.73	02/04 02/03	0.43 0.35	22.9%	61.4 55.1	36.2% 35.3% 11.4%	22.2 19.4	14.2%	1.57 1.29 21.7%			27.3	47.20 06/15/04	85.7	20.0 16.0 12.0	10.0	273.3	0.0-	.2	18.8	46.4
0.68	PFIZER INC	1.9	1.03	03/04 03/03	0.40 0.41	-2.4%	12,487.0 8,506.0	34.9% 38.9% 46.8%	4,363.0 3,307.0	31.9%	0.92 1.58 -41.8%			34.2	35.28 06/15/04	98.4	20.0 16.0 12.0	12.0	285.3	0.0-	-.1	10.8	31.8
B	C	D	E	F G H I	J		K	L M	N	O	P		Q	R	S T U	V	W X	Y	Z	AA	AB

- **Est EPS**—Column E is the estimated EPS twelve months in the future, which is used to calculate the Current PE ratio, the five-year forecast high price, and other valuation measures such as relative value, upside-downside ratio, and total return.

- **EPS Qtr End**—Column F shows the ending dates for the most recent quarter and the corresponding quarter for the previous year.

- **EPS $**—The letter identifier for Column G at the bottom of the PERT Report doesn't line up with the values in the report. Column G shows the EPS in dollars for the most recent quarter and the corresponding quarter for the previous year. In *Investor's Toolkit*, the EPS dollar values appear on the right side of the EPS area.

- **EPS % Chg**—Column H shows the percent change between the two values in column G. In *Investor's Toolkit*, the percent change value appears below the quarterly EPS dollars. This column is one of the measures you evaluate for signs of deteriorating fundamentals.

- **Sales Mill $**—Column I shows sales in millions for the quarters listed in Column F.

- **Sales % Chg**—Column J shows the percent change in sales for the most recent quarter compared to the corresponding quarter for the previous year. In *Investor's Toolkit,* the percent change value appears below the quarterly sales dollars. This column is another measure you evaluate for signs of deteriorating fundamentals.

OPTIONS FOR ESTIMATING EPS FOUR QUARTERS OUT

Because stock prices incorporate investors' expectations of the future, measuring valuation based on historical EPS can make stocks appear overvalued. Therefore, the PERT report uses EPS 12 months in the future to calculate the projected PE and other valuation measures. By default, NAIC SSG software uses the future EPS growth rate you projected on the SSG to calculate the EPS 12 months in the future.

An alternative to this mechanical approach is to use a one-year forecast EPS based on industry and economic outlook as well as analysts' estimates. Numerous sources provide estimated quarterly and annual EPS. For example, Barron's publishes EPS for the previous fiscal year along with an analysts' consensus estimate for the next two fiscal years. The Analyst Estimates link on Yahoo! Finance stock pages (http://finance.yahoo.com) shows estimates for the next two quarters and the next two years. You can use these to calculate an estimate of the EPS for the next 12 months regardless where the company is in its fiscal year. For example, Home Depot's fiscal year ends on February 1. Suppose it is the end of May, which means the current fiscal year has eight months to go. To calculate the next 12 months of EPS, you use eight months worth of this fiscal year's estimate and four months of the next fiscal year's estimate:

Projected EPS = (Current Year Est. EPS * 8)
                    + (Next Year's Est. EPS * 4) / 12

Home Depot Proj. EPS = ((2.15 * 8) + (2.45 * 4)) / 12 = 2.25

In Investors' Toolkit, you can replace the default calculated estimated EPS. To do this, you must turn on the option Enable Advanced PERT Estimates in the Preferences dialog box. Then, with a PERT Report open, choose Options_Enter Estimated EPS and enter the EPS you want to use.

- **Pre-tax Profit Mill $—**
Column K shows the pre-tax profit in millions for the most recent quarter and the corresponding quarter for the previous year.

- **Pre-tax Profit % Sales—**
Column L is reserved for the pre-tax profit margin on sales for the most recent quarter and the corresponding quarter for the previous year. In *Investor's Toolkit,* the pre-tax profit margins appear on the right side of the pre-tax profit area underneath the % Chg heading.

- **Pre-tax Profit % Chg—**
Column M is reserved for

the percent change in pre-tax profit for the most recent quarter compared to the corresponding quarter for the previous year. In *Investor's Toolkit,* the percent change value appears below the quarterly pre-tax profit dollars. This column is the measure you evaluate for the earliest warning signs of deteriorating fundamentals.

- **Trailing 12 Mos EPS $—**
Column N contains the EPS for the trailing twelve-month period for the quarters in Column F and the corresponding quarters of the previous year. In *Investor's Toolkit,* the trailing

12 Mos EPS values appear below the % Chg heading.

- **Trailing 12 Mos EPS % Chg—**Column O contains the percent change in trailing 12-month EPS for the most recent quarter compared to the corresponding quarter for the previous year. In *Investor's Toolkit,* the percent change value appears below the trailing 12-month EPS dollar values.

- **Cur P/E—**Column P is the PE ratio calculated by dividing the current price in Column Q by the estimated EPS 12 months out in column E. (Although the column heading indicates the current PE, the numbers in this column are projected PE ratios. Also, note that this is not the same current PE that you see on the SSG.)

- **Price—**Column Q shows the current price and date of the price quote.

- **RV—**Column R is the relative value calculated by dividing the current PE in Column P by five-year future average PE ratio in Column T. This is not the relative value that you see on the SSG. If you do not eliminate outliers in the PE ratios in Section 3 of the SSG, this relative value does not provide a meaningful picture of valuation. The relative value column is one of the valuation measures to check on the PERT Report.

- **5 Yr Ave P/E Ratio—** Columns S and U contain the five-year future high and future low PE ratios from Section 4 of your SSG. Column T is the average of columns S and U.

SuccessTip!

You should eliminate PE outliers in Section 3 of your SSGs to produce average PE ratios that you consider representative of the company's past performance. Otherwise, some of the valuation measures in the PERT Report will not reflect your view of the company.

- **Est Growth Rate EPS—** Column V contains the EPS growth rate you projected in Section 1 of the SSG.

- **P/E As % of Growth Rate—** Column W is the PEG ratio calculated by dividing the projected PE in Column P by your projected EPS growth rate in Column V.

Column X is blank on the PERT Report.

- **US/DS—**Column Y is the upside-downside ratio based on the high, low, and current price shown on the PERT report. Although you calculate it the same way you calculate the upside-

downside ratio on the SSG, the value on the PERT report is not necessarily the same as the one on your SSG. When you are looking for stocks that are overvalued, look for values less than 1.0 in the upside-downside ratio column.

- **% Compd Annual Rate of Return—**Column Z is the potential total return based on the price information in the PERT report. This is a key measure to evaluate when looking for overvalued stocks that are dragging down the return of your overall portfolio.

- **Est Five Years Low Price—** Column AA contains the low price you selected in Section 4 of your SSG.

- **Est Five Years High Price—** Column AB is not the high price from Section 4 of your SSG. Instead, this high price is calculated by compounding the estimated EPS in column E

for four more years using your projected EPS growth rate in Column V, and then multiplying those EPS by the future high PE ratio in Column S. You only compound the EPS in Column E for four years because the estimated EPS in Column E are already projected for 12 months in the future.

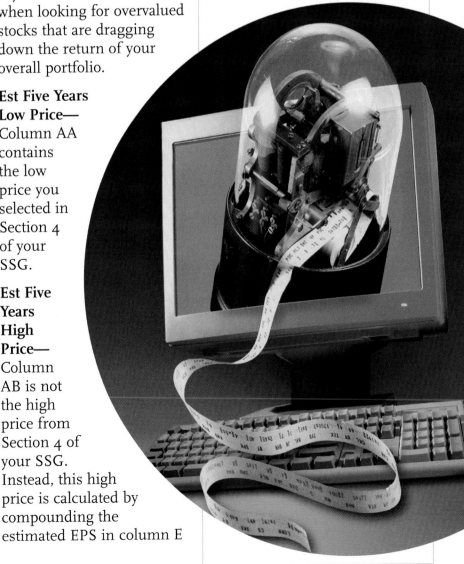

Portfolio Trend Report

Like the PERT Report, the Portfolio Trend Report shows growth and value measures for every company in a portfolio, but it doesn't intermingle measures with the underlying data, as shown in Figure 11-05. In addition to cleaning up the presentation of defensive and offensive criteria, the Portfolio Trend Report includes a few additional features. It shows percent change in growth rates for two quarters so you can spot potential adverse trends. It also includes the number of shares, dollar value, and what percentage the market value of each stock represents in your portfolio. The data and key measures shown in the Portfolio Trend Report come from basic data and results from your SSGs. If you prepare the Portfolio Trend Report manually, use the following guide to find the information you need:

- **Ticker**—The ticker symbol for the stock.

FIGURE 11-05: THE PORTFOLIO TREND REPORT SPOTLIGHTS GROWTH TRENDS, VALUATION MEASURES AND DIVERSIFICATION.

INVESTOR'S TOOLKIT

Portfolio Trend Report

Page: 1 of 1
Portfolio: PM_Sample
Prepared using The NAIC Investor's Toolkit

Date _____ 05/16/2004 _____

TICKER	COMPANY NAME / Size	PERCENT CHANGE				EST. E/S GROWTH	PROJECTED AVG. RET.	TOTAL RETURN	NUMBER OF SHARES	DOLLAR VALUE	% OF PORTFOLIO	PMGuide RECOM.
		QTR. SALES	QTR. PTP	QTR. EPS	12 Mo. EPS							
BBBY	BED BATH & BEYOND INC	23.7%	37.0%	34.29%	31.00%	20.0%	13.8%	20.5%	50	1921.5	1.4%	Buy
	Large	25.5%	33.8%	32.00%	27.96%					38.43 06/15/04		
CHS	CHICOS FAS INC	55.8%	70.4%	70.59%	50.65%	25.0%	11.1%	19.3%	300	13194.0	9.8%	
	Medium	53.4%	83.7%	77.78%	45.45%					43.98 06/15/04		
PLMD	POLYMEDICA CORP	18.4%	3.4%	1.20%	8.33%	20.0%	12.3%	17.9%	350	11035.5	8.2%	
	Medium	19.6%	30.9%	27.03%	13.27%					31.53 06/15/04		
HD	HOME DEPOT INC	14.5%	37.7%	40.00%	19.87%	11.4%	7.0%	13.1%	500	17980.0	13.3%	
	Large	14.7%	21.0%	25.00%	11.46%					35.96 06/15/04		
HDI	HARLEY-DAVIDSON INC	5.2%	11.6%	11.48%	21.33%	15.0%	8.1%	12.0%	200	12220.0	9.0%	
	Large	13.0%	22.8%	22.45%	31.75%					61.10 06/15/04		
SNV	SYNOVUS FINANCIAL CP	10.6%	16.5%	13.33%	5.56%	10.0%	7.1%	10.5%	700	17878.0	13.2%	
	Medium	2.8%	2.7%	-2.86%	4.03%					25.54 06/15/04		
MDT	MEDTRONIC INC	14.7%	11.2%	14.29%	15.56%	15.0%	3.4%	7.9%	100	4979.0	3.7%	
	Large	14.4%	14.2%	14.71%	16.15%					49.79 06/15/04		
CAKE	CHEESECAKE FACTORY INC	27.6%	30.6%	28.00%	16.50%	16.6%	1.6%	7.9%	300	12357.0	9.1%	
	Medium	23.0%	14.1%	15.38%	14.14%					41.19 06/15/04		
MSFT	MICROSOFT CORP	17.1%	50.3%	45.00%	26.76%	10.0%	-0.2%	3.0%	300	8247.3	6.1%	
	Large	18.9%	-17.6%	-22.22%	19.12%					27.49 06/15/04		
FDS	FACTSET RESEARCH SYSTEMS INC	11.4%	14.2%	22.86%	21.71%	10.0%	-3.8%	0.4%	600	28320.0	20.9%	
	Small	12.2%	17.9%	18.18%	22.13%					47.20 06/15/04		
PFE	PFIZER INC	46.8%	31.9%	-2.44%	-41.77%	12.0%	-3.8%	0.0%	200	7056.0	5.2%	
	Large	51.8%	-25.7%	-51.06%	-40.38%					35.28 06/15/04		

Small: 20.9%   Medium: 40.3%   Large: 38.8%   Total Dollar Value: $135,188

- **Company**—The name of the company from the SSG and size of company based on sales.

- **Percent Change Qtr Sales**—This column shows the percent change in quarterly sales between one quarter and the corresponding quarter of the previous year. The most recent quarter results appear above those for the next most recent quarter.

- **Percent Change Qtr PTP**—This column shows the percent change in quarterly pre-tax profit for two consecutive quarters from quarterly data in your SSG. The most recent quarter results appear above those for the next most recent quarter.

- **Percent Change Qtr EPS**—This column shows the percent change in quarterly EPS between one quarter and the corresponding quarter from the previous year. The most recent quarter results appear above those for the next most recent quarter.

- **Percent Change 12 Mos EPS**—This column shows the percent change in EPS for 12-month periods. The top number is the percentage change in EPS for the most recent 12 months, for example, the EPS from the second quarter of 2003 through the first quarter of 2004 compared to the EPS from the second quarter of 2003 through the first quarter of 2003. The bottom number is year-over-year percentage change one quarter earlier—the EPS for first quarter of 2003 through the fourth quarter of 2003 compared to the first quarter of 2002 through the fourth quarter of 2002.

- **Est E/S Growth**—This column contains the EPS growth rate you projected in Section 1 of the SSG.

- **Projected Avg Ret**—This is the projected total return you would achieve if you purchased at the current price and the stock reached a price based on a projected average PE instead of the projected high PE. In *Investor's Toolkit,* you can see this value in Section 5 of the SSG. To display Total Return and Projected Average Return on your SSGs, click Preferences. Click the Stock Study tab and then turn on the "Display the Projected Average Return on SSG Back" check box.

- **Total Return**—This is the total return from Section 5 of your SSG and is not necessarily the same value as % Compd Annual Rate of Return on the PERT Report.

FIGURE 11-06: THE PORTFOLIO SUMMARY SHOWS VALUATION MEASURES FOR YOUR PORTFOLIO MANAGEMENT OFFENSE.

PORTFOLIO SUMMARY

NAME: 05/16/04

TICKER	COMPANY NAME	DATE	PRICE	P/E	TOT RET	REL VAL	U / D	BUY BLW	SELL ABV	% Port	REC
BBBY	BED BATH & BEYOND	06/15/04	38.43	29.3	20.54	88.5	3.2	39.2	78.3	1.42%	Buy
CHS	CHICOS FAS INC	06/15/04	43.98	37.9	19.28	181.3	2.1	37.0	83.1	9.76%	
PLMD	POLYMEDICA CORP	06/15/04	31.53	18.0	17.93	120.0	2.8	30.9	57.4	8.16%	
HD	HOME DEPOT INC	06/15/04	35.96	19.2	13.09	62.1	1.7	30.3	53.2	13.30%	
HDI	HARLEY-DAVIDSON IN	06/15/04	61.10	23.9	11.96	84.5	1.7	52.7	88.0	9.04%	
SNV	SYNOVUS FINANCIAL	06/15/04	25.54	19.2	10.45	83.5	1.1	20.8	31.7	13.22%	
MDT	MEDTRONIC INC	06/15/04	49.79	31.9	7.93	76.9	0.8	35.2	58.7	3.68%	
CAKE	CHEESECAKE FACTORY	06/15/04	41.19	34.3	7.92	104.6	0.7	25.9	48.8	9.14%	
MSFT	MICROSOFT CORP	06/15/04	27.49	30.5	2.97	69.6	0.2	17.3	26.6	6.10%	
FDS	FACTSET RESEARCH S	06/15/04	47.20	30.1	.39	94.4	0.0	25.7	39.5	20.95%	
PFE	PFIZER INC	06/15/04	35.28	38.3	-.01	110.1	0.0	16.1	26.6	5.22%	

- **Number of Shares—** This column contains the number of shares that you own of the stock.

- **Dollar Value—** This column shows the market value of your stock holding based on the number of shares and the current price. In *Investor's Toolkit,* the current price and the date of the current price quote appear below the dollar value.

- **% of Portfolio—** This column shows what percentage the market value of the stock represents compared to the total market value of your portfolio.

- **PMGuide Recom.—** This column includes buy or sell recommendations based on the current PE and price.

You'll see "Buy" if the current PE is less than the five-year average PE (from Section 3 of the SSG) and the current price is in the buy zone (from Section 4 of the SSG). If the current PE is greater than 150% of the five-year average PE

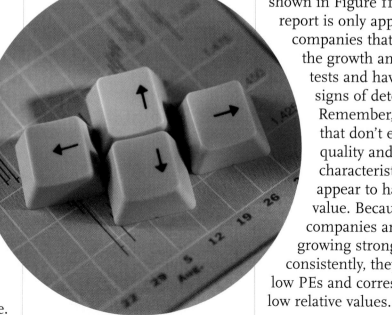

and the current price is in the sell zone, you'll see "Sell." For all other cases, the box is blank.

Portfolio Summary

The Portfolio Summary is a bare bones view of the valuation measures for the stocks in your portfolio, as shown in Figure 11-06. This report is only appropriate for companies that have passed the growth and quality tests and have no signs of deterioration. Remember, companies that don't exhibit quality and growth characteristics often appear to have attractive value. Because the companies aren't growing strongly or consistently, they often have low PEs and correspondingly low relative values.

Furthermore, if the stock price is low and you haven't reduced your forecasts on the SSG, the total return and upside-downside ratio could look attractive. By removing companies with poor fundamentals from your portfolio, the valuation measures on the Portfolio Summary are better indications of stocks that might represent good value.

- **Ticker**—The ticker symbol for the stock.

- **Company**—The name of the company from the SSG.

- **Date**—The date of the price quote.

- **Price**—The price as of the date in the previous column on the report.

- **P/E**—Unlike the PE ratio calculated in the PERT Report, this is the current PE ratio shown in Section 3 of your SSG.

- **Total Return**—This is the total return from Section 5 of your SSG.

- **RV**—This is the relative value that you see on the SSG. If you do not eliminate outliers in the PE ratios in Section 3 of the SSG, this relative value does not provide a meaningful picture of valuation.

- **U/D**—This is the upside-downside from Section 4 of your SSG.

- **Buy Blw**—This column shows the top of the buy range on your SSG. You can also decide whether a stock is a good value by checking total return.

- **Sell Abv**—This column is the bottom of the sell range on the SSG. You can also decide whether a stock is a good value by checking total return.

- **% of Portfolio**—This column shows the percentage that the stock represents in your portfolio based on the calculations in the Portfolio Trend Report.

- **Rec**—This column includes buy or sell recommendations based on the current PE and price.

CHAPTER TWELVE:

Finding the Right Type of Stocks

Drinking from the Fire Hose

Whether you are looking for a stock to buy with new contributions or to replace a stock you plan to sell, the problem isn't finding ideas for stocks to study; the problem is finding stocks to study that are suitable for the NAIC methodology. Everybody seems to have a stock recommendation or two or twelve. Newspapers, magazines, television shows, and many Web pages are great resources for investing, but the torrent of information could pin you to your sofa or office chair.

When you first start looking for ideas, you can whittle down the options by using resources that focus on NAIC-style investments. Then, when you've studied all those stocks, you can move onto other sources of ideas.

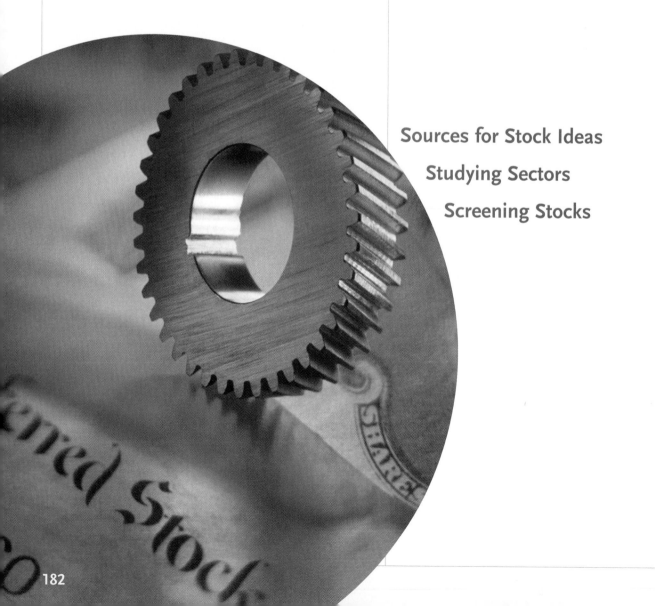

Sources for Stock Ideas

Studying Sectors

Screening Stocks

Sources for Stock Ideas

The different sources of stock study ideas might appeal to you depending on how you prefer to retrieve information and what sort of information you want to find. If you're looking for suggestions for stocks to study and plan to fill in all the blanks on your own, just about every source in this section will do. However, resources that focus on stocks that fit the NAIC methodology can prevent you from wasting time chasing down data for stocks that aren't appropriate for your portfolio. For beginners, sources that include opinions, judgment, and discussion about the stocks in question can help highlight key characteristics to study. The following sections list sources with an NAIC bent first.

Lists

Lists of investment recommendations are as ubiquitous as take-offs on David Letterman's Top 10 lists, but many of them aren't very useful to the NAIC-style investor. You must be careful to choose lists based on fundamental analysis. For example, Value Line's Timeliness ranking rates stocks based on their potential

for price movement in the next six to 12 months, which doesn't say anything about a stock's long-term growth potential. The following lists are sources for stock study ideas based on fundamental analysis.

- **The NAIC Top 100 list** is the result of an annual survey of the companies most widely owned by investment clubs that report their holdings to NAIC. Popularity in NAIC circles is an indication that a company has passed the

growth and quality tests of at least a few investment clubs. For example, companies with classic railroad track SSGs such as Pfizer, GE, Home Depot, and Bed Bath and Beyond all appear in the top 20. Unfortunately, being on the list doesn't guarantee that a stock will be perfect for your portfolio, your financial objectives, or risk tolerance. And, it definitely doesn't mean that the stock is a good value at its current price. Use this list for ideas but prepare your own SSG to determine whether the stock works for you and is a good value.

Success Tip!

Stocks new to the Top 100 or moving up significantly in the rankings show that clubs are buying or adding to their positions, which often indicates that the stock is not only a quality growth candidate but has recently sold at a good price. In addition, new stocks in the next 100 (from 101 to 200) might be up and coming contestants in the growth and quality arena.

- **Value Line lists** appear in the Summary & Index section, and the Selection & Opinion booklet, which are updated weekly. The Highest Growth Stocks list ranks stocks by Value Line's Estimated three–five Year Price appreciation and includes the current PE ratio as of the publication date. Although short-term price movement isn't the key criterion to an NAIC investor, the lists of Timely Industries can suggest industries to study. Likewise, if you find a stock from the Highest Growth Stocks list also appearing on the Timely Companies in

Timely Industries list, the stock has good growth prospects and is also on sale.

- **Other "best of" lists** on the Web can provide additional ideas or perhaps confirm suggestions you found elsewhere. The Forbes Web site (*http://www.forbes.com*) presents the Best 400 Big Companies in America, known as the Platinum 400, which focuses on large companies with the best scores for both long- and short-term financial returns as well as other measures. Forbes also taps one company as the best managed in each of the 26 industries it evaluates. If it's small companies you want, check out Forbes' Best 200 Small Companies in America. You can sort this list by several criteria including five-year average ROE and market value. MSN Money offers Jubak's 50 Best Stocks in the World (*http://money.msn.com/ articles/invest/jubak/fifty.asp*) for long-term buy and hold investors. Morningstar now offers star ratings on stocks, similar to its well-known mutual fund star rating.

Success Tip!

Before you decide to use a list as a source for ideas, make sure the inclusion criteria supports a long-term strategy of purchasing quality growth companies.

Magazines and Newsletters

Investment magazines and newsletters often overflow with investment suggestions, but you must take these ideas with a grain of salt. Print magazines and newsletters must go through publication, printing, and distribution, which means that the information could be two to three months out of date by the time you read it. In addition, to cater to investors' focus on buying, magazines and newsletters often provide buy recommendations but don't talk about selling something they recommended. The bottom line: you must study any stock recommended in these resources to determine whether it is appropriate for your portfolio and selling at a good price.

Before you spend money on magazine subscriptions that you could otherwise invest in growth stocks, spend a few hours at your local library reading different magazines and newsletters to see which ones you prefer. Most magazines and newsletters these days publish a Web site where you can read some articles without subscribing or request a free trial copy.

- ***Better Investing* magazine** has two features that focus on stocks you can study. Each month, the aptly named Stock to Study article provides an in-depth discussion of a company selected by *Better Investing's* Editorial Advisory and Securities Review Committee. Companies in the Stock to Study feature aren't always perfect. In fact, sometimes these companies have some warts to show you what problems look like. The Undervalued Feature examines stocks that might increase 20 percent in investment value (price appreciation plus dividend payout) within 18 to 24 months. Stocks that fit this criterion don't always possess the growth and quality that NAIC investors look for. Their return comes primarily from selling at a large discount compared to the projected EPS growth rate. Be sure to prepare your own SSG on any companies discussed in these articles so you can decide for yourself.

- ***BITS* magazine** is an online feature published on the NAIC Web site *(http://www. better-investing.org/articles/ bits)* that is available to Online Premium Services subscribers. *BITS* often includes stock studies complete with analysis and judgment by knowledgeable NAIC members. In addition to finding stocks to study,

you could pick up a few tips on studying stocks from the masters. *BITS* also publishes the NAIC Growth Screen, which includes companies that Value Line projects to double earnings in the next five years, have doubled earnings in the past five years, have a PEG ratio of 110 percent or less (based on Value Line's projected earnings growth rate), and have Value Line safety ratings of average or better.

- *Business Week,* as you might expect, is published weekly and often features more in-depth analysis of companies than other investment magazines.

- *Forbes, Fortune,* and *Smart Money* are popular investment magazines, each with its own style and slant.

- *Money* and *Kiplinger's Personal Finance* are targeted to beginners and cover a broader range of investing and personal finance topics than other magazines.

- *Wired* and *MIT's Technology Review* are not investment magazines, but they publish interesting articles on new technology or current research. If you're still interested in technology after the big sell-off in the early 2000s, these magazines talk about

companies working on what could be the next big thing.

- **Financial newsletters** often make more money for the publishers than they do for the readers. Before you subscribe to an investment newsletter, read the *Hulbert Financial Digest* first. It, too, is a newsletter, but it tracks the performance of portfolios recommended by other financial newsletters. To obtain a sample of the newsletter, or to subscribe, navigate to *http://cbs. marketwatch.com/Hulbert.*

Media Sources

With newspapers and television, chaff can overwhelm the wheat, but taking note of companies in the news doesn't hurt. Although the media often focuses on short-term results, news stories can highlight factors that might affect a company's long-term growth for better or worse. *The Wall Street Journal* is still the premier business newspaper, but the business section of your local paper reports news about individual companies and industry trends, too. In fact, local newspapers might be your best source for information about companies in the paper's area. Many financial Web sites, such as MSN Money (*http://money.msn.com*), Reuters Investor (*http://investor.reuters.com*), and Yahoo! Finance (*http://finance.yahoo.com*) include links to company and industry news.

Sharing Within the Community

E-mail lists and online forums about investing are everywhere, but NAIC itself is a huge community of like-minded investors. What's more, many of the most knowledgeable investors generously share their expertise with others.

- **I-Club-List** is an NAIC-oriented e-mail list dedicated to discussing how to study stocks, the analysis of individual companies, and the use of software tools for stock study. NAIC members from around the country interact through this list, so you can obtain advice and opinions from experienced investors no matter where you live. I-Club-List is a prolific group; receiving individual e-mails submitted to the list or even e-mails in digest form can be overwhelming. If you have specific questions you want to ask, you can post a message to the list and then access the list through the Web interface to check for responses. You can also search the messages posted to I-Club-List. For instance, if you would like to study companies in the pharmaceutical industry,

you can search for "pharmaceutical" to see what company names show up. To access or subscribe to I-Club-List, navigate to *http://www.better-investing. org/subjects/community/* and click I-Club-List.

- **The NAIC Compuserve forum** has interesting discussions available nowhere else. Anyone can access this forum for free through the Web. To learn how, click NAIC Forum (Compuserve) on the same page as the I-Club-List link.

- **Meeting with other NAIC members** is a great way to expand your pool of stocks to study. Classes, educational events, and Investors Fairs offered by local NAIC chapters; and regional and national NAIC events such as CompuFest and the *BI* National Convention (BINC) bring NAIC members together sometimes by the hundreds. Not only do you

learn from the classes and seminars you attend, but you can talk to other NAIC members to see what stocks they are studying and what they like or dislike about them. The NAIC home page (*http://www.better-investing .org*) includes links to information for CompuFest and the *BI* National Convention. To find out what's going on in your area, check the chapter

section in *Better Investing* magazine or click the Chapters link on the NAIC home page.

Industry and Sector Studies

Buying into an industry that stands to gain from demographic and other trends might boost the performance of your portfolio. Buying a quality growth company at the right price produces an attractive return. But when the industry is growing as well, your investment might grow for decades without running out of market. For example, Home Depot's revenues were $7 million in its first year. In 2003, Home Depot's sales were $64 billion. To have half a chance to continue growing its sales, the market for that industry must be large enough to support those sales. Home Depot estimates the market for home improvement merchandise and services to be $900 billion, providing plenty of room for continued growth.

For some investors, starting your quest for stocks by studying industries or sectors might be a little less intimidating. Compared to the thousands of publicly traded stocks you can buy, there are only about a dozen sectors and about 100 industries. You can start by finding industries with good growth prospects and then look for the best-managed growth stocks within that industry as potential investments.

Success Tip!

Different financial data providers categorize sectors and industries differently. To keep things simple and consistent, use information from the same data provider as you work your way down from sector to industry to company.

Business models differ from industry to industry. Some are capital-intensive and require high levels of debt to build factories, stores, or other types of infrastructure; other industries count on high volume and low profit margins, such as grocery stores and discount retailers; others use high levels of research and development to produce new products that can deliver higher profit margins and EPS. Spend some time learning about the opportunities and challenges that the industry faces. Look at industry average measures to understand how most companies in the industry operate.

Success Tip!

Some investors always seem to be looking for emerging, or "hot", industries. In many cases, these industries are filled with start-up companies that might not produce any earnings for several years. You should avoid getting caught up in the latest fad and instead focus on the fundamentals.

Many Web sites, including the following, provide industry overviews and news.

- Reuters Investor (*http://www.investor.reuters.com*) provides key developments, industry average ratios, and the companies within each industry it follows. The site provides industry research reports—some for free and some for a price.

- MSN Money (*http://money.msn.com*) stock pages provide key financial ratio results for a company and the corresponding industry.

- Standard & Poor's, First Call, Vickers, Argus, and Market Guide produce industry reports that analyze industry prospects and discuss the characteristics of companies in those industries. Brokers often offer these industry overviews to their customers, but the price tag might depend on the size of your account. Investors with higher asset levels receive reports for free, whereas the investors with smaller accounts might pay a fee.

- Industry Web sites and trade publications are great resources for learning about an industry. The business and reference sections at public libraries often carry industry-related reference material such as Value Line. Some industry and trade Web sites require a subscription, but many provide at least a few articles to the public. The Business.com Web site provides an easy way to find trade associations. Navigate to *http://www.business.com*. In the Business Directory list, click the link for the industry you are studying. On the industry page, click the Associations link.

Success Tip!

Keep track of the industries you've studied and make a point of studying a new one every so often. After you become comfortable analyzing industries that work with more typical financial ratios, branch out into industries with special requirements.

For example, many neophyte NAICers avoid banks and REITS, but these industries provide investment opportunities, particularly when interest rates trend down. You can find articles that explain how to study banks, REITS, and other industries on the NAIC Web site.

Screening Stocks

Thousands of companies are publicly held corporations, but only a small percentage of those meet the criteria NAIC investors seek. By weeding out the companies that don't grow fast enough or are too expensive, you can narrow the field of stocks to study dramatically. As you manage your portfolio, diversification makes you look for companies in specific industries or with a particular level of annual sales, which narrows the field even further.

Building an effective stock screen is as much art as science. Stock screening tools follow the criteria you specify—companies pass the test or they don't. If you specify EPS growth greater than 15 percent, a company growing at 14.99 percent won't show up. Don't try to build a stock screen to find the one stock you should buy! Evaluating financial performance includes too much judgment and qualitative analysis to delegate responsibility to an automated tool. For example, a stock screen can filter through companies to find those that grew 15 percent a year for the past five years, but it can't screen business outlook to determine which companies are best positioned to continue that growth rate in the future. By keeping your screening criteria more relaxed, you can shoot for four to 16 stocks and then scan a few financial ratios to decide which ones to study in detail.

Online Screening Tools

Online screening tools come in all shapes and sizes. Many Web sites try to help by defining stock screens for you; click a link and retrieve the results. Other online tools offer basic screening fields, so the tools are easy to use but limited in what they can do for you. More sophisticated tools combine more fields of data with arithmetic and logical operators, so you can define the criteria you want. Of course, these more powerful screening tools sometimes require a bit more effort to learn and sometimes carry a price tag to boot.

Sample Stock Screening Criteria

Regardless whether you use a simple screening tool or a sophisticated one, most of your stock screens will share a few fundamental criteria. Because many of the online screening tools enable you to save stock screens, you can save a stock screen and modify if for your more specialized searches. For example, if you want to screen within a specific industry, add a criterion for the industry to the list. The criteria in Table 12-01 are available in many, but not all, online tools. The stock screen in Table 12-1 shows criteria you might use to find a large-cap company for your portfolio:

- You might set the minimum growth rates to 7 percent, because large companies usually grow more slowly than smaller enterprises.

- For return on equity, you might want to see more return on the equity you own in the company and set the minimum to 12% or so.

- On the other hand, you might want a company with a debt to equity ratio below the corresponding industry's average, say 25%.

- In addition, you might limit the maximum PE and PEG ratio to find companies that might be selling at a reasonable price.

TABLE 12-01: SAMPLE CRITERIA FOR SCREENING STOCKS		
Criteria	**Minimum**	**Maximum**
Five-year sales growth rate	7%	
Five-year EPS growth rate	7%	
Last quarter EPS growth rate	7%	
Return on equity ratio	12%	
Debt to equity ratio		25%
PE trailing 12 Months		20
PEG ratio		100%

Easy Online Screening

In mid-2004, Quicken.com revamped its Web site and eliminated its stock screening tools, which were both easy and effective. Here are some easy to use stock screening tools that you can use instead.

- Morningstar (*http://screen.morningstar. com/StockSelector.html*) offers some interesting predefined screens, such

as Classic Appeal, which uses criteria very close to those for a basic NAIC screen. Morningstar's basic customizable Stock Screener offers very limited criteria for building your own stock screen. If you subscribe to Morningstar's Premium membership, you can develop screens using dozens of fields.

- Yahoo! Finance (*http://screener.finance.yahoo. com/newscreener.html*) offers predefined stock screens, a basic screening tool, and a more sophisticated screening tool. The basic HTML screener doesn't include all the criteria you need. To access the more sophisticated screener, click Launch Yahoo! Finance Stock Screener. You can define criteria from scratch or open a predefined stock screener and modify its criteria.

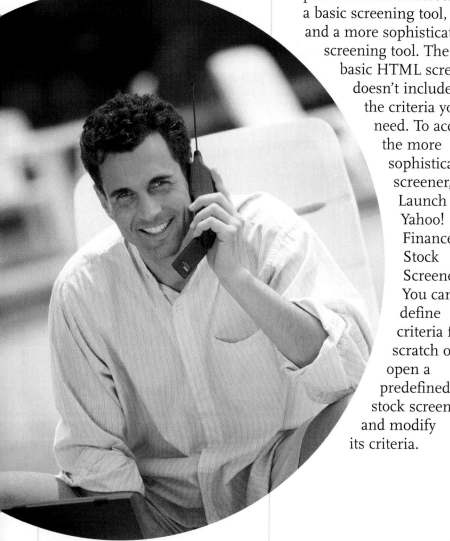

Stock Screens with Bells and Whistles

Some of the Web sites in the previous section offer additional stock screening tools with bells and whistles. However, if you want to harness the power of a sophisticated tool, you might as well use one of the best. MSN Money and Reuters Investor both offer sophisticated stock screening tools with predefined screens, powerful customization features, and the ability to save the results on the Web site or to a spreadsheet.

MSN Money Deluxe Screener (*http://money.msn.com/investor/ finder/customstocks.asp*) provides hundreds of financial measures and ratios for screening. Select financial measures, comparison operators, and criteria values by choosing from pull-down menus or typing values in boxes. You can specify a criterion value to be a number, the industry average, or a prompt that asks you to enter a value when you run the screen. For example, if you screen for different growth rates based on the size of the company, you can use prompts for the company size and the growth rate instead of saving multiple screens. This screener gets one negative mark because it doesn't include five-year EPS growth as a field.

You can start with a predefined screen, modify its criteria, specify the financial measures that appear in the results table, and then save your customized screen to run again. If you want to include a company that doesn't appear in the results, type the ticker symbol for the missing company in the Compare With box. By exporting screen results to an Excel spreadsheet or comma-delimited file, you can quickly evaluate financial measures beyond the ones you used for the screen. You can also create a watch list by exporting the symbols for the companies that passed the screen to MSN's Portfolio Manager.

When you first click the Stock Screener link, MSN Money displays the basic stock screener. To load the Deluxe Screener, click the Deluxe Stock Screener link at the bottom right of the Web page and follow the instructions to load the software on your computer. A graph appears on the download Web page to signify that the installation completed successfully.

The following steps describe the creation of a stock screen using the MSN Money Deluxe Screener. Web sites do change, so these instructions might require some modification when you access the MSN Money Web site.

1. Select Investing on the top-level menu bar, then select Stock on the next menu bar. Click Stock Screener in the navigation bar in the left margin and click Custom Search if necessary.

2. To start with a predefined screen, click File_Open in the Deluxe Screener menu bar.

3. Expand Pre-defined Stock Searches by clicking its plus sign, and then click one of the searches, such as Contrarian Strategy. Click the Open and Edit button to display the criteria for the screen. To see the results of the predefined screen before you edit it, click Run Search.

4. To delete a criterion, right-click within the criterion row and choose Delete Row from the shortcut menu. For example, you can delete the Dividend Yield criterion if you don't care whether the company pays a dividend.

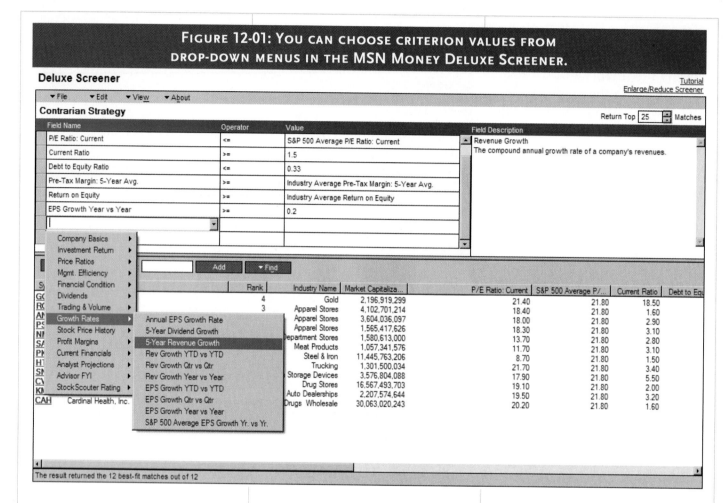

FIGURE 12-01: YOU CAN CHOOSE CRITERION VALUES FROM
DROP-DOWN MENUS IN THE MSN MONEY DELUXE SCREENER.

5. To add a criterion, click in the first empty Field Name cell, and select the category and the field you want, such as Growth Rates and 5-Year Revenue Growth shown in Figure 12-01. Then, click the Operator box in the same row and select the operator, such as >=. Finally, click the Value box in that row and choose the value for the test. For example, to find stocks whose sales are growing greater than 7 percent, select Custom Value in the drop-down list and then type .07.

6. To modify a criterion, click the box with the item you want to change and choose the value you want.

7. To view the results of your custom screen, click the Run Search button. By default, the columns in the results are the fields you used to screen the stocks.

8. To view additional fields, right-click any column heading and choose Customize Column Set from the shortcut menu. To remove a field, select the

TINKERING WITH RESULTS IN A SPREADSHEET

If you want to look at the results of a stock screen in different ways, download screen results to a spreadsheet. With the results in a spreadsheet, you can sort the rows, filter the results in different ways, or perform calculations with the values, such as calculating an average for the companies in the screen.

Within Excel, you can sort or filter the stock screen results. For example, click Data_Sort and then choose a field such as 5-Year Revenue Growth. To view the highest growth rates at the top, sort the rows in descending order. If the stock screen resulted in numerous companies, you can filter the rows to hide some of the results. For example, if the results include several companies from the same industry, you can filter the list for only that industry to compare the company values side by side. Click Data_Filter_AutoFilter. Click the down arrow in the Industry column and choose the industry name in the list.

field name in the Displayed Column list and then click the Remove button. To add a field, expand a category in the Available Columns list, select the field name, and then click Add. Click OK when the list includes the columns you want.

9. To download the results to an Excel spreadsheet, click File in the Deluxe Screener menu bar, choose Export Results to Excel, and click OK in the Export Screener Data dialog box. The spreadsheet appears in Excel, but you must use File_Save As to save the file to your computer.

Reuters Investor Power Screener *(http://www.investor. reuters.com/nscreen/builder.asp)* is more powerful than the MSN Money Deluxe Screener, but it isn't as easy to use. In PowerScreener you can even define your own variables by developing formulas using multiple financial measures and operators. For example, you can add the PEG ratio as a user-defined variable by dividing the built-in PE ratio variable by the built-in EPS growth variable. You can define criterion that include more than one test, so you can, for example, look for companies whose EPS growth and ROE are both greater than 12 percent. When you customize the columns in the results, you can save the columns and their order as a

layout so you can change the columns you view simply by switching layouts.

NAIC Stock Prospector

If you subscribe to NAIC's Online Premium Services, you might want to consider NAIC *Stock Prospector* for your stock screening. It currently costs $59, but you might not mind the price because of the features it offers. Because *Stock Prospector* works with Online Premium Services data, your stock screens use up to date data, not to mention the same data that you use to prepare your SSGs. In addition, *Stock Prospector* makes it easy to scan screening results for stocks that fit the NAIC mold.

- **Built-in NAIC screens** help identify NAIC-style stocks. *Stock Prospector* includes a wizard that helps you use predefined screens or define your own customized criteria. The NAIC 2 screen, shown in Figure 12-02, looks for historical EPS growth greater than 15 percent, projected EPS growth greater then 15 percent, a PEG ratio less than 1.0 and total return greater than 15 percent.

- **Weighted criteria** place more emphasis on the criteria you consider most important. For example, if you consider quality of earnings more important

than high growth, you can increase the weighting on the stability of EPS (the R-squared value of historical EPS shows the volatility) and decrease the weighting on the EPS growth rate.

- **Running totals** show you how many companies were filtered out by each criteria in the screen. For example, in Figure 12-02, filtering by historical 5-year EPS growth greater than 15 percent alone, the screen reduces the number of companies to 359. After using all four criteria, the list is down to 77 companies. Running totals are helpful if you want to revise your criteria to

FIGURE 12-02: *STOCK PROSPECTOR* INCLUDES NAIC-ORIENTED SCREENS.

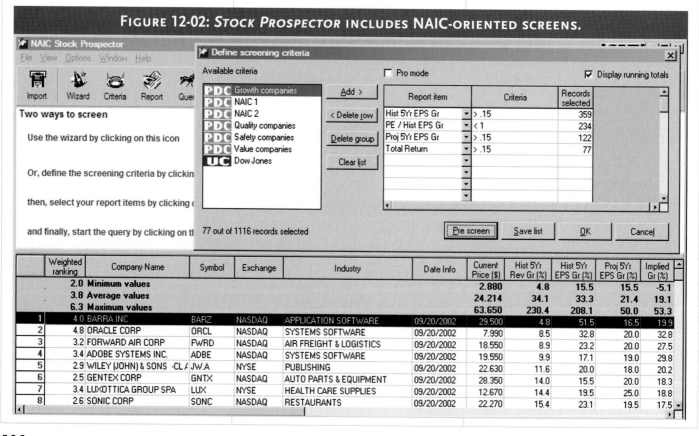

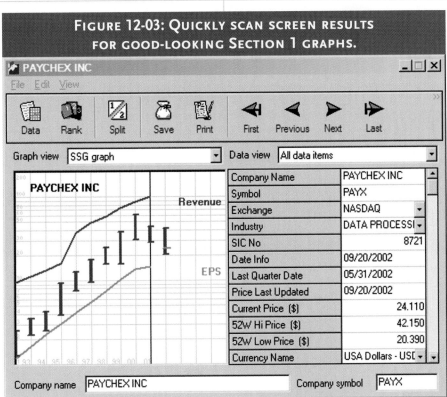

FIGURE 12-03: QUICKLY SCAN SCREEN RESULTS FOR GOOD-LOOKING SECTION 1 GRAPHS.

Success Tip!

If you want to screen for companies within a specific industry, define the first criterion to restrict the industry. Not only do you screen only the stocks in that industry, the running total for the first criterion tells you how many companies are in the industry and how many are eliminated by the other criteria.

include more or fewer companies. For example, you can select a criterion that filters out too few and make it more restrictive. In Figure 12-02, the total return greater than 15 percent filtered out 50 stocks, but left 77 remaining. To reduce the results, try increasing the total return criterion to greater than 20 percent.

- Previewing SSGs in Stock Prospector displays a miniature view of the SSG for the company you select, as illustrated in Figure 12-03. A separate window opens in which you can view the Section 1 graph as well as other SSG information. To quickly

review the SSGs for all the companies in your screen, click the Previous or Next button in the toolbar. You can quickly scan these SSG previews to apply your own judgment to choose the companies you want to study further. To find interesting companies to study in an industry, build a stock screen with relatively relaxed criteria that weed out the real dogs. Then, as you find railroad track SSG graphs among the resulting companies, add them to your short list for an industry study.

CHAPTER THIRTEEN:

Comparing Companies

The Devil is in the Details

When you prepare SSGs for companies, you begin to develop a sense of the quality and growth characteristics of those companies. The more you study the companies you're considering, the more ingrained your understanding becomes. The Stock Comparison Guide summarizes the results of several SSGs side by side, which often confirms what you already know. By following up your Stock Comparison Guide with a comparison of additional financial ratios, you can strengthen your confidence about the winner you select. When you invest in a taxable account, you must consider the impact of taxes and commissions before making your final decision.

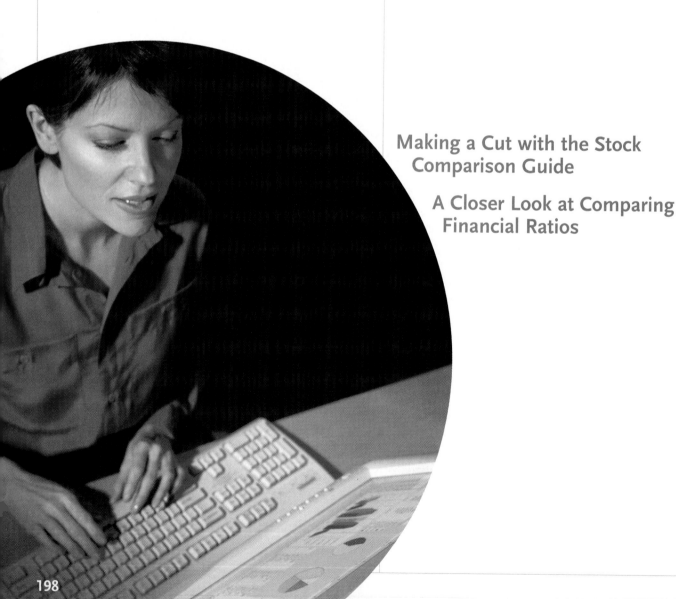

Making a Cut with the Stock Comparison Guide

A Closer Look at Comparing Financial Ratios

Making a Cut with the Stock Comparison Guide

Stocks must pass a number of tests before they find a home in your portfolio. First, they must survive the stock screening process. Then, Sections 1 and 2 of the SSG and your background check on the underlying business must look good enough that you continue on to Sections 3, 4, and 5. A stock must pass the value tests in those sections of the SSG to stay in the running. The Stock Comparison Guide (SCG) is the next step in choosing the stock you want to add to your portfolio.

The Stock Comparison Guide lines up the results from SSGs you've completed for up to five companies. (Make sure that the SSGs you compare in a Stock Comparison Guide use the most recent data and include your updated judgment.) Instead of shuffling through SSG pages or switching between windows on your computer, you can review basic performance parameters at a glance. If you haven't dismissed a company while preparing the SSG, the disparities that might appear when you compare contenders in the Stock Comparison Guide might change your

mind. Remember that the Stock Comparison Guide is more meaningful if you compare companies within the same industry. Otherwise, you are comparing apples to oranges.

Success Tip!

This comparison should be the beginning of your assessment, not the end. Just as a stock screen can't filter a list of stocks down to one winner for you, the Stock Comparison Guide doesn't look

at many of the financial ratios that provide important clues about a company's prospects. Nor can the Stock Comparison Guide judge many of the qualitative characteristics that mold a company's future.

Choosing Stock Comparison Guide Criteria

The SCG includes several comparison categories and numerous individual comparisons, but these aren't all equal in importance. For example, the average pre-tax profit margin (listed as % Profit Margin Before Taxes on the SCG) is more important than the PE ratio measures. Pre-tax profit margin tells you about the quality of

management and potential growth. You might rather wait for the PE ratios to reach the right level than accept a company with a less attractive pre-tax profit margin.

Success Tip!

Investor's Toolkit 5 provides weightings for the measures on the SCG, so you can emphasize important criteria and reduce the effect of less critical measures.

The number of measures in each category can also throw the vote. There are only two management comparisons that cast votes in the software version of the SCG, but both are core measures of a company's quality. On the other hand, the SCG includes nine price comparisons. Without choosing the measures on the SCG wisely, a company might appear to win just because it's price is very low. In addition, when you use NAIC software, some of the measures on the SCG don't

get a vote, even though you care about those values. If you use NAIC software to prepare an SCG, don't accept the software's conclusions. Use your own judgment to decide which company is the winner.

Success Tip!

By clicking each row you can override the computer selection and choose for yourself the winners in the rows you want to evaluate.

Growth Comparisons

Because growth and quality must come before value, the measures in the Growth Comparisons section carry more weight than price measures. The growth rates in the Growth Comparisons section come directly from the historical and projected rates that you enter in Section 1 of the SSG. If you use NAIC software, the highest growth rate is the winner in each comparison. In reality, choosing the winners can be more complicated. For example, consider five stocks that all grow at 14 percent, but two are large-cap stocks; two are mid-caps; and one is a small-cap. There is no clear winner in this example.

- **Historical % of Sales Growth** and **Historical % of Earnings per Share Growth** are the average historical growth rates that you see in Section 1 of the SSG. The historical growth rates aren't as important as the projected growth rates, because you want to know what the company can do for you in the future. However, the past growth rates indicate whether a company has delivered sufficient growth in the past. This measure doesn't take into account the quality of the historical growth—how consistent growth has been in the past. It also doesn't evaluate the historical growth based on the size of the company. A small company's growth could blow away the performance of a large company, but the added risk might not be worth it. You don't have to eliminate these measures from the SCG, but you also shouldn't weight them as heavily as the projected growth rates. For example, in the Stock Comparison Guide in Figure 13-01, Hot Topic wins in every growth category, but the bottom line is that Hot Topic and Pacific Sunwear tie at 20 percent on the measure that matters the most; the projected EPS growth.

FIGURE 13-01: CONSIDER ELIMINATING SOME OF THE MEASURES FROM THE SCG TO PLACE EMPHASIS ON THE MORE CRITICAL MEASURES. IN THIS FIGURE, THE X TO THE LEFT OF ROW 11 SHOWS THAT THE INVESTOR REMOVED THE HIGHEST PE DURING THE LAST FIVE YEARS AS A TEST IN THE SCG.

GROWTH COMPARISONS
(From Section 1 of the NAIC Stock Selection Guide)

	ABERCROMBI ANF	HOT TOPIC HOTT	PACIFIC SU PSUN
(1) Historical % of Sales Growth	28.3 %	48.5 %	33.1 %
(2) Projected % of Sales Growth	12.0 %	25.0 %	22.0 %
(3) Historical % of Earnings Per Share Growth	31.6 %	59.2 %	38.1 %
(4) Projected % of Earnings Per Share Growth	12.0 %	20.0 %	20.0 %

MANAGEMENT COMPARISONS
(From Section 2 of the NAIC Stock Selection Guide)

		ABERCROMBI ANF	HOT TOPIC HOTT	PACIFIC SU PSUN
(5) % Profit Margin Before Taxes (Average for last 5 Years)	(2A) Trend	21.0 DOWN	13.4 EVEN	10.6 UP
(6) % Earned on Equity (Average for last 5 Years)	(2B) Trend	30.9 DOWN	20.6 EVEN	17.4 UP
(7) % of Common Owned by Management		1.0	0.5	4.0

PRICE COMPARISONS
(From Section 3-5 of the NAIC Stock Selection Guide)

			ABERCROMBI ANF	HOT TOPIC HOTT	PACIFIC SU PSUN
(8) Estimated Total Earnings Per Share For Next 5 Years			15.16	8.84	9.85
(9) Price Range Over Last 5 Years	High (3A)		8.00~50.80	1.40~32.30	5.10~24.60
	Low (3B)				
(10) Present Price			37.13	20.59	20.79
X	Price Earnings Ratio Range Last 5 Years	(11) Highest (3D)	36.50	29.70	33.30
		(12) Average High (3D7)	23.90	25.20	27.40
X		(13) Average (3-8)	16.80	18.30	19.50
		(14) Average Low (3E7)	9.60	11.30	11.60
X		(15) Lowest (3E)	5.20	4.60	9.60
X	(16) Current Price Earnings Ratio (3-9)		17.43	20.80	18.84
	Estimated Price Zones	(17) Lower-Buy (4C2)	14.97~26.75	11.20~23.08	11.00~23.98
		(18) Middle-Maybe (4C3)	26.75~50.32	23.08~46.83	23.98~49.93
		(19) Upper-Sell (4C4)	50.32~62.10	46.83~58.70	49.93~62.90
	(20) Present Price Range (4C5)		-Hold-	-Buy-	-Buy-
	(21) Upside Downside Ratio (4D)		1.13	4.06	4.30
X	(22) Current Yield (5A)		0.67	0.00	0.00
	(23) Total Return (5C)		11.69	25.26	26.87

OTHER COMPARISONS

		ABERCROMBI ANF	HOT TOPIC HOTT	PACIFIC SU PSUN
(24) Number of Common Shares Outstanding		94.61	46.98	76.65
X	(25) Potential Dilution from Debentures, Warrants, Options	None	None	None
X	(26) Percent Payout (3G7)	0.00	0.00	0.00
	(27) Earnings Stability (R2)	84.1 %	92.1 %	87.7 %
	(28) Relative Value	103.8 %	113.7 %	96.6 %

Topic and Pacific Sunwear, which doesn't automatically brand it a loser. But, the downward trends in both profit margins and ROE combined with the slow growth rates are enough to remove it from the running.

- **% Profit Margin Before Taxes (Average for last 5 Years)** is the average profit margin from Section 2 of the SSG. If all the stocks in the SCG meet your basic growth rate criteria, you might look for the highest profit margin that is trending up to spot the stronger competitors.

Success Tip!

Declining profit margins are your earliest warning signal of lower EPS growth in the future, so this measure is a critical component in your decision. The SCG doesn't show the consistency of profit margin performance over the years, which is an important indication of the quality of company management. You should weed out companies with inconsistent profit margins as you evaluate their SSGs. If a company doesn't meet your basic criteria for growth, quality, and value, you should not add it to a Stock Comparison Guide.

- **Projected % of Sales Growth** and **Projected % of Earnings per Share Growth** are your forecasts for growth for the next five years. Not only do these values look at future performance, but they also include any adjustments you made due to the quality of historical growth. You should not ignore these measures under any circumstances.

Management Comparisons

The SCG pulls the five-year average values and trends for profit margin and ROE from Section 2 and grabs the percentage of stock that management owns from insider ownership in the SSG header. *Investor's Toolkit* shows any even or upward trends as winners, whereas *NAIC Classic* and *Stock Analyst Plus!* pick one winner per row. Regardless which method you use to choose winners, consider eliminating a company from the SCG if it doesn't win in the management comparison section. For example, in Figure 13-01, Abercrombie & Fitch grows more slowly than Hot

- **% Earned on Equity (Average for Last 5 Years)** is the average ROE from Section 2 of the SSG with any outliers you select removed from the calculation. Higher ROE and consistent or increasing values indicate that management provides the shareholders with sufficient return on their investment in the company, so this is an important measure of management quality. However, consistency and above-industry-average values are important as well. Furthermore, if the debt levels vary significantly between the companies you're comparing, ROE isn't a true measure of management quality; ROA (return on assets, described in Chapter 8) is a better measure in this situation. To evaluate companies for these measures, you must go beyond the SCG (see Chapter 8.)

- **% of Common Owned by Management** indicates whether management's interests are aligned with those of the shareholders, but this measure doesn't have a vote in the automated SCG. Significant ownership varies based on the size of the company, so reviewing the dollar values of insider ownership in the annual report is the best way to gauge management's interests.

Success Tip!

NAIC Online Premium Services don't include insider ownership, so be sure to update your SSG data with insider ownership from another source. For example, Yahoo! Finance stock pages, include a Major Holders link which includes insider and institutional ownership.

Price Comparisons

The price measures in the SCG actually compare measures from Sections 3, 4, and 5 of the SSG. This section compares EPS, PE ratios, price zones, upside-downside ratios, yields, and more. The number of measures related to price could tip the scales to a low-priced stock even if another company won the growth and management competitions. To keep things balanced, you can select the most important of the price measures to receive a vote. In addition, winning values for some price comparisons aren't immediately apparent.

Read the following descriptions to make sure you choose the price measures you want.

- **Estimated Total Earnings Per Share For Next Five Years** adds up the estimated EPS for the next five years, but the winner is actually the company with the lowest PE ratio calculated by dividing the current price by the total EPS for the next five years. The measure looks at how quickly a

company could "repay" its purchase price with the EPS that it generates. For example, Hot Topic's ratio of price to five-year total earnings is 2.3. Pacific Sun's ratio is 2.1.

In the Price Comparisons section of the SCG in Investor's Toolkit, the Price Range Over Last 5 Years, Present Price, and Estimated Price Zones measures appear for reference only.

- **Price Earnings Ratio Range Last 5 Years** includes five separate measures. The highest value for each measure is the winner based on the theory that investors are willing to

pay more for quality growth companies. Although Benjamin Graham used this theory to invest successfully, five votes might be excessive. If you want to use only one of these measures, consider the average PE or the average high PE.

Success Tip!

PE ratios for the last five years can be misleading if the economy has been particularly hot or cold. For example, in 2000, PE ratios for the five previous years were often inflated. In many cases, the higher the PE ratio, the more the price dropped when the bear market arrived.

- **Current Price Earnings Ratio** is based on the current price divided by the trailing four quarters EPS in Section 3 of the SSG. If you think that the PE ratios from the past five years aren't indicative of a company's future, consider eliminating this measure.

- **Present Price Range** indicates whether the stock is a buy, hold, or sell at its current price. The Upside Downside Ratio tells you the same thing and more, so this measure is redundant.

- **Upside Downside Ratio** indicates whether a company is a buy as well as the risk of a price drop compared to the potential price increase. A loser in this comparison isn't the end of the world. If a company wins in growth and quality, you can wait until the price drops.

- **Current yield** is the percentage return you receive from dividends based on the stock's current price. (This value changes along with the current price.) If you focus on current income, the winner will be the company with the highest yield. If you care only about long-term growth, this measure is less important than total return or projected average return.

If you use NAIC software such as *Investor's Toolkit,* you can choose between combined estimated yield, total return, or projected average return for the measure on line 23.

- **Total Return** is the estimated compound annual return from both price appreciation and dividend yield over the next five years.

- **Projected average return** is the estimated total return over the next five years based on selling the stock at the forecast average PE instead of the forecast high PE.

- **Combined estimated yield** is the sum of the average price appreciation and average dividend yield. Although this result doesn't take compounding into account, the winner is the largest number.

The final section of the SCG is a mixture of measures. The SCG contains two lines for optional measures. To select the criteria, consider the type of companies you are studying. For example, for high-growth companies with high PEs, the PEG ratio, listed as P/E: Projected Growth Rate (PEG) in *Investor's Toolkit,* is helpful. For companies that carry debt, consider the debt to equity ratio (Debt/Capital Ratio). Relative value and projected relative value measure the current or projected PE to the

five-year historical average PE. Earnings Stability (R-squared) is a measure of how consistently EPS have grown over the past 10 years.

- **Number of Common Shares Outstanding** can indicate the size of a company. In *Investor's Toolkit,* this measure doesn't get a vote, but you can place emphasis on this measure if you are looking for a particular size of company.

- **Potential Dilution** is the potential effect on EPS due to shares that could be issued for stock options, warrants, and convertible bonds. If you use EPS from a data source that already takes dilution into account, you can eliminate this measure.

- **Percent payout** shows the percentage of earnings paid as dividends. The winner for this measure depends on whether you are looking for growth or income.

For growth, the winner is the lowest percent payout. For income, the winner is the highest percent payout.

A Closer Look at Comparing Financial Ratios

After comparing SSG performance with the Stock Comparison Guide, the next step is a closer look at additional financial ratios for each company you are considering. As described in Chapter 8, these measures help you understand how companies operate and can flag brewing problems.

Comparing financial ratios to industry averages indicates whether a company is a strong competitor in its market. Comparing financial ratios to specific competitors helps you identify the strongest of the bunch.

Many financial ratios have guidelines for acceptable values, but you must use these with care. Some business models invalidate the typical rules of thumb. For example, the current ratio is a measure of company liquidity—whether the company has enough current assets to cover its current liabilities. The rule of thumb for a satisfactory current ratio is a value of at least 2 or greater. Companies that work on high volume, low profit margins, and cash transactions can have very low current ratios. These companies often receive cash payments for goods long before they must pay their suppliers.

With a thorough analysis of the SSG, financial ratios, and qualitative characteristics such as business outlook, your gut feel for the companies you've studied might tell you which one is the winner without any extra tools. Until you develop that level of experience, not to mention confidence, a tool similar to the Stock Comparison Guide can help.

FIGURE 13-02: A FINANCIAL RATIO SPREADSHEET FROM BOB ADAMS THAT HELPS YOU INTERPRET COMPANY RESULTS.

ANALYZING THE ANNUAL REPORT --   **HOME DEPOT INC   HD   2003**   Millions of dollars - except today's price

The cheaper the paper, the more valuable the information -- Peter Lynch   (Company)   (Symbol)   (Year of report)

Press Ctrl+D to delete current data.   Ctrl+I to insert OPS data.   See the bottom of the form for instructions

1	$2,852	Cash (see Balance Sheet)	
2		Marketable Securities or Investments	

Accounts Receivable   Change: -21% OK!, Right direction (Decreasing)

Days waiting for payment this year= 6

Days waiting for payment prior year= 9

Below 60 is good - below 45 is superb

3	$1,097	Accounts Receivable this year
3	$1,386	Accounts Receivable prior year
4	$9,076	Inventories current year
4	$9,264	Inventories prior year

Inventories   Change: -2% YES! - Right direction (Decreasing)

Inventory Turnover Days this year = 57   Both Accts Rec. & Inventories are decreasing, that's positive.

Compare with other companies in the industry

5	$13,328	Total Current Assets
6	$20,063	This Yr. Total Property Plant & Equip.
6	$17,168	Prior Yr. Total Property Plant & Equip.

Sales or Revenues   Change: 11% Way to GO! (Increasing)

Sales to Accts Receivable Ratio.............   OK (Sales growing faster than Accts Receivable)

Sales to Inventories Ratio...................   This ratio is OK (Sales growing faster than Inventories)

7	$9,554	Total Current Liabilities
8	$856	Long-term Debt this year
8	$1,321	Long-term Debt prior year

Plant & Equipment   Change: 17% OK - (Sales should grow as fast)

(Sales should be increasing as fast or faster).   Oops - Sales aren't growing as fast

9	2,262	Common Shares Outstanding this Yr.
9	2,293	Common Shares Outstanding prior Yr.
10	$22,407	Total Stockholders Equity
		(see Consolidated Statement of Earnings)

Long-term Debt   Change: -35% Right direction (Decreasing)

A small change isn't considered a serious negative.

Debt to Equity Ratio is OK

| 11 | $64,816 | Total Sales or Revenues this Year |
| 11 | $58,247 | Total Sales or Revenues prior Year |

Total Interest Coverage   Pretax exceeds interest X times   109 Large numbers aren't as useful as small.

[Pretax Profit + Total Interest Paid / Total Interest Paid]   This company appears to be in good shape financially.

Any number below 5 is worrisome. A number below 3 is very worrisome

11a	$57,973	Cost of Sales this Year
11a	$52,375	Cost of Sales prior Year
11b	$6,843	Income before Taxes

Number of shares outstanding trend: Even   -1% No significant change

[Curr. Yr. Shares/Prior Yr. Shares]   A small change of up to about 2% isn't considered too consequencial

| 11d | $4,303 | This Yr. Net Income |
| 11d | $3,657 | Prior Yr. Net Income |

Cost of Sales   Up   11% Caution - Why is it increasing?

[Cost of sales this year/Cost of sales prior year as a % change]   Good - Sales increasing faster than Cost of Sales

| 11e | | Total Interest Paid on Debt (from Ann. Rpt) |

Cashflow Growth   -19% Cashflow should increase at the same rate as Sales - or greater

[Curr. Yr. Cash from Operations/Prior Yr. Cash from Operations]   Caution - Cashflow is not increasing at or better than the Sales rate

| | 109.1 | Total Interest Coverage (from OPS) |
| | | (see Statement of Cash Flows) |

Free Cash Flow Margin   2% Anything over 10 is Great - Substantially over 10 is EXCELLENT

[Free Cash Flow / Sales]

| 12 | 4,802 | This Yr.-Net Cash provided by Operations |

Earnings Confidence Rating -- Measures quality of Earnings   0.90 Generally the closer this is to 1, the higher the quality of Earnings

[Net Income/Net Cash from Operations]

| 12 | 5,963 | Prior Yr. -Net Cash provided by Operations |
| 14 | $2,749 | Acquisition of Property Plant & Equipment |

Net Income   Net Cash

Compare - Net Income with Net Cash   18%   -19% Oops - Net Cash is growing at a slower rate than Net Income

Net Income is growing   Caution - Net Cash is declining

13	$492	Total Dividends paid (if any)
	$36.99	Today's Price per Share
18-Mar-04		Date of Price quote

Cash Position per Share: $0.88 per share in cash beyond debt.   Great! This represents actual cash included in the price of each share of stock.

[Net Cash / Shrs outstanding]   Offers price support in falling market if positive.

CAUTION: Check for accuracy if using OPS data

LT Debt to Equity Ratio: 4% debt to equity.   Long-term Debt is in normal range

[Long-term Debt / Total Equity]   Normal Long-term Debt -- Less than 25% debt.

NOTE: Ratios are more meaningful if compared to other companies in the same industry.

Quick Ratio: 0.4 to 1   About 1:1 is normal. The higher the better.

[Cash+Markable Securities+Accts Rec. / Total Liabilities]   This is a relatively severe test of a company's liquidity and its ability to meet short-term obligations.

Working Capital Ratio: 1.4 to 1   About 2:1 is normal for manufacturer. 1:1 normal for Utilities.

[Total Current Assets / Total Current Liabilities]

| Danger |
| Caution |
| Good |
| Very Good |

Inventory Turnover Ratio: 6.4 to 1   The higher the ratio the better. Indicates quality merchandise & proper pricing.

[Cost of Sales / Inventory]   Also note the number of days Inventories are held before they become a product and sold (See "Inventories" above).

bob-adam@attbi.com

Web site - http://www.homestead.com/bobadams/bobsite.html

Tools for Evaluating Financial Ratios

Calculating financial ratios doesn't have to be difficult. In fact, you can analyze ratios without warming up your calculator, although you might exercise your computer keyboard entering some data from annual reports. A few NAIC members have created excellent Excel spreadsheets to assist your financial analysis.

Bob Adams, director for the Puget Sound chapter and a director on the national Computer Group Advisory Board, offers two spreadsheets on his personal Web site *(http://bob-adams.home.comcast.net)* that help you analyze financial ratios: one for most companies and one specifically for banks. The spreadsheets work with one company at a time, but comparing companies is easy by placing hard copies side by side. Cells in the spreadsheets include comments with hints for interpreting company results. In addition, warnings or atta-boys appear depending on the ratio values, as illustrated in Figure 13-02. The spreadsheets include macros so you can automatically download data from NAIC Online Premium Services.

Several NAICers collaborated on a ratio analysis spreadsheet *(http://www.better-investing.org/articles/web/8764)* that shows the results for multiple companies simultaneously. Look in the "related files" section of this article. You must manually enter values from company annual reports or Sec 10-Ks on the Input Data worksheet. The Output Results worksheet categorizes ratios as profitability measures, capital structure, and turnover ratios. As demonstrated in Figure 13-03, the spreadsheet shows the formula for the ratio in column B, provides a guideline for good results in column C, and color-codes the ratios themselves to flag good, bad, and in-between values. Remember to take the color-coding with a grain of salt because different business models might invalidate a hard and fast guideline.

FIGURE 13-03: A SPREADSHEET THAT POSITIONS THE RATIO RESULTS FOR SEVERAL COMPANIES SIDE BY SIDE.

	A	B	C	BB	BC
1	profit				
2	Measure - Unhide Col. B for detail	See"How to Input Data & Interpret	Good User Criteria	HD 2/3/2002	HD 2/3/2003
3	**Profitability Measures**				
4	Pretax Profit Margin	% Pretax profit margin=(Pretax profit / sales)	>15%	9.3%	10.1%
5	Net Profit Margin (Profitability)	% Net profit margin = (Net Profit / Sales)	>10%	5.7%	6.3%
6	Asset Turnover(Efficiency)	Sales / Avg Annual Assets	Chk Chgs	2.24	2.07
7	Financial Leverage(Gearing)	Avg Annual Assets / Avg Shareholder Equity	Chk Chgs	1.44	1.49
8	Return on Equity	% Return on Equity= (Net Profit / Average Equity)	>15%	18.4%	19.3%
9	Retained to Common Eqty	% ROE x (earnings - dividends)/ earnings	>= Grth Rt	16.0%	16.7%
10	Growth of Debt	% Growth of annual debt	< ROE	NA	5.3%
11	Return on Invested Capital	ROIC = (Net Profit) / (Avg. Equity + LTD)	>15%	17.1%	18.1%
12	Return on Total Assets	Return on total assets = (Net Profit / total assets)	Cmp Ind	11.5%	12.2%
13	Cash from Operations/Net Income %	(Net Cash from Operating Activities(NCO)/Net Income)-1	> 0%	95.6%	31.1%
14	EPS	Net Income / Weighted Average Shares	> Prior Yr	1.29	1.56
15	Cash From Operations/Per Share	Net Cash from Operations / Avg Weighted Shares	>EPS	2.53	2.05
16	Growth in Cash from Operations/Share %	(CFO/share CY - CFO/share PY) /CFO/Share PY	>EPS Gr	NA	-19.0%
17	Quality of Earnings	(NI-NCO)/(Total Assets CY+Total Assets PY)/2	< 3%	-12.2%	-4.0%
18	Impact on NI of Expensing Stk Options	(NI if Stk Opt Expensed-NI)/NI	>-5%	-8.0%	-6.8%
19	Retained Earnings/Shareholder Equity	Retained Earnings/Shareholder Equity	SGR	70.8%	80.7%
20	Free Cash Flow ($M)	Net Cash from Operations - CAPEX	> Prior Yr	2560	2053
21	Free Cash Flow Margin %	(NCO-CAPEX-Dvds)/Sales	>10%	4.0%	2.7%
22	Operating Cash Flow Margin	%OCF Margin=Net Cash from Operations/Revenue	> 15%	11.1%	8.2%
23	Operating Cash Flow Coverage	NCO / (Absolute Value (NCI+NCF)	> 0.9	1.64	0.94
25	**Capital Structure**				
26	Total Debt to Equity Ratio	Total debt to equity ratio = total debt / equity	<. 33	0.07	0.07
27	Total Debt/ NCO	Total Debt /Net Cash from Operating Activities(NCO)	<3.3	0.21	0.28
28	LTD / 2x Last Years Earnings	Long Term Debt / 2 times last years Net Income	<1	0.21	0.18
29	Share Buyback/(Dilution)	(# shares last year - # shares this year) / # shares last year	> 0.0%	-0.04%	0.38%
30	Stk Option Shares/Total Shares %	Stk Opt Sh Granted/Total Shares	<5%	2.95%	3.55%
31	Net C&E+STI+MS-Total Debt	Cash & Equiv.+Sh Tm Inv.+Marketable Securities-Total Debt	>0	1288.00	932.00
32	Net C&E+STI+MS-Total Debt per Sh	Cash & Equiv.+Sh Tm Inv.+Marketable Securities-Total Debt/Shares	>0	0.55	0.40
33	C&E+STI+MS vs Debt Ratio	(Cash & Equiv+ Sh Tm Inv+MS) / Total Debt	> 1.5	2.0	1.7
34	C&E+STI+MS Ratio CY/PY %	Cash & Equiv+Sh Tm Inv+Marketable Securities CY/Same for PY	> 0%	1336.7%	-11.5%
35	Interest Coverage Ratio	(Pretax Profit + Interest Expense) / Interest Expense	> 5	178.0	159.7
36	Current Ratio	Current ratio= Current Assets / Current Liabilities	> 2.0	2.52	1.48
37	Quick Assets Ratio	Quick Assets Ratio= (C&E+STI+MS+AR) / Current Liabilities	> 1.0	0.5	0.4
38	Foolish Flow Ratio	Foolish Flow Ratio = (CA-C&E)/CL-STD)	<1.25	2.13	1.20
39	**Turnover Ratios**				
40	% Change in Accounts Receivable(AR)	AR CY / AR PY	< 0%	10.2%	16.5%
41	Change in Sales %	Sales CY / Sales PY	>12%	17.1%	8.8%
42	% Change in AR vs Sales	Chg AR% - Chg Sales%	< 0%	-6.9%	7.8%
43	Days Sales Outstanding CY	AR CY / (Sales CY / 365)	< PY	6.3	6.7
44	Days Sales Outstanding PY	AR PY / (Sales PY / 365)		6.7	6.3
45	Inventory Turnover Rate (CY)	COG CY / Inv CY	> PY	5.6	4.8
46	Inventory Turnover Rate (PY)	COG PY / Inv PY		4.9	5.6
47	% Change in Inventory	INV CY / INV PY		2.6%	24.0%
48	% Change in Inventory vs Sales	Chg Inv% - Chg Sales%	< 0%	-15%	15%
49	Plant Turnover Ratio	Sales CY / PP&E	Incr YTY	3.5	3.4
50	CEO Pay as % of Net Income	CEO Total Compensation /Net Income		0.78%	0.55%
51	Cash Conversion Cycle(CCC)	CCC=DIO+DSO-DPO (From Fool)	Ind Cmp	38	41

How to Input Data & Interpret / Input Data / **Output Results** / Criteria /

Ranking Competitors

If only there was one size to fit all investors. Because financial objectives differ, so do the desirable characteristics for investments. Therefore, your list of criteria might vary depending on the financial goal you're saving for, your stage in life, your tolerance for risk, and other factors. Furthermore, the list can grow or shrink depending on your experience in investing.

A shorter checklist such as the Stock Comparison Guide helps beginners focus on key criteria. As you learn more, you can add more measures to the list and assign importance to each criterion.

You don't need a fancy spreadsheet; a checklist can suffice. However, if you use a spreadsheet to calculate financial ratios, adding a checklist worksheet to your file makes it easy to access the values you need. For example, the spreadsheet checklist in Figure 13-04 includes criteria from the SSG (see Chapter 7), financial ratios (see Chapter 8), and a few qualitative measures (also in Chapter 8).

Each company has two columns of information. The first includes financial ratios for your judgment of performance. For example, both Home Depot and Lowe's receive a "Yes" for consistent historical and recent quarter growth. On the other hand, the cells for Projected EPS growth (for company size) show the values from the SSG: 10 percent for Home Depot and 17 percent for Lowe's.

The second column is your rating for the result: 1-Good, 2-OK, or 3-Poor. This checklist doesn't use formulas to rate the results. The process of looking at the company results, comparing them to industry averages and other competitors, and choosing a rating helps you understand the companies and make your decision. In Figure 13-4, the ratings are color-coded so you can spot any troublesome areas. Home Depot and Lowe's are clearly quality growth companies. Home Depot's measures might have a slight edge on Lowe's, but its upside-downside ratio and total return are less than Lowe's. An investor with lower tolerance for risk might decide to wait for Home Depot to drop in price. Another investor could choose Lowe's as a quality growth company with an attractive total return.

Chapter 10 discusses Investor's Toolkit 5 Smart Challenger, which helps you search for companies that meet or exceed the quality, growth, and valuation measures of your current holding.

FIGURE 13-04: COMPARE ALL THE CRITERIA YOU EVALUATE WITH A CHECKLIST.

	A	B	Home Depot (C) Value	(D) Rating	Lowe's (E) Value	(F) Rating	(G) Value	(H) Rating
3	SSG	Insider ownership	1.0%	1-Good	1.0%	1-Good		
4	Section 1	Institutional ownership	61.0%	1-Good	79.0%	2-OK		
5		Sufficient historical growth for company size	20.0%	1-Good	20.0%	1-Good		
6		Consistent historical and recent quarter growth	Yes	1-Good	Yes	1-Good		
7		EPS growth close to sales growth	Yes	1-Good	Yes	1-Good		
8		Sustainable growth	16.2%	1-Good	16.8%	1-Good		
9		Projected EPS growth (for company size)	10.0%	2-OK	17.0%	1-Good		
10		Correlation of price bars to growth trend		2-OK		1-Good		
11		Trends in Preferred Procedure (costs, taxes, preferred dividends, n		1-Good		2-OK		
12		Price volatility		2-OK		2-OK		
13		Regular stock splits		2-OK		2-OK		
14	Section 2	Trend in pre-tax profit margin	Up	1-Good	Up	1-Good		
15		Above industry average profit margin	10.6%	1-Good	9.7%	1-Good		
16		Trend in ROE	Up	1-Good	Up	1-Good		
17		Above industry average ROE	18.9%	1-Good	17.7%	1-Good		
18	Section 3	PE ratios steady or increasing		3-Poor		3-Poor		
19		Payout ratio	13.8%	2-OK	4.7%	2-OK		
20	Section 4	Current price not close to forecast low		1-Good		1-Good		
21		Relative value between .85 and 1.1	0.63	2-OK	0.899	1-Good		
22		Upside-downside ratio 3.0	1.4	3-Poor	6.1	1-Good		
23	Section 5	Sufficient total return for risk	11.9%	2-OK	22.8%	1-Good		
24	Financial Ratios	ROA	10.8%	2-OK	9.2%	2-OK		
25	Profitability	Return on Invested Capital	19.1%	1-Good	13.5%	2-OK		
26		Cash From Operations/Per Share	$2.89	1-Good	$4.00	1-Good		
27		Growth in Cash from Operations/Share %	36.0%	1-Good	17.0%	2-OK		
28		Free Cash Flow Margin %	4.0%	2-OK	115.0%	2-OK		
29	Capital Structure	Current Ratio	1.4	1-Good	1.5	1-Good		
30		Quick Ratio	0.4	1-Good	0.4	1-Good		
31		Debt to Equity Ratio	5.7%	1-Good	26.7%	1-Good		
32		Interest Coverage Ratio	124.2	1-Good	16.8	1-Good		
33	Turnover Ratios	Inventory Turnover	6.4	1-Good	6.1	1-Good		
34		Change in Inventory vs Sales	Down	1-Good	Down	1-Good		
35		Receivables Turnover	59	1-Good	235	1-Good		
36		Change in Receivables vs Sales	Down	1-Good	Down	1-Good		
37		Days Sales Outstanding	6	1-Good	2	1-Good		
38		Asset Turnover	2.6	1-Good	2.9	1-Good		
39	Qualitative Analys	Industry Outlook		1-Good		1-Good		
40		Business Outlook		1-Good		1-Good		
41		Management Strategies		1-Good		1-Good		
42		Trustworthiness		1-Good		1-Good		

Sheet1 / Sheet2 / Sheet3 /

Managing Mutual Funds with NAIC Tools

The Ball is STILL in Your Court

Mutual funds are managed by professional fund managers, so why would you have to keep tabs on your mutual fund investments? If you think that mutual fund companies and managers always do the right thing for the shareholders or that they can possibly know what the right thing is for you, some people would like to sell you some land. Truth be told, mutual fund companies are in it to make money for themselves. Making money for investors

is simply the carrot that persuades shareholders to pay the mutual fund company fees and expenses.

To buy the right mutual funds in the first place, you must know what you need, read the mutual fund prospectus to see if the fund fits your criteria, and then choose the best fund for the job. Although you don't have to watch funds as frequently as you do the stocks in your portfolio, a regular checkup is in order.

Mutual Fund Red Flags

On Watch with the
Fund Trend Report

Screening for Funds

Comparing Mutual Funds

Mutual Fund Red Flags

With stocks, the reasons to sell are often the opposite of the reasons to buy. Mutual funds work the same way. Although you aren't likely to evaluate all the companies in a mutual fund to see whether their returns might drop in the future, funds provide warning signs that performance is about to fly south. By checking fund trends, you can decide whether to replace a fund before it hurts your portfolio.

Success Tip!

Similar to your decisions with stocks, you might decide to sell a mutual fund for reasons other than red flags in the fund performance. If your financial objectives or tolerance for risk change, current mutual fund holdings might not meet your new criteria.

In some respects, mutual funds are easier to evaluate than stocks. To truly understand a stock investment requires thorough study of the company's financial performance and business prospects. With a mutual fund, you still want good returns for the risks you take, but you don't have to evaluate nearly as many measures.

- **Investment philosophy—** Mutual funds typically follow an investment theme. Some themes are based on company size and investment strategy such as large-cap growth funds. Others focus on investment goals such as capital appreciation or income. If a mutual fund changes its approach, the results could throw your portfolio diversification off or make the risk level unsuitable for your risk tolerance. For example, if you own a small-cap growth fund for the higher-return higher-risk portion of your portfolio, a switch to medium or large-cap companies would decrease your potential risk but also decrease your potential returns.

- **Return and Risk—**The returns that a mutual fund achieves depend to some extent on the investment philosophy that the fund follows. Large-cap funds typically generate lower returns with less volatility

because the underlying large-cap stocks generate lower returns with less volatility. Small-cap funds might provide higher average returns, but they might come with serious volatility from year to year. With the advent of index mutual funds, you can choose low-cost mutual funds that emulate stock market indexes if you are satisfied with the average return for the index that the fund follows. When you invest in actively managed funds, you want returns that are worth the higher fees you pay the fund manager for his or her expertise.

- **Taxes**—When you hold funds in a taxable account, the taxes you pay can make a big dent in your returns. When you invest in funds in a taxable account, the tax-adjusted returns are the bottom line.

- **Expenses**—The mutual fund industry possesses an arsenal of fees and expenses that funds might charge you. Regardless what names they go by, fees and expenses mean more money for the fund company and lower annual returns for your portfolio. Because it is the rare fund manager who can consistently and significantly beat the market, you're better off with lower-cost funds.

- **Turnover**—Frequent changes to the makeup of the fund portfolio can have significant effects on the returns you earn from a fund. For funds held in taxable accounts, fund turnover means higher tax bills for you and more short-term gains taxed at higher rates. Even in tax-advantaged accounts, high turnover costs you money in brokerage commissions and other trading fees—and these costs don't appear in the annual returns that mutual fund companies publish.

- **Management Tenure**— You pay fund expenses in return for a fund manager managing your money. Since your evaluation of fund performance mostly relies on past performance, it's more reassuring to know that the same manager that produced past returns is still steering the ship. Of course, a manager new to one fund can have an illustrious reputation from previous assignments, so you can't go entirely by the numbers you see.

OBTAINING MUTUAL FUND DATA FOR TREND REPORTS

Morningstar mutual fund reports are the best-known source for comprehensive mutual fund data. Even Web sites that offer mutual fund data frequently present Morningstar data with a few tweaks. Morningstar publishes updated online reports every month or two. The hardcopy reports are updated every five months. If you subscribe to NAIC's online Mutual Fund Resource Center, you can access Standard & Poor's data for over 17,000 mutual funds and the online mutual fund forms automatically populate with data when you enter a ticker symbol.

On Watch with the Fund Trend Report

The NAIC Stock Fund Trend Report, shown in Figure 14-01, summarizes the fund criteria you use when choosing a fund, but shows values for several periods side by side. You can scan the most recent fund results to look for undesirable values, such as excessive turnover or high expense ratios. The Stock Fund Trend Report also emphasizes trends that can warn you about impending problems. Here's a guide to the sections of the Trend Report and how to use them to spot problems.

Portfolio Composition

Portfolio composition shows you the percentages of assets held in cash, bonds, stocks, and other types of investments. To maintain the proper diversification for your overall portfolio, make sure that your **stock** funds are invested primarily in **stocks** and that **bond** funds are invested primarily in **bonds.** If you use portfolio diversification and time as your guards against risk, you don't need a fund manager storing up cash to try to time the market. In Figure 14-01, the Mairs & Power Growth Fund shows cash holding steady at about three percent. Mutual funds typically keep some cash on hand to cover fund redemptions, but you might find funds that are

FIGURE 14-01: THE STOCK FUND TREND REPORT SUMMARIZES THE CRITERIA YOU USE TO SPOT SELL SIGNS.

FUND INFORMATION ⑦

Fund Name: Mairs & Power Growth Fund   **Symbol:** MPGFX
Category: Domestic Equity   **Style:** Equity All Cap Value

Filter Data: No Filter ▾ [Filter] **Earliest Available Date:** 12/31/2002

Portfolio Analysis Date			12/31/2002	06/30/2003	09/30/2003	12/31/200
Portfolio Composition		Cash	0.00%	3.16%	3.22%	2.72ᶜ
		Bonds	0.00%	0.00%	0.00%	0.00ᶜ
		Stocks	100.00%	96.84%	96.78%	97.28ᶜ
		Other	0.00%	0.00%	0.00%	0.00ᶜ
Company Size (from sales)		Large	54.62%	55.07%	51.59%	51.47ᶜ
		Medium	38.97%	37.44%	41.49%	45.24ᶜ
		Small	6.41%	7.49%	6.92%	3.29ᶜ
P O R T F O L I O	**S E C T O R S**	Consumer Discretionary	8.9%	8.6%	8.2%	4.6ᶜ
		Consumer Staples	11.4%	11.4%	11.4%	11.4ᶜ
		Energy	0.0%	0.0%	0.0%	0.0ᶜ
		Financials	15.6%	15.6%	15.6%	15.6ᶜ
		Health Care	19.4%	19.4%	19.4%	19.4ᶜ
		Industrials	24.7%	24.7%	24.7%	24.7ᶜ
		Information Technology	7.5%	7.5%	7.5%	7.5ᶜ
		Materials	12.3%	12.3%	12.3%	12.3ᶜ
		Telecommunication Services	1.2%	1.2%	1.2%	1.2ᶜ
		Utilities	0.0%	0.0%	0.0%	0.0ᶜ
Number of Stocks			34	37	37	3
Total Assets ($M)			1,023.5	1,060.1	1,197.5	1,234.
Sales Growth			10.0%	11.3%	10.2%	9.7ᶜ
Trailing Earnings Growth			11.4%	12.4%	11.4%	10.1ᶜ
P/E Ratio			17.9	19.7	19.5	21.
M A N A G E M E N T	**Management Change?**		No	No	No	N
	Total Return % - 10-Year		16.12	16.55	16.55	16.5
	Total Return % - 5-Year		8.48	9.67	9.67	9.6
	Total Return % - 3-Year		8.48	8.64	8.64	8.6
	Taxes % - 10-Year		1.31	1.33	1.33	1.3
	Taxes % - 5-Year		1.27	1.28	1.28	1.2
	Taxes % - 3-Year		1.35	1.35	1.35	1.3
	5-Yr Average Turnover %		7	7	7	
C O S T	**Expense Ratio**		0.78%	0.78%	0.78%	0.78ᶜ
	12b-1 Fee		-	-	-	
	Load: Front / Back		0.00% / 0.00%	0.00% / 0.00%	0.00% / 0.00%	0.00% 0.00ᶜ
	Redemption Fee		0.00%	0.00%	0.00%	0.00ᶜ

100 percent invested—many index funds included—and there isn't anything wrong with that.

If you use NAIC's Mutual Fund Resource Center, the Stock Fund Trend Report includes the Portfolio Composition section. The paper form does not.

Company Size (Market Capitalization)

The percentage of companies of different sizes is important if you want to keep your overall portfolio diversified between large, medium, and small companies. If a mutual fund indicates an investment philosophy in its name, such as the Power to the People

Small-cap Growth fund, the SEC requires that the fund invest at least 80 percent in small-cap growth companies. Without representative names, funds have leeway in what they buy. Small-cap mutual funds that don't close to new investors often gravitate toward larger and larger companies as the level of fund assets makes it more difficult to purchase enough shares in small companies. In addition, many of their small-cap winners grow into mid- to large-cap companies.

Watch for increasing representation in a company size category that doesn't fit your plans. You might be

headed for higher risk or lower returns than you had expected. For example, the Mairs and Powers Growth Fund in Figure 14-01 is categorized as an all-cap equity fund, but the small-cap percentage had dropped to only three percent by the end of 2003.

The online Trend Report uses Large, Medium, and Small categories with categories based on annual sales. The paper Trend Report includes Giant, Large, Medium, Small, and Micro categories, defined by market capitalization.

Sectors

Another aspect of fund philosophy is the level of diversification and the sectors invested in. Some funds focus on only one sector such as financial services or healthcare, whereas others invest in a number of sectors with good prospects. You don't have to have strong opinions about sector allocations to use this portion of the Trend Report. The idea is to make sure that the fund isn't building up too much of a stake in one sector. Many funds "stocked up" on information technology stocks during the dot-com boom. Just as you work hard to protect your portfolio from dependence on one sector, your mutual funds should maintain their diversification as well.

Number of Stocks

One of the reasons mutual funds are popular is the instant diversification that they offer. There's no "right" number of stocks, but many funds own 100 or more. Higher numbers of stocks can lead to index-like performance.

Total Assets

Changes in fund assets can be problematic. Success can be the undoing of small-cap stock funds. If a small-cap stock fund does well, investors want a piece of the action resulting in a big increase in the fund's assets. As assets increase, the fund managers have a harder job finding good small-cap companies to buy and lose the nimbleness that led to success in the first place. If you own a mutual fund with good performance and low total assets, dramatic increases in total assets can lead to average performance. Ideally, funds close to new accounts to protect performance for current shareholders.

Declining fund assets present a different set of problems. When shareholders redeem shares, the fund manager might have to sell investments to pay for the redemptions. If stocks have done well, the sales can generate capital gains distributions to all shareholders, not just those redeeming shares. When the number of shareholders decreases significantly, fund expenses might increase for those that remain, when the fund must allocate its expenses among a smaller number of shares.

Growth Rates and PE

The Fund Trend Report shows the overall results for sales growth, trailing EPS growth, and PE ratio for the entire fund portfolio. Just as NAIC investors look for quality growth companies, a mutual fund that invests in the strongest companies is positioned to deliver above average performance. Nevertheless, trends in sales and EPS growth can be due to the economy or factors other than problems in individual investments within a fund. Compare the growth and PE values produced by the fund to the growth and PE for a comparable market index. If the growth rates for the fund's portfolio are above those of the index while the PE ratio is below, the fund has what it needs to outperform its benchmark index.

Success Tip!

MSN Money is a good place to compare information about growth rates and PE ratios. On a mutual fund page, click the Returns link to display a fund's annual and average returns and the percentage difference compares to the fund category and the corresponding index. Click the Portfolio link to see the PE ratio for the fund and the fund category.

Management Changes

Fund managers make or break actively managed funds. When a new manager takes over, not only have you lost the manager who produced past returns, but the new manager could drastically increase turnover as he replaces the previous manager's companies with his favorites.

Manager changes aren't necessarily bad. Sometimes, the primary manager leaves, but a long-time assistant manager who knows the ropes takes over. Or, a manager with a winning record from other funds takes on a new fund. When the Stock Fund Trend Report shows a management change, do some research on the new manager to see whether you should be concerned.

Returns

Certainly, the returns that a fund achieves are important, but one or two years of astronomic returns doesn't mean that the fund will continue to deliver at that pace. In fact funds with incendiary past performance are often poised to plummet just as quickly. Funds that provide more consistent returns over longer periods, through both good times and bad, are more likely to continue that performance in the future. The Stock Fund Trend Report shows average total

returns for the past three-, five-, and 10-year periods. And, because the Trend Report shows returns over several reporting periods, you can get a sense of the fund's performance for even longer than 10 years.

With index funds so prevalent these days, the real crucible for a fund is beating the comparable market index over long periods of time. Although the market index return doesn't appear on the Fund Trend Report, the Total Returns section of Morningstar mutual fund reports includes annual and long-term total return for the fund and its corresponding index. In addition, Morningstar reports, the Morningstar web site *(http://www.morningstar. com)*, and Yahoo! Finance *(http://finance.yahoo.com)* compare fund returns to both the category average and a corresponding index. If your fund has lagged its peers and its benchmark index for more than two years, start looking for a new fund—or move your money into a low expense fund that follow the corresponding index. For example, the Mairs and Powers Growth Fund in Figure 14-01, shows a steady 10-year average return of approximately 16 percent, which exceeds the 10-year average return for the corresponding S&P 500 index by about 6 percent a year.

Success Tip!

Although risk doesn't appear on the Stock Fund Trend Report, the Sharpe ratio is a statistical measure that indicates the return you earn for each unit of risk. If you start looking for a new fund, look for higher Sharpe ratios so you earn more return for the risk you assume.

If you hold a fund in a taxable account, check the percentage that would be lost to taxes in the Management section of the Trend Report. Opt for funds that manage their portfolio to limit the tax costs. For example, in Figure 14-01, over longer periods the fund gave up about 1 percent per year to taxes.

Turnover

Turnover measures the level of trading that a fund does and lots of trading does two things—both bad. First, every time a fund buys or sells a holding, it incurs brokerage costs, which reduce the returns you receive. Second, when a fund sells holdings with gains, those gains show up in fund distributions, which mean higher tax bills if you hold the fund in a taxable account.

Turnover often increases when a new manager shows up, keen to remake the fund. The Fund Trend Report shows the five-year average turnover rate as a percentage of fund assets.

Stock funds with an average annual turnover rate of 20 percent or less are desirable, although funds that invest in small-cap stocks often tend toward higher turnover than large-cap funds. Bond funds have higher turnover than stock funds, because managers must buy and sell bonds not only for fund purchases and redemptions, but also to replace bonds that mature. Look for bond funds with an average annual turnover rate of 100 percent or less.

Success Tip!

Index funds have an advantage in the turnover department. Because an index fund follows an index, the manager has to buy or sell holdings only for changes in the index (and purchases and redemptions in the fund.)

Expenses

Mutual fund expenses are a huge drag on fund returns and one of the main reasons that many actively managed funds perform worse than their index counterparts. As shown in Table 14-01, even small differences in annual fund expense ratios can make noticeable differences in the money you obtain. But, some of the high expense ratios charged by actively managed funds can suck the wind out of your investment. To keep your money working for you, look

TABLE 14-01: IMPACT OF EXPENSES ON A 10-YEAR $10,000 INVESTMENT			
Expected annual return %	Expense Ratio %	Final value	Total % Expenses Paid
11	0.2	$27,831	2.0
11	0.5	$27,006	4.9
11	1.25	$25,038	11.8

for funds with annual expense ratios less than 1 percent and try to avoid funds with sales loads altogether.

If fees started out low, small increases aren't too great a concern, but bear watching nonetheless. Be wary of increasing fund fees when the fund already charges above average rates.

Screening for New Funds

If you decide that a fund in your portfolio needs to go, the NAIC fund screening tools help you find funds to fill the upcoming hole in your portfolio diversification plan. Of course, if your money is in a 401(k) plan or other account with limited fund selection, you can skip the fund screening to compare

BOND FUND TRENDS

The Bond Fund Trend Report includes characteristics typical to all funds, such as portfolio composition, number of holdings, total assets, total return, management change and expenses. But this report also includes some metrics that are specific to bond funds. The Average Effective Duration calculates the average length of time for the entire portfolio of bonds to mature, which is one measure of the risk level of the fund. The longer the duration, the greater the change in the net asset value of the fund in response to interest rate changes. When interest rates increase, the price of bond funds drops. The Average Credit Quality is another measure of bond fund risk, showing the financial strength of the companies that issue the bonds in the portfolio. The lower the credit quality, the higher the risk of default. When you use the NAIC online Trend Reports, the appropriate Trend Report appears depending on whether you enter a ticker symbol for a stock or bond fund.

your options, as explained in the next section "Comparing Mutual Funds". NAIC fund screening uses the same S&P mutual fund data that appears in the Trend Reports.

Several online fund screening tools provide dozens of screening criteria and don't charge a fee. If you already subscribe to the NAIC Mutual Fund Resource Center, the fund screening feature focuses on the essentials, as shown in Figure 14-02.

- **Category**—Specify the category of fund that you want, such as domestic equity or global equity for stock funds and domestic taxable fixed income for bond funds. Because you usually want a fund whose risk and return aligns with your financial goals, you

should choose a category as one of your criteria.

- **Style**—Style breaks down categories into finer divisions. For example, you can use the Style criteria to specify large-cap growth, large-cap value, small-cap growth, or even funds that focus on the healthcare or information technology sectors.

- **Family**—If you are looking for a new fund in an account with limited choices (i.e. a 401(k) account), you can specify the fund family to search.

- **Five-year sales growth**—For stock funds, you can specify the average annual sales growth achieved by the entire fund portfolio over the last five years. If you run a screen and

FIGURE 14-02: SPECIFY CRITERIA TO NARROW THE FIELD OF FUNDS.

MUTUAL FUND
EDUCATION AND RESOURCE CENTER

FUND SCREENING

Category	Domestic Equity
Style	Equity Small Cap Growth
Family	Any
5 yr. Sales Growth	Any
5 yr. EPS Growth	>= 12%
Manager Tenure	>= 5 years
Avg. Annual Return 3-Year	Any
Avg. Annual Return 5-Year	Any
Avg. Annual Return 10-Year	>= Style Index
5-Year Average Turnover	Any
Expense Ratio	<= 1.5%
Load	No Load
Minimum Purchase	<= 1000
Avg. Credit Quality	Any
Average Duration (years)	Any

Search   Start Over

receive fewer results than you want, eliminate this criteria and focus on the five year EPS growth or the average annual returns.

- **Five-year EPS growth—** For stock funds, you can specify the average annual EPS growth achieved by the entire fund portfolio over the last five years. For example, you might search for funds with portfolio annual EPS growth exceeding 12 percent over the last five years. Many mutual funds tune their portfolios to perform well in up markets and take a beating when the economy is poor.

- **Manager Tenure—** Search for funds whose managers have directed their funds for more than five years. If a screen returns too few funds, eliminate this criteria and then evaluate the managers for each fund. For example, funds that are run by new managers with good reputations from previous assignments are acceptable even though

their tenure at the current fund is less than five years.

- **Average Annual 3-, 5- and 10-year Returns—** For large-cap funds, you can select >= S&P 500 Index to find funds that beat their corresponding index. For other types of funds, you're better off choosing >= Style Index to find funds that beat the average performance for the fund style.

- **5-year Average Turnover—** This criterion has two choices: Any and < 20 percent. Because few funds deliver turnover less than 20 percent, choose Any for your first pass. If the results return too many funds, you can use turnover to reduce the field.

- **Expense Ratio**—Choose a value to limit the expense ratio that funds charge. Remember that small-cap and international funds tend to have higher costs and therefore higher expense ratios, so you might start by limiting those to less than 1.5 percent. For most stock funds, look for funds with less than 0.5 percent expense ratios.

If the results include too few or too many funds, relax or tighten up your expense ratio criteria.

- **Load**—Choose No Load unless you like to spend more money for the same results. Very few funds with loads and high expense ratios beat their low-cost counterparts over the long term.

- **Minimum Purchase**—If you have a fixed amount of money to invest in a fund, there's no point finding a great fund that requires an initial purchase of $100,000. Choose the amount that is closest to the amount you have to invest. Alternatively, you can eliminate this criterion and see if the funds that the screen returns accept smaller amounts if you sign up for an automatic monthly investment plan.

Success Tip!

When you screen for bond funds, you can specify the Average Credit Quality and Average Duration.

Comparing Mutual Funds

After you find funds that meet your basic criteria, you can use NAIC's mutual fund Comparison Guide to inspect and rank the features of two funds side by side. The fund Comparison Guide doesn't break new ground; it uses the same measures provided by the Check List and the Trend Report.

If you use the Comparison guide in the NAIC Mutual Fund Resource Center, each fund has two columns: the first displays the performance values for the fund and the second enables you to rank the fund as the winner or loser, as illustrated in Figure 14-03.

For example, you might rank one fund first because the manager has been running the fund longer, but rank it second because its turnover ratio is higher. As demonstrated in Figure 14-03, the online tool keeps track of your first and second place votes so you can see which fund comes out ahead in the initial voting. In reality, some criteria are more important than others so you should scan the performance measures and judge for yourself. For a fund in a taxable account, you might place more emphasis on the turnover ratio, the tax cost percentages, and the expense ratio than you do on the number of stocks and total assets.

FIGURE 14-03: THE ONLINE COMPARISON GUIDE TRACKS YOUR RANKING OF EACH FUND.

Better Investing

National Association of Investors Corporation

biaforenaic@wispertel.net logout | help

| JOIN NAIC | Search: ___ Go | START A CLUB |

NAIC
HOME
ABOUT
MEMBERSHIP
CHAPTERS
CORPORATE MEMBERS
NAIC STORE
SITE SEARCH

MEMBER RESOURCES
MEMBER SERVICE
PUBLICATIONS
COMMUNITY
EDUCATION
CLUBS
YOUTH
SOFTWARE
GREEN SHEETS

PREMIUM SERVICES (OPS)
BITS ONLINE
COMPANY REPORTS

PREMIUM SUBSCRIPTIONS
MUTUAL FUND RESOURCE CENTER
IAS ONLINE

VOLUNTEER RESOURCES
ARTICLES
FILES
Beta Links:
  Stock Check List
  Preferred Procedure (Flash)
  Preferred Procedure (HTML)
  BETA?

Issue Archives:
  Better Investing
  BITS
Article Archives:
  Better Investing
  BITS
  Web Articles
Author Archives:
  Authors

MUTUAL FUND EDUCATION AND RESOURCE CENTER

Get a new report:
Ticker: ___ Go Find Ticker

Stock Fund Comparison Guide
| Mairs & Power Growth Fund | Vanguard 500 Index/Inv | Print View | Comparison Guide Help |

Fund Name		Mairs & Power Growth Fund (MPGFX) remove	RANK	Vanguard 500 Index/Inv (VFINX) remove	RANK
Style Name		Equity All Cap Value		Equity Large Cap Blend	
Portfolio Composition	Cash	2.78%		0.68%	
	Bonds	0.00%		0.00%	
	Stocks	97.22%		99.32%	
	Other	0.00%	· ·	0.06%	· ·
Company Size (from sales)	Large	50.20%		84.29%	
	Medium	42.00%		15.61%	
	Small	7.79%	· ·	0.09%	· ·
SECTORS	Consumer Discretion	5.1%		10.8%	
	Consumer Staples	11.4%		10.9%	
	Energy	0.0%		5.9%	
	Financials	15.6%		20.4%	
	Health Care	19.4%		13.2%	
	Industrials	24.7%		10.8%	
	Information Technology	7.5%		17.6%	
	Materials	12.3%		3.0%	
	Telecommun Services	1.2%		3.4%	
	Utilities	0.0%	· ·	2.6%	· ·
Number of Stocks		37	· ·	508	· ·
Total Assets ($M)		1,595.6	· ·	76,820.3	· ·
Sales Growth		8.0%	· ·	8.8%	· ·
Trailing Earnings Growth		7.8%	· ·	7.5%	· ·
P/E Ratio		21.8	· ·	21.3	· ·
Management Tenure		24.4	· ·	16.7	· ·
Total Return % - 10-Year		17.45	· ·	11.26	· ·
Total Return % - 5-Year		10.88	· ·	-1.58	· ·
Total Return % - 3-Year		9.47	· ·	-2.25	· ·
Taxes % - 10-Year		1.62	· ·	0.76	· ·
Taxes % - 5-Year		0.03	· ·	0.87	· ·
Taxes % - 3-Year		0.69	· ·	0.55	· ·
5-Yr Average Turnover %		7	· ·	6	· ·
Expense Ratio		0.75%	· ·	0.18%	· ·
12b-1 Fee		·	· ·	·	· ·
Load: Front / Back		0.00% / 0.00%	· ·	0.00% / 0.00%	· ·
Redemption Fee		0.00%	· ·	0.00%	· ·
		1st 2nd		1st 2nd	

(Left margin vertical labels: PORTFOLIO, MANAGEMENT, COST)

Back to Top

☒ Denotes Member Content
☒ Denotes Premium Content

Search: ___ Go

Member Service
Privacy Policy

Making the Most
of Special Situations

Keeping Your Interests at Heart

Sometimes, the stock market seems more like a square dance than a place of business. Companies combine, part ways, and reunite with regularity. Shareholders might be the owners of publicly-held companies, but that doesn't mean that the results of these organizational changes are in the shareholders' best interest. When you're faced with organizational changes in a company you own, the key question is "What's in it for me?" The same holds true for other types of investment offers. The sales pitches might sound good; they're sales pitches after all. For the right person at the right time, it could be the ideal investment. You must do your homework because no one else can decide if it is right for you.

Mergers and Acquisitions

  Spin-Offs

    **IPOs and Start-ups:
    Investing or Gambling?**

    **Can You Make Money with
    Cyclical Stocks?**

    **Making the Most of Your
    Fixed-Income Investments**

Mergers and Acquisitions

You work hard to find companies you want to invest in, so it's frustrating when a company you purchase changes shape. Does the new configuration have the same characteristics as the company you bought or will the executives make more from the deal than the shareholders? Proposed changes aren't always in your best interest, so unquestioning acceptance of an organizational change is not a good idea. When a company you own is involved in a merger, acquisition, spin-off, or another more esoteric reconfiguration, evaluate the resulting company as a new entity to decide if it works for you.

The Pros and Cons of Acquisitions

Many companies make the acquisition of smaller competitors a steady part of their diet. In addition to growing business internally, companies increase their growth by taking over the customers and market share from the competitors they acquire. When a company acquires a less-efficient competitor, it can streamline the added operations and increase EPS not only from the additional customers but from improving the profit margins for the acquired operations. For example, Lincare Holdings regularly acquires smaller competitors in the home oxygen-therapy market. Because many patients who require oxygen therapy are on Medicare, some competitors in this market struggle with complicated third-party reimbursement requirements. Lincare uses proprietary computer systems to manage these third-party reimbursements and has a long history of successfully integrating its acquisitions.

When a company makes one substantial acquisition, the costs of the acquisition temporarily depress the pre-tax profit margin and EPS, as illustrated in Chapter 7 in Figure 7-03. As long as these measures get back on track the following year, you can evaluate the company as you would normally. But, what

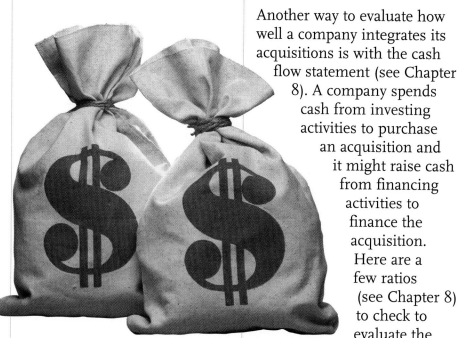

Another way to evaluate how well a company integrates its acquisitions is with the cash flow statement (see Chapter 8). A company spends cash from investing activities to purchase an acquisition and it might raise cash from financing activities to finance the acquisition. Here are a few ratios (see Chapter 8) to check to evaluate the success of company acquisitions:

- **Cash from operating activities**—Ultimately, the acquisition should generate enough cash from operating activities to make everything worthwhile, so look for increasing cash from operating activities.

- **Cash from operating activities and EPS growth**—Look for cash from operating activities growing at a similar or higher rate than EPS. Otherwise, the company is obtaining more cash from financing or investing, which could mean the business isn't sustainable.

- **Return on invested capital**—If a company uses debt and/or equity (new shares of stock) to finance

about companies that make numerous acquisitions every year? If you use normalized data such as Value Line, read the notes at the bottom of the stock page to see if acquisition costs are removed. If so, the EPS performance probably looks better than it really is. NAIC's Online Premium Services data doesn't remove acquisition costs. If the pre-tax profit margin and EPS graphs look good in Section 1 using OPS data, the company makes its acquisitions a profitable part of the business.

acquisitions, look for stable or steadily increasing return on invested capital (ROIC), which shows that the acquisitions are good investments of capital.

If you own a small company that is going to be acquired by a much larger company, you might end up with a very small number of shares in the new endeavor. You should evaluate the percentage that the new holding will represent in your total portfolio. If you are comfortable with the new holding's growth prospects and value, you might choose to purchase additional shares to increase the size of the holding in your portfolio. If you feel that the new holding will be too insignificant a percentage and offers too little in value and growth, you can sell your shares before or after the merger. If your current shares have appreciated in price, be sure to evaluate the capital gains you might owe before making your decision.

Mergers: Be Careful When Elephants Dance

Since the Financial Accounting Standards Board (FASB) eliminated the pooling of interest method, every merger of two companies represents one company purchasing another. Whether you own the company being acquired or the one doing the acquiring, after the merger you might own shares in a combination of the two companies. Companies merge for any number of reasons, many of which don't benefit you the shareholder. To determine whether you should hold onto your shares or sell, you must analyze the two companies as well as the results of their merger.

When two strong companies merge, the results are usually good. If one company is strong and well-managed and the other is poorly-managed, the result might depend on the relative size of the two partners. When the larger partner is strong, the acquisition could work to your advantage as the acquired operations improve their performance. If the larger partner is the weak link, the chances of the merger being successful for the smaller company's shareholders are slim.

Success Tip!

Merging a weaker company into a stronger one is a risky endeavor. Management might turn the operation around, but then again, the weak link might be beyond repair. To be safe, see if the larger partner has a history of successfully integrating smaller, less-efficient operations.

Review the SSG of the Acquiring Company

If you bought a company's stock based on the NAIC methodology and it's being purchased by another company, prepare an SSG on the proposed acquirer to determine what type of company it is and whether it meets your requirements. If the proposed partner is cyclical, slow growing, or generates poor profit margins and ROE, consider selling your shares.

If your initial analysis indicates that the acquiring company is attractive, you can wait several weeks (or sometimes months) to see pro forma financial statements issued to shareholders. Pro forma statements combine the two entities with some complex accounting treatment. Other alternatives include requesting a recent stock report from your full service broker, or purchasing a report for a fee on the merger from the many on-line investment research firms available.

Share Price and Tax Considerations

When a merger is announced, the stock price of the purchaser usually drops because the costs of the acquisition decrease earnings for a short time. The stock price for the company being acquired usually goes up, because the shareholders in that company would not accept an offer that decreased the share price.

Acquiring companies often use stock to buy an acquisition if the PE ratio for their stock is high. A high PE means that shares of stock are much cheaper than paying cash or assuming debt to finance the acquisition.

When a company that you own is acquired, the transaction doesn't trigger a tax event if the transaction is a stock for stock deal. Your cost basis in your original stock is the cost basis in the stock of the merger. For example, if your original cost basis in company A was $1,000, the cost basis for merged company B would still be $1,000. If the new shares don't divide evenly into the old shares, you might receive cash as payment for a fractional share. You must treat this as a sale of that fractional share.

Tender Offers

When a company or individual wants to acquire a part or even an entire company, he makes a tender offer for your shares. You should evaluate the offer before you decide to deliver your shares in exchange for the compensation described in the tender offer. Sometimes, a tender offer is a better deal for the company or individual making the offer than it is for you, a current shareholder.

Tender offers can comprise cash, cash and stock, or some combination of cash, stock, preferred stock, debt, and other items. If a tender offer includes stock, prepare an SSG for the company making the offer. If you have no interest in owning that company, sell your shares. If a tender offer pays for only some of your shares, decide whether the remaining shares are worth keeping. For example, if accepting a tender offer leaves you with shares that represent a minute fraction of your portfolio, it's better to sell all your shares.

Spin-offs

Just as you might sell a stock that no longer fits your requirements, company management or the board of directors might decide that a business unit or division no longer fits the company strategy. There's no guarantee that a spin-off will be a worthwhile investment. A division freed from the bureaucracy of a parent company might blossom and deliver far better than its former parent. Or, it could stumble trying to make it on its own.

In many cases, management decides to spin off a company for reasons that will make you want to spin those shares off from your portfolio. With a spin-off, consider the reasons management provides. Go back and read the annual reports from previous years for information about the segment being spun off. For example, General Motors is by no means a growth powerhouse: its historical sales growth is a meager 2 percent and its historical EPS growth tends to stay in the negative numbers. In 1998, GM spun-off Delphi Corporation, a division that sold auto parts. Since the spin-off, Delphi has outdone its parent in underperformance with an average annual sales "growth" of negative 1 percent and an average EPS growth rate of negative 13 percent.

Success Tip!

Spin-offs frequently deliver a very small number of shares in the new company, which could represent a fraction of a percent in your portfolio. Why spend time studying a company whose shares won't affect your portfolio performance in any meaningful way? Unless you want to purchase more shares of the spin-off, it's better to sell these shares.

Initial Public Offerings and Start-ups: Investing or Gambling?

Companies conduct initial public offerings (IPOs) to raise equity capital. Although most IPOs provide financing for start-up companies, some IPOs raise money for major expansions to an existing business. IPOs for start-up companies fall into the high-risk, high-reward category. Sure, you might get in on the ground floor of the next Microsoft, but you're more likely to end up with stock certificates for papering your powder room. Start-up companies have no earnings—that's why they often use IPOs to raise money. And without earnings, the stock price is purely speculation.

Read the Prospectus

The SEC requires a company to distribute a prospectus describing the IPO, so that investors can make an informed decision. A prospectus includes a description of the business plan, past financial performance of the organization, and the risks involved in the IPO.

If you consider investing in an IPO, first read the prospectus carefully. Make sure the business plan makes sense. Is there a market for the products or services the company offers?

THE DOT-COM FRENZY

In the late 1990s, plenty of technology companies took advantage of investors' irrational exuberance to finance their ideas. Unfortunately, many of these companies had only that—ideas. NAIC investors know that earnings growth is the basis for stock price appreciation. But, other investors with more greed than sense paid good money for dot-com stories. When earnings did not materialize, the stock prices collapsed costing these investors a lot of money.

Do you think the company is likely to make money? How long before the company turns a profit? What will the company use the IPO capital for? If the business or the business plan confuses you, stop right here. Look for management with a successful track record. If the IPO is for a start-up, has management nurtured successful start-ups in the past?

Pricing IPOs and Start-ups

Company management or the investment bankers they work with want to retain as much ownership as they can, while raising the capital the company needs. To sell the least number of shares, management tries to get the best price for each IPO share that it can. For start-ups, IPOs come out when the stock market is upbeat. For existing businesses, IPOs are offered when company profits look good and the stock market is healthy.

Review an IPO prospectus to see if the company generates any earnings. If it does, you can evaluate the deal by calculating a PE ratio based on the most recent earnings and the IPO price. If a start-up has no earnings, you can't use the PE ratio to determine a reasonable buy price. In these situations, consider the price to sales ratio

USING THE PRICE TO SALES RATIO

The Price to Sales Ratio is the price of a share divided by the sales per share. Most data sources don't provide sales per share, but you can calculate it by dividing the company's sales for the most recent four quarters by the number of outstanding shares at the end of the last quarter.

You can use the Price to Sales Ratio in similar ways to the PE ratio. For example, you can compare a company's Price to Sales ratio to the Price to Sales ratio of the corresponding industry. Or you can compare a company's current Price to Sales ratio to its historical trends.

On MSN Money (http://money.msn.com) stock pages, you can click the Financial Results link and then the Key Ratios link to find price ratios. For example, the Price to Sales ratio for the S&P 500 is approximately 1.5. But the biotech industry Price to Sales ratio is almost 10.

as a substitute—assuming you really want to risk investing in a company with no earnings. Because sales are the source of earnings, the sales per share can act as a stand-in for EPS,

albeit a riskier one, during the early years.

Can You Make Money with Cyclical Stocks?

The profits for cyclical stocks fluctuate with the health of the economy or the prices of raw materials. For example, auto manufacturers are cyclical because people shy away from buying new cars when times are bad and reward themselves with new cars when times are good. Commodity industries such as steel, oil, and metal also fall into the cyclical category based on the fluctuation in commodity prices.

EPS in cyclical companies generally don't show a steady, upward trend, so you can't use the standard approach to an SSG to forecast future price. To try to make money investing in a cyclical stock, you buy the stock when times are bad and sell when times are good. For cyclical stocks dependent on the economy, such as a car maker, you buy when the economy is bleak (ideally when it's the bleakest, but that's market timing) and then sell when the economy is strong. When the economy is bad, earnings are low, which pushes the PE ratio higher. When the economy is good, earnings are high, which brings the PE ratio down. For cyclical stocks, desirable PE ratios are the exact opposite of what you look for in growth stocks.

The investment timeframe for cyclical stocks is at most half of the business cycle—from the lowest point of the economy to the highest. Since you can't predict when these will occur, your timeframe is much shorter, perhaps only a year or less, which could mean your gains are taxed at the ordinary rate instead of at the capital gains rate. Using a super-discount broker and a tax-advantaged account gives you a fighting chance. Yes, you can make money from cyclical stocks, but it's risky, costly, and requires far more work than investing in growth stocks.

Making the Most of Fixed-Income Investments

No matter what stage of life you're in, fixed-income investments could play a role in your portfolio. Fixed-income investments pay lower returns than stocks over the long-term and, used correctly, offer less risk than stocks. The key is to purchase fixed-income investments for the right reason, allocate the right amount of your portfolio to them, and invest in them so you receive the return and risk you want. Chapter 2 talks about why you should purchase fixed-income investments and provides some ideas about how much you should invest in them. But, after you've decided that fixed-income investments belong in your portfolio, the following sections can help you earn the return you want with the risk you expect.

Analyzing Annuities

Many investors hear pitches for annuities and buy them because of their tax deferral characteristics. By understanding how an annuity works and what to look for, you can decide whether an annuity is right for you and whether the annuity you're looking at is a good investment.

When you purchase an annuity, you give a lump sum to an insurance company, who in return pays you an amount on a regular schedule, typically for the remainder of your life.

Insurance actuaries use statistics to calculate your life expectancy based on how long large populations with similar characteristics have lived. The insurance company then invests in fixed-income securities to produce the money it needs to meet its contractual annuity payments. This sounds like a no-muss, no-fuss way to receive income without spending time buying and managing a portfolio of stocks and bonds. It is, but the convenience comes with a price:

- **Commercial annuities are tax-deferred, not tax-deductible.** Some annuities are tax-deductible, but most are only tax-deferred. The lump sum you contribute is paid with after-tax dollars. Your money compounds tax-deferred within the annuity and you pay taxes on the payments you receive.

- **The return isn't guaranteed over the long term.** Insurance companies usually advertise an attractive annual return, but this rate is only guaranteed for a specific period of time, sometimes as little as one year. Then, the insurance company can change the annual rate as often as they want. They make payments to you based loosely on the return they earn on that money. To determine what kind of

rate changes you might be in for, ask the salesperson for a report of the annuity's historical interest-rates. If the salesperson won't provide the report, don't invest in the annuity. Also, ask what rates new buyers received compared to the rates paid for renewals to existing customers after the rate guarantee ran out. New buyers shouldn't receive more than 1 percent higher rates than a renewing customer when interest rates have remained the same.

- **You're paying for life insurance on the owner of the annuity.** Not all of the money the insurance company earns comes back to you in your regular payments. Part of the investment returns pay for life insurance to guarantee that the beneficiaries receive the nominal value of the original lump sum.

- **You're paying a commission to the salesperson.** Part of the original lump sum goes to paying the salesperson's commission. Between life insurance that you might not need and a salesperson's commission, you can probably get a better return investing the money elsewhere.

- **You pay a penalty to leave early.** Annuities carry a surrender charge that you must pay to cancel the annuity contract. Typical surrender charges are 7 percent declining one percentage point a year, but some charges can last for decades. If you purchase an annuity and then realize that the returns are sub-par, you have to pay even more to get your money out so you can put it in a better investment. Read the contract and compare the surrender charge to the industry average. Don't accept an above-average surrender charge and do not accept a contract that lowers your interest rate from your sign-up date if you leave early.

If you do purchase an annuity, stick to a fixed interest rate annuity (even though the interest rate really isn't fixed). Variable annuities provide payments based on stock investments. In some cases, you can choose the investments; for others, the insurance company manages the money. Either way, insurance companies charge high fees for this type of annuity, which means you're usually better off purchasing mutual funds or stocks on your own.

Success Tip!

Do not buy an annuity in a tax deferred account. All you do is pay extra fees and potential penalties for a benefit provided by the investment account itself.

Laddering Fixed-Income Investments

Fixed-income investments such as bonds and certificates of deposit are often a balance between interest rates and accessibility. You earn a higher interest rate for a longer-term bond or CD, but then your money is tied up. With certificates of deposit, you pay a penalty for early withdrawal. With bonds, the bond coupon rate is fixed until maturity (and the bond doesn't default.) If you want higher interest rates AND access to your money more frequently, a strategy called laddering lets you have your cake and eat it too.

You build a fixed-income ladder by placing money in fixed-income investments that mature at regular intervals. For example, if you have $100,000 for the next five years expenses, you can invest $20,000 into a CD or bond that matures each year for the next five years. Once a year, you can withdraw the money in the investment that matured or roll it into a new investment. If you keep the

principal in your fixed-income investments, your ladder eventually comprises five, five-year CDs or bonds.

A ladder also helps you manage interest rate risk. Even if interest rates change, the ladder averages out those changes so you receive a steadier flow of income whether current rates are high or low. You can adjust your ladder to take advantage of interest rate trends. When rates are low, reinvest maturing investments in shorter-term CDs or bonds. As rates move higher, you reinvest at higher rates. When rates are high, reinvest in longer-term investments to lock in the higher rates for longer periods.

If you need money every month, stick with an annual ladder to keep the number of CDs or bonds manageable. Then, withdraw money when an investment matures and place the proceeds in a money market or savings account for easy access until the next maturity date.

Keeping Records

The Right Tool for the Job

Investments don't come in shoe boxes, so why do people store their investment information in them? With the IRS such a stickler for documentation, you don't need the additional stress of trying to find the paperwork that proves your deductions during an audit.

Keeping track of buys, sells, dividends, spin-offs, and other types of transactions can be a struggle.

For example, when you keep records of purchases by hand and a stock splits, you must adjust the records for every purchase to reflect that split. Knowing what's important keeps your work to a minimum. But, computer-assisted record keeping can reduce the pain of the job and help you determine both how your portfolio is doing and how you could do better.

What's Important?

Tracking Investment Information

Record Keeping Tools

Record Keeping and the Investment Club

Understanding Performance Measures

What's Important

Your financial well-being goes beyond your investments, so the first order of business is to make sure that you not only keep ALL your necessary financial papers, but that you store them in the right place. You should organize your papers so that everything is easy to find; you'll appreciate being able to locate what you need when you need it—and your heirs will appreciate it as well.

Legal Papers

You must store legal papers such as your will in the right place or they won't be available when they are needed.

- **Will**—Leave your will with your lawyer or store it somewhere else that is safe yet accessible, such as a fireproof safe in your house

or a safety deposit box. If your safety deposit box can't be opened immediately upon your death, give the will to your executor or a family member other than your spouse for storage in their safety deposit box. Regardless, make sure that your executor knows where the will is.

- **Living will**—If you use a living will, store one copy in your fireproof safe and provide copies to the people who will follow the

instructions you outlined in the living will.

- **Power of attorney**—Store your power of attorney in a fireproof safe in your house. Better yet, give it to the person assigned power of attorney for storage in his or her safety deposit box. They will know where it is and have access to it when it's needed.

- **Life insurance policy**— Because your life insurance policy becomes important

Preparing a household inventory is well worth your time. Otherwise, you must document your possessions from memory and no one remembers everything they own. To simplify the job, don't write things down—take pictures of everything, including the contents of every drawer, closet, and storage receptacle in your home or elsewhere. Digital cameras make it easy to store the pictures to a CD for safe storage.

Financial Papers

Taxes are one of many reasons to keep financial papers, but financial documentation comes in handy as proof to creditors, ex-spouses, or for insurance claims. At the very least, you should keep records long enough to reconcile your accounts so you can correct any mistakes. Most of these papers can stay in your filing cabinet, which is good because they would quickly fill even the largest fireproof safe or safety deposit box. However, the ones that should go into a fireproof safe or safety deposit box are identified as such in the following list.

- **Proof of ownership—** Keep deeds, titles, proofs of ownerships, and descriptions of the property you own in your fireproof safe or safety deposit box.

when you die, you should store your policy in your safety deposit box only if your beneficiary can access it immediately upon your death. Otherwise, store it in your fireproof safe. If you sign up for any other type of life insurance, such as mortgage-life insurance or life insurance obtained by purchasing travel with a credit card, keep records of this coverage with your regular life insurance policies.

Personal Papers

You can be as fussy as you want with your personal papers. Store personal sapers

in a fireproof safe or in your safety deposit box. These records include your birth certificate, social security card, marriage certificate, divorce papers, adoption papers, passports (even old ones), military service records, and other documents relating to the major events in your life. Keeping records of health care such as vaccinations and operations can come in handy as well. Store copies of all your insurance policies (health, disability, homeowners', auto) in your filing cabinet, but keep additional copies in your safe or safety deposit box.

- **Tax records**—Store tax returns along with supporting documentation for the last six years. (If the IRS comes after you for fraud, there is no statute of limitations.) In addition, retain any tax returns that show capital gains that you carry forward on your house, which you need when you sell. Retain tax returns showing non-tax-deductible contributions to IRA accounts.

- **Bank records**—A few years of bank statements and canceled checks can come in handy to track down vendors or create a budget. Otherwise, you can eliminate older statements. The important tax-related documentation such as interest paid or received should go with your tax records.

- **Credit card statements**—Two or three years of credit card statements help track down vendors or resolve erroneous charges.

- **Loan records**—Store the records for current loans and mortgages in your filing cabinet. Store proof of paid-off loans and notes for money owed to you in your fire-proof safe or safety deposit box.

- **Receipts**—Retain receipts for high-value items that might trigger a query from your insurance company for your claim.

Success Tip!

When you decide to throw out old financial records, it's a good idea to shred them before putting them out with the rest of your trash. Otherwise, identity thieves could piece together enough information to obtain access to your accounts or open new accounts in your name.

Calculating Your Net Worth

Similar to the shareholders' equity in a company, your net worth is what's left over after you subtract liabilities from your assets. To keep tabs on how you're doing overall, calculate your net worth once a year. If you use software such as *Quicken* and store information about all your assets and liabilities in its database, you can check your net worth any time you want.

To calculate net worth, you need to know how much you have in assets and liabilities. **Assets** include the following:

- Cash in checking, savings, and money market accounts and funds

- Market value of investments including stocks, bonds, mutual funds, and ownership in an investment club

- Cash value of insurance policies

- Market value of easily sellable personal property such as jewelry and cars

- Vested value of retirement benefits and current value of retirement accounts

- Market value of your home and other real estate

- Market value of other personal property such as antiques, art, or boats

- Market value of a private company you own

Liabilities include all the money you owe:

- Current bills

- Credit card debt

- Auto and other loans

- Life insurance loans

- Mortgage balance and home equity loans

  - Student loans

    - Margin loans

For example, if your total assets add up to $1,257,500 and your liabilities are $334,800, your net worth is:

Net worth = $1,257,500 − $334,800 = $922,700

Investment Information

Some investment information is reference material, which comes in handy when you want to find out how to redeem mutual fund shares

or evaluate the accuracy of management performance predictions. Other investment information is essential not only for tax purposes but for tracking your portfolio performance and making decisions about changes to your portfolio.

Reference Material

Keep the reference material that you receive from mutual funds or brokerage accounts in your filing cabinet. This includes investment account agreements, mutual fund prospectuses, and letters with rule changes. In addition, take notes when you speak to your broker or investment account representative and store those with your account information. Develop a habit of putting your instructions in writing. If you have a problem with the broker's handling of your account, your records support your case.

Investment Certificates

Store stock certificates in your safe or safety deposit box, or store them in "street name" with your broker for convenience. Otherwise, keep a list of the certificate numbers, CUSIP numbers, and what securities those numbers represent in your safe or safety deposit box.

Investment Records

Whether your records are for tax returns or portfolio management, the information you need to know is similar:

- **Cost basis**—How much your investment cost to purchase. This can change due to mergers, acquisitions, and spin-offs. If you use average cost for taxes, the cost basis per share changes due to stock splits, multiple purchases, or purchases via reinvested dividends.

- **Interest and dividends**—The interest and dividends paid by your investments. In addition to paying taxes on these if you hold investments in taxable accounts, the income you earn contributes to the total return on your investment.

- **Capital gains or losses**—The amount of money you gained or lost from an investment you sold. Mutual funds distribute to shareholders the capital gains from the sales of investments within the fund portfolio, but retain capital losses to offset future gains.

Success Tip!

Unrealized capital gains and losses are the gains and losses in your investments based on their current value. You can use these values to decide whether to buy or sell investments to reduce your tax bill.

- **Expenses**—Commissions and fees that you pay to buy and sell investments, which you can deduct when calculating your capital gains and losses.

- **Current value**—The current value of investments you still own, which is used to calculate the total return you have earned so far on an investment. The value of your investments also determines your portfolio diversification.

To keep track of this information, keep the following transaction records:

- **Trade confirmations**—To calculate capital gains for your tax return, you must know the security you bought or sold, the price you paid or received, the commission you paid both to buy and to sell, any additional fees, and when the transactions occurred.

- **Monthly statements and annual statements**—Use the monthly statement to reconcile your account. If the annual statement summarizes your transactions, you can then throw out the monthly statements.

cash, *NAIC Portfolio Record Keeper (PRK),* developed by Quant IX Software, not only organizes and tracks all your investment transactions, but also helps you analyze tax and diversification issues before you buy or sell. *PRK* can also track investments in both your individual and investment club accounts.

Quicken, Microsoft Money, *and other personal finance software applications track portfolio transactions, produce investment and tax-related reports, and integrate with tax preparation software. But, these applications fall short on portfolio management features— particularly when you use the NAIC methodology to gauge potential performance.*

In addition to speeding up your tracking efforts, using *PRK* removes some of the burden of knowledge from your shoulders. For example, *PRK* provides forms for entering pertinent transaction information for purchases and sales, dividends and interest, dividend reinvestments, investment expenses, stock splits (which apply to shares you own in more than one portfolio), spin-offs and mergers, tenders and exchanges, returns of capital, and security transfers. Similarly, you can track lot assignments if you use first-in first-out, last-in last-out, average cost, or specific identification of share lots to manage your tax bill.

- **Reinvestment statements—** If you receive reinvestment statements from a mutual fund or dividend reinvestment program, retain these to track your cost basis per share.

- **Reorganization data—** When one company spins off another, you end up with stock in the original company plus shares in the new one. Keep the information that the original company provides about how to allocate acquisition or purchase costs to the two stocks. Likewise, retain records of mergers and acquisitions. When a company acquires a company that you own, you retain the cost basis of your shares as the cost of the merged companies.

Record Keeping Tools

Between the complexities of some potential investment transactions and the added intricacies of tax ramifications, record keeping isn't for the faint of heart. Keeping your papers organized so you can find them easily is only the beginning. Knowing what to do with the information is another matter. If you invest in a variety of investments, including stocks, bonds, mutual funds, options, and

Predefined reports simplify collecting information for taxes or portfolio management. For taxes, you can create reports of realized gains or losses, income received, capital gains distributions, and other tax-related information. To analyze your portfolio, you can produce reports of portfolio diversification by investment, company size, type of asset, and more. *PRK* tracks categories for stocks and mutual funds, so you can see the diversification of your entire portfolio. Performance reports help you decide which investments to focus on. When you hold investments in taxable accounts, unrealized gain and loss reports help you decide whether you can reduce your tax bill by choosing specific investments to sell. In addition, you can create customized reports to suit your requirements. For example, you can combine the holdings from multiple portfolios in a single report to evaluate your retirement investments even though they reside in multiple retirement accounts.

PRK Version 4 integrates with NAIC's Online Premium Services, which means you can quickly add or update stocks to your portfolios. For example, you can import measures such as price, earnings per share,

projected earnings per share, projected earnings growth rate, dividends per share, book value per share, cash flow per share, beta, rating, industry, sector, and company size. Then, you can view performance and ratios calculated with these measures, such as the price to book value per share or price to free cash flow per share.

PRK can import data and prices from other NAIC analysis applications, prices from the Internet, and past investment transactions from Quicken.

When you use a ready-made application such as *PRK,* you usually get other helpful features that you would never put together on your own. The Home Page shown in Figure 16-01 summarizes the information for a portfolio. For example, *PRK* also provides price alerts, a calendar for recording important dates, and a diary for logging activities or to-dos.

Record Keeping and the Investment Club

Investment clubs are much like mutual funds. Multiple members pool their money and share in the performance of the portfolio. In addition to keeping records for taxes and portfolio management, investment clubs must track contributions, payouts, and ownership for each member in the club. Because of this,

investment clubs must perform additional calculations and produce a few more reports than the individual investor. This section introduces some of the record keeping requirements for investment clubs.

Success Tip!

To learn more about the ins and outs of club accounting, order the Accounting Manual from NAIC or purchase NAIC's Club Accounting software. For more specific information, search the NAIC Web site for articles about club accounting or attend a club

accounting class offered by a local NAIC chapter.

Tracking Club Valuation and Unit Value

Mutual funds track ownership by selling shares to investors. The value of a share is called the net asset value and is calculated by dividing the total value of the portfolio (minus

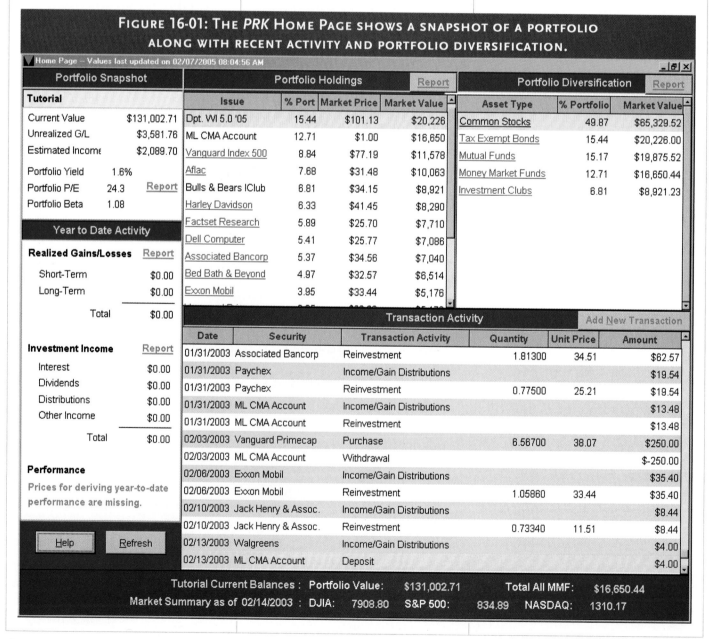

FIGURE 16-01: THE *PRK* HOME PAGE SHOWS A SNAPSHOT OF A PORTFOLIO ALONG WITH RECENT ACTIVITY AND PORTFOLIO DIVERSIFICATION.

Home Page -- Values last updated on 02/07/2005 08:04:56 AM

Portfolio Snapshot

Tutorial

Current Value	$131,002.71
Unrealized G/L	$3,581.76
Estimated Income	$2,089.70
Portfolio Yield	1.6%
Portfolio P/E	24.3 Report
Portfolio Beta	1.08

Year to Date Activity

Realized Gains/Losses Report

Short-Term	$0.00
Long-Term	$0.00
Total	$0.00

Investment Income Report

Interest	$0.00
Dividends	$0.00
Distributions	$0.00
Other Income	$0.00
Total	$0.00

Performance

Prices for deriving year-to-date performance are missing.

Help   Refresh

Portfolio Holdings   Report

Issue	% Port	Market Price	Market Value
Dpt. WI 5.0 '05	15.44	$101.13	$20,226
ML CMA Account	12.71	$1.00	$16,650
Vanguard Index 500	8.84	$77.19	$11,578
Aflac	7.68	$31.48	$10,063
Bulls & Bears IClub	6.81	$34.15	$8,921
Harley Davidson	6.33	$41.45	$8,290
Factset Research	5.89	$25.70	$7,710
Dell Computer	5.41	$25.77	$7,086
Associated Bancorp	5.37	$34.56	$7,040
Bed Bath & Beyond	4.97	$32.57	$6,514
Exxon Mobil	3.95	$33.44	$5,176

Portfolio Diversification   Report

Asset Type	% Portfolio	Market Value
Common Stocks	49.87	$65,329.52
Tax Exempt Bonds	15.44	$20,226.00
Mutual Funds	15.17	$19,875.52
Money Market Funds	12.71	$16,650.44
Investment Clubs	6.81	$8,921.23

Transaction Activity   Add New Transaction

Date	Security	Transaction Activity	Quantity	Unit Price	Amount
01/31/2003	Associated Bancorp	Reinvestment	1.81300	34.51	$62.57
01/31/2003	Paychex	Income/Gain Distributions			$19.54
01/31/2003	Paychex	Reinvestment	0.77500	25.21	$19.54
01/31/2003	ML CMA Account	Income/Gain Distributions			$13.48
01/31/2003	ML CMA Account	Reinvestment			$13.48
02/03/2003	Vanguard Primecap	Purchase	6.56700	38.07	$250.00
02/03/2003	ML CMA Account	Withdrawal			$-250.00
02/06/2003	Exxon Mobil	Income/Gain Distributions			$35.40
02/06/2003	Exxon Mobil	Reinvestment	1.05860	33.44	$35.40
02/10/2003	Jack Henry & Assoc.	Income/Gain Distributions			$8.44
02/10/2003	Jack Henry & Assoc.	Reinvestment	0.73340	11.51	$8.44
02/13/2003	Walgreens	Income/Gain Distributions			$4.00
02/13/2003	ML CMA Account	Deposit			$4.00

Tutorial Current Balances : Portfolio Value: $131,002.71   Total All MMF: $16,650.44

Market Summary as of 02/14/2003 : DJIA: 7908.80   S&P 500: 834.89   NASDAQ: 1310.17

FIGURE 16-02: THE VALUATION STATEMENT SHOWS THE TOTAL VALUE AND UNIT VALUE IN A CLUB.

Valuation Statement as of 12/31/04

Security	Ticker, DRP	First Buy or Valuation Date	Shares Owned This Date	Cost Per Share	Total Cost	Price Per Share This Valuation	Total Value This Valuation	% of Total	Tot Ret SINCE	CA Ret 12/28/89
American Intl Group Inc	AIG	06/24/04	30.000000	72.8450	2185.35	65.6700	1970.10	1.58	−9.65%	−17.72%
American Power Conversion	APCC	08/21/00	100.000000	24.1745	2417.45	21.4000	2140.00	1.72	−9.68%	−2.31%
Amgen Incorporated	AMGN	10/28/04	70.000000	56.5250	3956.75	64.1500	4490.50	3.61	13.49%	105.89%
Applebee's Intl	APPB	11/19/97	337.000000	6.4896	2187.00	26.4500	8913.65	7.17	315.48%	22.16%
Bed Bath and Beyond	BBBY	03/27/00	260.000000	18.8794	4908.65	39.8300	10355.80	8.33	122.64%	18.29%
Bright Horizon Family Sltns	BFAM	12/17/03	50.000000	39.6590	1982.95	64.7600	3238.00	2.60	63.29%	60.21%
Cheesecake Factory	CAKE	05/22/03	120.000000	21.6413	2596.95	32.4700	3896.40	3.13	50.04%	28.61%
Cobiz Inc.	COBZ	05/22/00	450.000000	7.5742	3408.40	20.3000	9135.00	7.34	245.90%	30.89%
Doral Financial	DRL	02/26/04	70.000000	34.0207	2381.45	49.2500	3447.50	2.77	46.23%	56.70%
Ethan Allen Interiors	ETH	05/16/01	80.000000	36.5344	2922.75	40.0200	3201.60	2.57	21.02%	5.40%
Fiserv, Inc.	FISV	03/25/04	100.000000	36.7245	3672.45	40.1900	4019.00	3.23	9.44%	12.44%
Harley Davidson, Inc	HDI	12/23/04	75.000000	60.7460	4555.95	60.7500	4556.25	3.66	0.01%	0.30%
Home Depot	HD	03/19/97	230.000000	17.3367	3987.45	42.7400	9830.20	7.90	232.82%	16.70%
Johnson Johnson	JNJ	04/28/93	120.000000	27.8668	3344.02	63.4200	7610.40	6.12	1106.15%	23.77%
Lincare Holdings	LNCR	04/25/00	300.000000	18.9863	5695.90	42.6500	12795.00	10.29	203.09%	26.71%
Medtronic Inc	MDT	08/26/04	50.000000	51.8290	2591.45	49.6700	2483.50	2.00	−4.01%	−11.10%
NBTY, Inc	NBTY	11/18/98	500.000000	10.8562	5428.08	24.0100	12005.00	9.65	219.05%	20.88%
O'Reilly Automotive Inc	ORLY	08/06/04	75.000000	37.7060	2827.95	45.0500	3378.75	2.72	19.48%	55.61%
Pfizer	PFE	10/16/02	100.000000	31.1150	3111.50	26.8900	2689.00	2.16	−17.03%	−8.10%
Roper Industries, Inc.	ROP	08/19/98	140.000000	26.0354	3644.95	60.7700	8507.80	6.84	202.55%	18.99%
Sysco	SYY	07/17/03	65.000000	29.9869	1949.15	38.1700	2481.05	1.99	29.19%	19.18%
Walgreen Company	WAG	08/26/04	50.000000	37.1990	1859.95	38.3700	1918.50	1.54	3.29%	9.76%

Total this date — 71616.50 — 123063.00 — 98.92 — 796.86% — 20.67%

Security returns from Start or Switchover to this Date — 1215.83% — 19.18%

Cash in Bank	738.21	738.21	0.59
Cash in Broker	585.99	585.99	0.47
Cash in Suspense	0.00	0.00	0.00
Cash in WD Liability Account	0.00	0.00	0.00
Total Cash Accounts this Date	1324.20	1324.20	1.06
Total Securities and Cash Accounts this Date	72940.70	124387.20	100.0
Total number of Valuation Units to Date		2388.287691	
Value of Each Unit This Date		52.08	
Number of Units Each $24.41 will Purchase		0.468683	

Print date: 01/19/05

expenses) by the number of shares owned by shareholders. For investment clubs, the unit value performs the same duty.

The Valuation Statement, shown in Figure 16-02, is a report that shows the performance of each stock in a portfolio, the performance of the club portfolio as a whole, as well as the calculation for the unit value of an investment club.

The formula for unit value is as follows:

Unit value = Total portfolio value / Total number of valuation units

The total portfolio value is the sum of the value of all the securities in the club portfolio and the cash accounts for the club. The total number of valuation units comes from the Members Status Report, which is described in the next section. For example, if a portfolio is worth $124,387.2 and members own 2388.29 valuation units, the new unit value is:

Unit value = $124,387.2 / 2388.29 = $52.08

Typically, the Valuation Statement shows the number of units that $10.00 will purchase, so that the club treasurer can calculate the new units bought with each member's subsequent club contribution. For the club used in the unit value example, the number of units purchased with $10.00 is:

Number of units = $10 / $29.811 = 0.33544

Tracking Member Status

Keeping track of a member's ownership in the club means tracking the money that the member contributed as well as the money the member withdraws. The Member Status Report shows each member's participation in the investment club over a period a time. The report shows the amount of money contributed, the value of contributions plus earnings, the number of units owned, and the current value of those units.

In addition, this report shows the return earned by each member. A member's return can differ significantly from the return of the club as a whole, depending on when the member began contributing and how much he or she paid in on any given date. For example, a club could have an average annual compound return of 18 percent, while a member who began contributing during the bear market of 2000-2001 might show an average annual compound return of 2 percent. Two members beginning at the same time that put in the same amount of money (but contributed different amounts each month) will also see different compounded returns.

When Club Members Leave

When a member in an investment club resigns, requests a partial withdrawal of his account value, or passes away, the club can pay the member in cash or stock (depending on the terms of the partnership agreement). Each option has its advantages when used in the proper circumstances. The IRS never makes anything easy. The tax rules differ depending on whether a member withdraws part or all of their money. The NAIC Accounting Manual describes these rules and the recommended strategies in detail. The Member Withdrawal Report documents how the member is paid. Here's a basic guide to the best methods for distributing club dollars.

- **Stocks in the club portfolio that have increased significantly in value.** Transferring stock to a departing or withdrawing member has several advantages. First, by transferring stock that has appreciated in value to that member, the remaining members are not responsible for taxes on the capital gains on the value transferred. Second, the departing club member defers paying taxes on the capital gains of the appreciated stock until he decides to sell the stock. Third, the club can use the transfer of stock to reduce an overallocation in one or more stocks.

Success Tip!

Make the most of stock transfers by transferring the shares with the largest gains.

- **Stocks in the club portfolio that have lost value and the club wants to sell them.** Sell the stock and pay the member with the cash from the sale. The members in the club can use the loss from the sale to offset any realized capital gains.

- **The club portfolio diversification needs rebalancing.** Identify the stocks that comprise too much of the portfolio and use a stock transfer to pay the departing member and rebalance the portfolio at the same time. Suppose the departing member wants to withdraw $10,000 and 1,000 shares of Bed Bath and Beyond, which represents approximately 20 percent of the $200,000 club portfolio. If Bed Bath and Beyond is selling for $35 a share, the club could transfer 285 shares to the departing member and at the same time reduce the percentage of Bed Bath and Beyond to a less risky 12.5 percent of the portfolio (715 shares * $35 = $25,025).

Tracking Income

Investment club members must pay taxes on the income they receive from their investment club, just as they pay taxes on income for investments in their individual accounts. However, an investment club allocates the income to its members based on the number of units they own, so it must calculate the earnings per unit.

Earnings per unit = Total earnings / Number of units

The Distribution of Earnings Report shows the total values for different types of income, such as dividends, interest, capital gains, and expenses. It also shows how much of the earnings are allocated to each member.

Understanding Performance Measures

Comparing your portfolio return to your target is a snap—either the compound annual total return for your portfolio met or exceeded your target or it didn't. Because returns can vary depending on the economy and other external factors, many investors want to compare their portfolios to a benchmark and this requires

some care to achieve meaningful results. The total return you see in NAIC analysis software and *PRK* uses a calculation know as the internal rate of return, which takes into account the cash flows into and out of your portfolio to determine the compound average annual return. If you calculate return on your own and the cash flows for your portfolio are significantly different than the benchmark you use, then a comparison between your portfolio return and the benchmark won't tell you anything. Internal rate of return can get complicated, but here is a quick introduction to comparing apples to apples.

If the math in the following sections is more than you want to deal with, don't force yourself to work through the calculations. The performance report in Portfolio Record Keeper *calculates portfolio return as does* NAIC Club Accounting *software.*

One Initial Contribution

Suppose you rolled over a 401(k) plan into an IRA account and made no additional contributions. Your IRA account has one initial contribution and retains any earnings distributions in the account, reinvested in additional shares or kept in cash. Because index performance is typically based on an initial $10,000 contribution with earnings reinvested, you can compare your portfolio return with the return for a benchmark because the contribution and reinvestments are performed in a similar fashion. With the initial and ending value of your portfolio, you can calculate the average annual return for your portfolio using the following formula:

Compound average annual return in percent =

((Ending value / Initial value) ∧ (1 / # of periods) − 1) * 100

((48,000 / 20,000) ∧ (1/5) = 1.191358

(1.191358 − 1) * 100 = 19.1358 percent

Success Tip!

The ∧ in the formula represents raising the value ratio to an exponent.

If the period you are evaluating matches a calculated average return for the benchmark, such as three-, five-, or 10-year returns, you can compare your portfolio return to that value. Otherwise, you can use the annual returns for each year of the evaluation period to calculate the average annual return for the benchmark.

Average return =

(((1+rtn1)*(1+rtn2)*(1+rtn3)*(1+rtn4)*(1+rtn5))∧(1/5) − 1) * 100

Suppose a mutual fund delivered 10 percent, 11 percent, 8 percent, 5 percent, and 19 percent returns in five consecutive years. The funds average annual return for that period is:

Five-year avg annual return =

(1.10 * 1.11 * 1.08 * 1.05 * 1.19) ^ (1/5) = 1.105033

(1.105033 − 1) * 100 = 10.5 percent

SuccessTip!

The returns for low-cost index mutual funds are one way to obtain annual returns for benchmarks.

Additional Contributions

If you make additional contributions during a period, you can still compare your portfolio return to the benchmark IF your contributions are small compared to your initial value. The calculations aren't exact, but they work as approximations. For example, if an investment club has a portfolio worth $400,000, but the monthly member contributions are only $1,000, the approximation is fine. However, if you make significant contributions or withdrawals during the comparison period, your cash flows don't match the benchmark, and you can't compare your returns. In this situation, you would have to know every distribution made by your benchmark index including dividends and capital gains and model investments in the benchmark that match your portfolio.

Trying to compare the returns for different stocks in your portfolio also isn't meaningful unless you purchased both stocks at the same time. For individual stocks, you are better off studying a stock to understand why it didn't live up to your expectations, so you can improve your stock studies in the future.

SuccessTip!

NAIC Portfolio Record Keeper can calculate internal rate of return for your investments so that you can compare them to market indexes.

Investment Resources

A Quick Guide to Tools and Information

Good sources for investment tools, information, education, and data appear in every chapter of this book. This chapter categorizes and lists these sources *with a brief description so you can find what you need as quickly as possible.*

Screening Tools

Industry Information

Financial Statements and Annual Reports

Price Charts

Online Portfolio Tracking

Media, Magazines and More

Books

Education

Community

Software and Data

Screening Tools

Chapter 12 discusses how to use a stock screen. Chapter 14 provides a brief description of the NAIC mutual fund screening tool.

- Wall Street City *(http://www.wallstreetcity. com)* is easy to use but includes most measures you might want for stock screening criteria.

- Morningstar *(http://screen.morningstar. com/StockSelector.html)* offers predefined screens for stocks and funds, a basic customizable Stock Screener, and more robust features with its premium membership. You can also drill down through sectors until you find a stock to buy *(http://www.morningstar. com/Cover/Stocks.html)*.

- Yahoo! Finance *(http://screener.finance.yahoo. com/newscreener.html)* offers predefined stock screens for stocks and funds, a basic screening tool, and a more sophisticated screening tool.

- MSN Money Deluxe Screener *(http://money.msn.com/ investor/finder/customstocks. asp)* provides a basic online screener and a more robust tool that you download and run on your computer.

- Reuters Investor Power Screener *(http://www.investor.reuters. com/nscreen/builder.asp)* is more powerful than the MSN Money Deluxe Screener, but it isn't as easy to use.

Industry Information

Chapter 12 explains how industry information helps you find the right types of stocks.

- Standard & Poor's, First Call, Vickers, Argus, and Market Guide produce industry reports, which are available through your local library and possibly through your broker.

- Value Line industry reports provide a brief overview of industry opportunities, threats and performance.

- Industry Web sites and trade publications provide background and recent developments for industries. Type industry keywords into the Google search engine (*http://www.google.com*) to locate industry Web sites.

- The Business.com Web site (*http://www.business.com*) provides an easy way to find trade associations.

- Reuters Investor (*http://www.investor.reuters. com*) provides free and fee-based industry information.

- MSN Money (*http://money.msn.com*) stock pages provide key financial ratio results for a company and the corresponding industry.

- The Industry Center Web page at Yahoo! Finance (*http://biz.yahoo.com/ic*) provides a variety of industry information.

- Yahoo! Finance (*http://finance.yahoo.com*) stock pages include an Industry link in the navigation bar.

- Smart Money's Sector Tracker (*http://www.smartmoney.com /sectortracker*) shows sector and industry performance over different periods.

Financial Statements

When you want to examine company performance more closely, annual and quarterly reports and SEC filings provide the information you need.

- The SEC EDGAR database (*http://edgar.sec.gov/edgar. shtml*) enables you to search and download SEC filings.

- The Free Edgar Web site (*http://www.freeedgar.com*) provides the same SEC filings as the SEC's EDGAR site but is easier to use.

- Price Waterhouse Coopers (*http://edgarscan.pwcglobal. com/servlets/edgarscan*) offers downloadable *Excel* spreadsheets of EDGAR data.

- The PRARS Web site (*http://www.prars.com*) provides downloadable annual reports for many but not all companies.

Price Charts

Historical prices help you determine the value offered by a company at its current price.

- Yahoo! Finance (*http://finance.yahoo.com*) provides downloadable files of historical price data.

- Big Charts (*http:// www.bigcharts.com*) provides interactive price charts with numerous indicators.

- Stock Charts (*http://www.stockcharts.com*) provides interactive price charts with numerous indicators.

Online Portfolio Tracking

Online portfolios are one approach to keeping tabs on price and potential return.

- Yahoo! Finance (*http://finance.yahoo.com*) offers portfolio watch lists.

- Morningstar.com (*http://portfolio.morningstar. com/portasp/allview.asp*) provides a portfolio watch list for stocks and mutual funds.

- Bloomberg (*http://www.bloomberg.com*) and First Call (*http://www1.firstcall.com*) provide earnings release information.

Media, Magazines and More

Investment news, analysis, and informative articles are available through every type of media channel.

- *Better Investing* magazine is NAIC's magazine for stock and investing information.

- *BITS* magazine is an online magazine (*http://www.better-investing.org/articles/bits*) that focuses on investment education and computers in

investing. It is available to Online Premium Services subscribers.

- *Business Week* features more in-depth analysis of companies than other investment magazines.

- *Fortune* includes articles on investing and finance targeted for investors.

- *Forbes* discusses details of business operations and potential.

- *Smart Money* (*http://www.smartmoney.com /stocks*) covers personal finance and investing topics.

- *The Wall Street Journal* (*http://www.wsj.com*) is still the premier business newspaper, but also offers its business and investing news online for a subscription fee.

- CBS Market Watch (*http://cbs.marketwatch.com*) presents investing, finance, and stock market stories.

- CNN Financial (*http://www.cnnfn.com*) offers financial information on its Web site.

- *Barron's* (*http://www.barrons.com*) is another good investment newspaper with a Web site that charges a fee.

- CNBC television provides all-day coverage of the stock market.

- Yahoo! Finance (*http://finance.yahoo.com*) offers news from several sources and Web sites.

- The Street Web site (*http://www.thestreet.com*) offers a variety of investment information.

- The American Stock Exchange Web site is *http://www.amex.com*.

- The NASDAQ Exchange Web site is *http://www.nasdaq.com*.

- The New York Stock Exchange Web site is *http://www.nyse.com*.

- The OTC Financial Network Web site is *http://www.otcfn.com*.

Books

Investment books are a tremendous way to expand your knowledge of investing.

- NAIC has published a series of books describing various aspects of the NAIC methodology (*http://store. yahoo.com/ betterinvesting /educational- tools.html*): *NAIC Official Guide, NAIC Stock Selection Handbook, Mutual Fund Handbook, NAIC Computerized Investing & the Internet Handbook, Investing for Life Youth Handbook, NAIC Investment Club Operations Handbook,* and others.

- Learn from Warren Buffett's mentor by reading Benjamin Graham's *Security Analysis* (Graham and Dodd, McGraw-Hill, 2002).

- Learn how Peter Lynch approached the stock market with *One Up on Wall Street* (Simon & Shuster, 2000).

- For more book ideas from other NAIC investors, check out the list of favorite books at *http:www.better-investing. org/articles/web/4237*). In addition to the books mentioned in the previous list, other all-time favorites include *Bogle on Mutual Funds, Warren Buffett Way,* and *Stocks for the Long Run*.

Education

Improving your investment skills is a lifelong journey.

NAIC educational opportunities are published in Better Investing *magazine and on the NAIC web site* (http://www.better-investing.org).

- NAIC national conferences including Compufest and the *Better Investing* National Congress include several days of education and corporate presentations.

- NAIC chapters host Investors' Fairs and educational events that offer education and corporate presentations for incredibly reasonable prices.

- NAIC chapters teach classes on a variety of topics.

- The American Association of Individual Investors *(http://www.aaii.org)* is another source for investment education on a broad range of topics.

- The Motley Fool Web site *(http://www.fool.com)* offers light-hearted but thorough education on a variety of topics.

- About.com offers *(http://stocks.about.com)* education on all sorts of topics, including finance and investing.

- *Money* magazine *(http://www.money.com/money/101)* provides beginner-level education.

- Smart Money *(http://university.smartmoney.com)* offers courses on investing and personal finance.

Community

In addition to investment clubs, you can discuss investing with others online.

- I-Club-List *(http://www.better-investing.org/subjects/community)* is an NAIC e-mail list dedicated to discussing how to study stocks, the analysis of individual companies, and the use of software tools for stock study. The NAIC Compuserve Forum is another online discussion group.

- Yahoo! Finance includes message boards that discuss investment topics *(http://messages.yahoo.com/yahooBusiness_Finance/index.html.*

- The Motley Fool *(http://www.fool.com)* offers discussion boards for a variety of investment topics.

- Silicon Investor *(http://www.siliconinvestor.com/stocktalk)* includes discussion boards about tech industries and companies.

Software and Data

Analysis software and electronic financial data can speed up your stock studies, leaving you more time to add your own judgment, study more stocks, or learn new topics.

Fundamental Analysis Software

- NAIC *Stock Prospector* is a screening tool that can use data from Online Premium Services.

- *NAIC Classic* provides an introduction to NAIC fundamental analysis. When you grow more comfortable with the techniques you can switch from beginner to experienced mode.

- *NAIC Take Stock* is another approach to studying stocks as you learn the NAIC methodology.

- *NAIC Investor's Toolkit* includes NAIC tools for stock analysis and portfolio management based on the NAIC investment methodology with additional features to help you work your way through the steps in your investment process.

- *NAIC Stock Analyst* also includes stock analysis and portfolio management features, including a closer look at balance sheet measures.

- *Personal Record Keeper* helps you keep your investment information organized both for portfolio management and tax reporting purposes.

Data Files

- Data comes in many shapes, sizes, and price ranges.

- Online Premium Services from NAIC *(http://www.store.yahoo.com/ betterinvesting/280031.html)* offers Standard & Poor's Compustat data files for more than 4,000 stocks, which import directly into NAIC software applications. Data is original as reported, but standardizes some data.

- Standard & Poor's reports *(http://www.stockinfo.standard poor.com/sr.htm)* include as reported data and are often available for free or a small fee through brokers.

- Value Line *(http://www.valueline.com)* offers normalized data for 1700 stocks in its regular edition and for an additional 1800 companies in the expanded edition.

NOTES

Index

Pass on the Gift of Lifetime Investing!

Send a Free NAIC Investor's Kit to a Family Member or Friend

Help a family member, friend, neighbor or co-worker become a successful long-term investor... the NAIC Way! Send us their name and we will mail them a free NAIC Investor's Kit. This kit will include information introducing them to NAIC long-term investment methods, programs and tools. The kit will also explain the benefits of lifetime investing including guidelines for starting an investment program on your own or with an investment club.

To send a free NAIC Investor's Kit to someone you know—complete the information below and mail, fax or e-mail the information to NAIC, or contact NAIC by calling toll free: 1-877-275-6242.

Help others you know become successful long-term investors... *the NAIC way!*

Mail to:
NAIC
P.O. Box 220
Royal Oak, MI 48068

___ **YES, please send an NAIC Investor's Kit
to the following person:**

Name _____

Address_____

City_____**State**_____**Zip**_____

e-mail _____

FAX: 248-583-4880
e-mail: service@better-investing.org
NAIC Web Site: www.better-investing.org

Investment Education Since 1951

The National Association of Investors Corporation (NAIC) is a non-profit organization of individual investors and investment clubs, based in Madison Heights, Michigan. Founded in 1951, NAIC's mission is to increase the number of individual investors though investing in common stocks and equity mutual funds, and to provide a program of investment education and information to help its members become successful, long-term investors. NAIC helps investors start a lifetime investment program by following NAIC's Four Investment Principles:

1) *Invest a set sum regularly over your lifetime*

2) *Reinvest earnings and dividends*

3) *Buy growth stocks and mutual funds that concentrate on growth companies*

4) *Diversify your investments*

NAIC members who follow these investment principles have become successful investors over time.

To learn how to start a lifetime investment program using NAIC's proven methods, contact NAIC today.

National Association of Investors Corporation
711 West 13 Mile Road
Madison Heights, MI 48071
1-877-ASK-NAIC (275-6242)
www.better-investing.org